DICK VITALE

WITH

Charlie Parker and Jim Angresano
Foreword by John Saunders

A Division of Howard W. Sams and Company

Published by Masters Press (a division of Howard W. Sams)
2647 Waterfront Pkwy E. Dr, Suite 300, Indianapolis, IN 46214

Library of Congress Cataloging-in-Publication Data
Vitale, Dick.

   Dickie V's top 40 all everything teams / by Dick Vitale with
   Charlie Parker and Jim Angresano.
        p. cm.
   ISBN 1-57028-016-9 : $14.95

   1. Sports—United States—Miscellanea. 2. Sports teams—United
States—Miscellanea. I. Parker, Charles S., 1945- . II. Angresano,
James, 1946- . III. Title. IV. Title: Dickie V's top forty all everything
teams.

GV583.V58   1994   94-34362
796'.02--dc20   CIP

Credits:
Cover design by Phil Velikan
Front cover photo by Jeff Camp
Back cover photo courtesy of ESPN
Typography by Leah K. Marckel and Phil Velikan
Assistance provided by Misty York, Terry Varvel and Marke Foutch
Edited by Kim Heusel, Heather Seal and Holly Kondras

FOREWORD

Dick Vitale first came to my attention in 1982. As a college basketball fan living in Canada, my exposure to the game was limited, but when I first got a look and listen to Dickie V, I said this is the game for me. I had never heard such enthusiasm for the game...for any game...for anything for that matter. After moving to the U.S. I realized this was not just enthusiasm, it was a love for the game...not just the sport but the game...Dick loves the sound of the arena, the coaches, players, fans and his job. Paying Dick to sit courtside is like paying a rooster to crow.

Since 1986 I've worked side by side with Dick, in both the studio and courtside. If I was first impressed with his love of the game I am equally impressed with his passion for his job. For every *dipsy do dunkeroo*, *slam bam jam* or *PTPer* trumpeting from his head set, there is a lifetime of knowledge and hours of preparation poured into each game. It is just as important to Dick to explain as entertain.

As for Dick's immense popularity, you may not be able to understand it without understanding what makes any fan a fan. Those of us who love the world of sports are no strangers to screaming in amazement, joy or frustration. What Dick Vitale does on TV with ESPN and ABC is what most of us have done watching our favorite teams over the years; it's also what brings us back to the game and back to the TV set. We love the game and we love anyone who loves it along with us. That's what makes Vitale, Vitale. As a fan I enjoy it and as a colleague I'm happy to be part of it. Here's to plenty more, BABY!!!!!

John P. Saunders

PHOTO CREDITS

INTRODUCTION

Sports trivia is enjoyed by a growing number of people. Friends often challenge each other's knowledge of basketball, baseball and football—like trying to name the starting lineups in that classic January 20, 1968 Houston-UCLA game. Or the players who were on base that wild day in 1951 when Bobby Thompson hit his famous shot heard 'round the world. Or the final score of the football game won by the Immaculate Reception.

In this book I'm going to test your sports trivia in another way. I'm going to ask you to consider some mythical teams and then select sports personalities and famous moments to fit those teams. In all, I've come up with 40 teams and invite you to choose rosters for them by letting your imagination run loose.

Take my All-Ornithological Team. Know of any athletes whose birthname or nickname suggests some type of bird? I thought you would. Probably you've thought of Mister Celtic himself, Larry Bird. And Goose Gossage. Maybe even "The Bird," Mark Fidrych. Or Robin Yount. If you thought long enough about it, there are at least a couple of dozen more beaky-sounding athletes you might come up with.

After you've named as many birds as you can, you can go on to the next team in the book or skip ahead to my All-Fish Team— where Kevin Bass is swimming around—or All-Money and Banking Team—where you can bet your bottom dollar that you'll find both Norm and Dave Cash.

The organization of this book is easy to follow. After the eligibility for each team is described on a right-hand page, accompanied by a sample name or two, space is provided for you to select your own team. So I won't get in the way of your creative juices, my teams appear after each of the fill-in pages, along with some interesting tidbits about some of the players and events on my list. All of my selections are keyed into either some type of name play or some memorable aspect or event, as hinted by the eligibility requirements and the samples provided. Don't worry, it's easy to figure out. Take my word for it— you'll get the hang of it right away.

In the spirit of fun, the rules for playing the game are not hard and fast. Athletes may spell or pronounce their names differently than the team names might suggest (say, "Swann" instead of "Swan"). Also, the names you'd wish for in a perfect world may be part of a longer name (such as "Duck" buried in "Duckworth"). In some cases there are even greater stretches, so it's up to you and your friends to ultimately decide what works and what doesn't. It's sometimes a fine and sometimes a hazy line that separates a good stretch from a harebrained thought that taxes the imagination too much.

Each of my all-star teams includes about 20-40 members. Most are professional baseball, basketball and football players, but there are also several athletes from other sports, as well as coaches, play-by-play announcers and owners. As far as I'm concerned, any sport and any sports personality is fair game. If you find yourself laughing or saying "Why didn't I think of that?", you've found a great entry for a team.

Some of the names you come up with will be eligible for more than one team and will also be "double hits" on a single team. Take ex-footballer Trenton Jackson—he makes my All-U.S. Cities Team twice, since Trenton and Jackson are both cities. Come to think of it, he could also make my All-Presidents Team—remember "Old Hickory?"

You'll probably find as I did that it's impossible to come up with all the possible names on any given list. If, for my All-U.S. Cities Team, for instance, I had to write down every Jackson I could think of and cover every city in the atlas, I'd go nuts and the book would look like the Manhattan Yellow Pages. And an-

other thing—I'm human like you and miss names. Sometimes I'm driving in my car and—whammo—suddenly another player I didn't think of hits me. Or, I'll be settling into the booth ready to do a broadcast, foolishly patting myself on the back for the job I did on my All-Auto Team, and—wouldn't you know—some freshman named Studebaker Smith or Jack "The Ferrari Burlinetta" Martin shows up on someone's bench.

For those of you who want to challenge friends to a session of trivial recall, an appendix in the back of the book suggests ways for you to turn the book into a game. There's even a couple of suggestions for keeping score. In sports as in life, nothing faster decides an argument at who's better at something than a scoresheet. Numbers talk, baby, nobody walks.

Whatever way you use this book—by yourself or with a friend —enjoy your walk through sports trivia land. *Dickie V's Top 40* is a game that can be played sitting at home in an easy chair, at a party or at the beach, on a long car ride, or circling O'Hare airport for an hour or two waiting for your plane to land.

One final thing. After you read this book, see if the next time you watch anything having to do with sports on the tube you're not doing a scan job for catchy names and slotting them on mythical teams. Tim Raines? Definitely All-Weather Team. Slick Watts? All-Contours Team, baby. Bo Hickey? Well, you know.

Enjoy.

Table of Contents

1   All-Ornithology Team 1
2   All-Occupations Team 7
3   All-Colleges and Universities Team 13
4   All-Terrain Team 19
5   All-Foliage Team 23
6   All-Presidents Team 29
7   All-Colors Team 37
8   All-Fruits, Veggies, and Grains Team 43
9   All-Beverages Team 47
10 All-U.S. Cities Team 53
11 All-Countries and Nationalities Team 59
12 All-Extraterrestrial Team 65
13 All-Religious Team 69
14 All-Money and Banking Team 75
15 All-Mammals Team 79
16 All-Fish Team 85
17 All-Food Team 91
18 All-Foot Team 97
19 All-Anatomy 101
20 All-Doctors Team 105
21 All-Housing and Construction Team 111
22 All-Weapons and Ammo Team 115
23 All-Auto Team 121
24 All-Music Team 125
25 All-Auto Team 131
26 All-Royalty and Heads of State Team 137
27 All-Natural Materials Team 141
28 All-Calender and Time Team 147
29 All-Sizes, Measurements, and Distances Team 151
30 All-Military Team 157
31 All-Initials Team 163
32 All-Intelligence Team 169
33 All-Three Names Team 173
34 All-Two Sports Team 177
35 All-Shortest Name Team 183
36 All-Unofficial Teams Team 187
37 All-Bo and Mo Team 193
38 All-Two First Names Team 198
39 All-Water Team 203
40 All-Hollywood Team 207
Appendix: Keeping Score 213

When you talk about a guy who could deliver in spades when it counted—especially with the pressure cooker turned on high-you're talking about my man Larry Bird.

1 | ALL-ORNITHOLOGY TEAM

Eligibility: Each team entry must include a first name, last name, nickname or sports expression that suggests a bird, a type of bird or a part of a bird (such as a wing).

Samples: Larry Bird
Goose Gossage

And your nominees are ...

_____   _____

_____   _____

_____   _____

_____   _____

_____   _____

_____   _____

_____   _____

_____   _____

_____   _____

Dick's Picks
All-Ornithology Team

Larry Bird *BASKETBALL*

"The Bird," Mark Fidrych *BASEBALL*

Bird Averitt *BASKETBALL*

Birdie Tebbetts *BASEBALL*

Elvis Peacock *FOOTBALL*

Robin Roberts *BASEBALL*

Robin Yount *BASEBALL*

Rory Sparrow *BASKETBALL*

Junior Wren *FOOTBALL*

Goose Gossage *BASEBALL*

Goose Goslin *BASEBALL*

Lynn Swann *FOOTBALL*

Craig Swan *BASEBALL*

George Crowe *BASEBALL*

John David Crow *FOOTBALL*

Larry Finch *BASKETBALL*

Joey Jay *BASEBALL*

Sonny Dove *BASKETBALL*

Mack Herron *FOOTBALL*

"The Stork," George Theodore *BASEBALL*

"The Mad Stork," Ted Hendricks *FOOTBALL*

"The Penguin," Ron Cey *BASEBALL*

Don "The Duck" Chaney *BASKETBALL*

Kevin Duckworth *BASKETBALL*

Ken "The Hawk" Harrelson *BASEBALL*

Frank Quayle *FOOTBALL*

Billy Martin *BASEBALL*

Bruce Starling *FOOTBALL*

Eddie "The Eagle" Edwards *SKIING*

Solly Drake *BASEBALL*

Jose Cardenal *BASEBALL*

Meadowlark Lemon *BASKETBALL*

Paul Crane *FOOTBALL*

Ed Kranepool *BASEBALL*

Mike Parrot *BASEBALL*

Jeff Parret *BASEBALL*

Pete Falcone *BASEBALL*

Joe Falcon *TRACK & FIELD*

Harthorne Wingo *BASKETBALL*

Gerod Swallow *SKATING*

Ralph "The Roadrunner" Garr *BASEBALL*

"The Vulture," Phil Regan *BASEBALL*

"The Albatross," Michael Gross *SWIMMING*

Trivial Tidbits

Larry Bird BASKETBALL

Larry entered the NBA with Magic Johnson in 1979 and led the Celtics in scoring, rebounding and steals his first year--winning NBA Rookie of the Year Honors. When you think of Larry Bird, you think of the big three: Larry, Magic and Michael. The big three were so sensational that they were scintillating super and special. Larry could pass the rock and make the big hoop. When you needed a big one—he delivered. Larry was flat out Mr. Clutch.

"The Bird," Mark Fidrych BASEBALL

Nicknamed "The Bird" since he resembled Sesame Street's Big Bird, Detroit Tiger Fidrych gained fame his rookie season in 1976 by pitching a one-hitter on national TV, often talking to the ball before delivering his pitch. The crowd ate it up. He won 19 games, had a 2.34 ERA, and was named American League Rookie of the Year. Injuries cut short his very promising career, and he won only 10 more games thereafter. I ran into the Bird when I was coaching at the University of Detroit. In fact, America get ready for this, I offered him a full scholarship. I said, "Mark, baby, accept a scholarship during the off-season; come and play a little hoops." We know what he did in baseball. He was Mr. Personality, with charisma galore.

Birdie Tebbetts BASEBALL

Tebbetts—who managed the Reds and Braves for 11 years in the '50s and '60s—hit .270 lifetime and finished his career with exactly 1,000 hits. Tebbetts' high-pitched voice is what got him his nickname. He was one of my favorite catchers; I used to love the Boston Red Sox. I talked about the Red Sox in my sleep: Ted Williams, Dom DiMaggio, Mel Parnell, Johnny Pesky and Bobby Doerr...you name them. I used to know all their statistics inside and out. Mr. Tebbetts was like a manager behind the plate.

Elvis Peacock FOOTBALL

You gotta love his name, baby. This Sooner running back (talk about an acrobatic running style) strutted his stuff in Switzer's wishbone offense before his NFL career was cut short by injury in the early 1980s. In 1980 he rushed for 777 yards, averaging 4.7 yards per carry.

Robin Roberts BASEBALL

I used to emulate him. As a kid (not to give away your age, Robin baby), I pitched in the little league. It was his style that I wanted—that smooth delivery, smooth as can be. Robin Roberts was a control pitcher's control pitcher. He won 20 or more games for six consecutive seasons (1950-55). Most of his 19-year career was with the Philadelphia Phillies. He racked up 28 wins in 1952—10 more than any other National League pitcher that year. He finished his career with 286 wins.

Robin Yount BASEBALL

You talk about all-around ability, consistency and dedication; well, this guy had it all. Among Yount's boatload of achievements, besides beginning his professional career at age 18, are two MVP awards (1982 and 1989) and finishing in the top 15 on the major league all-time list for number of at bats, hits, games played, and doubles. He retired in 1993 after playing 20 seasons and over 2600 games—all with the Brewers.

Goose Gossage BASEBALL

One of the top AL stoppers of the '80s, the Goose was on the mound during that memorable moment in 1983, when George Brett hit what looked like a home run. I mean, it was back in the cheap seats. Yankee manager Billy Martin protested that Brett had excessive pine tar on his bat. The ump agreed with Martin and disallowed the dinger.

Goose Goslin *BASEBALL*

A Hall of Famer with speed, a strong throwing arm and a penchant for knocking 'em home—Goslin finished his career 19th on the all-time RBI list. He compiled a lifetime batting average of .316, playing mostly with Washington and Detroit.

Lynn Swann *FOOTBALL*

One of the best, ever. Period and exclamation point! A wide receiver with mercurial moves and leaping ability, Swann played for one NCAA National Championship team—U.S.C. in 1974—and four Super Bowl-winning Pittsburgh Steeler teams. In Super Bowl X, in which the Steelers ruined the day for the Cowboys, 21-17, Swann had a career performance by catching four passes for a monster 161 yards—a record that got him MVP honors.

Craig Swan *BASEBALL*

Swan played in "the show" for a dozen seasons, mostly with the New York Mets, in the '70s and '80s. His most prolific year was 1979, when he went 14-13.

George Crowe *BASEBALL*

Crowe played an average of about 70 games a year during his nine-year career, collecting 299 RBIs for four different clubs. His best year was with the Reds in 1957, when he hit 31 dingers—not bad for only 133 games—and batted .271.

Larry Finch *BASKETBALL*

You talk about a guy who loves Memphis! "Tubby" Finch's entire college and professional career has taken place in that one city. He started out playing alongside Larry "Dr. K" Kenon, who went to the glass to put up big numbers with the Memphis State Tigers in the late 60s, then went with the often renamed and short-lived Memphis Tams of the old ABA for a single season. Finch then came back to State again as coach.

Joey Jay *BASEBALL*

Traded to the Cincinnati Reds in 1961, this 13-year veteran responded by winning 21 games, a full dozen more than he did in 1960 for the Milwaukee Braves. In '62 he dittoed himself and won 21 again. How sweet it is, having guys like Frank Robinson, Vada Pinson and Gene Freese in the lineup. Joey Jay was the first Little Leaguer to make the majors.

Sonny Dove *BASKETBALL*

No, this is not the name of a beauty soap. An All-American at St. John's under Lou Carnesecca, Sonny Dove had success in the old ABA—where he averaged 14 points per game—then in his brief stint with the NBA's Detroit Pistons. He came to and went from the ranks of pro basketball in about the time it takes to get a college degree.

"The Stork," George Theodore *BASEBALL*

Born George Basil Theodore, he could make my All-Condiments Team, too. The gangly, six-foot-four Theodore's two-year career with the New York Mets (1973-74) included playing in the 1973 World Series where the Mets took the Oakland A's to seven games before Reggie Jackson, Catfish Hunter and company put up the W in Game 7.

"The Mad Stork," Ted Hendricks *FOOTBALL*

This six-time All-Pro, who never missed a game during his 13-year NFL stint with the Raiders and Colts, had four career safeties and 21 blocked kicks—both NFL records. His tallish height, thinnish frame and flailing arms are where the nickname comes from, but he could defend with the best of them. And talk about a student—he took courses like Electromagnetic Theory and Mathematical Analysis at Miami University.

Don "The Duck" Chaney BASKETBALL
Before being drafted by the Boston Celtics, where he starred defensively for many years, Chaney teamed with Elvin Hayes on the 1967-68 Houston Cougars' 31-2 team that upset UCLA in the regular season, 71-69, ending the Bruins 47-game winning streak. At the end of his playing career, Chaney began coaching in the NBA. He is presently head coach of the Detroit Pistons.

Kevin Duckworth BASKETBALL
This 7-foot strongman played center for the great, but day-late-and-dollar-short, Portland Trailblazers teams of the late 1980s and early '90s. This guy could produce numbers, averaging about 14 ppg since entering the NBA in 1987. He is now playing for the Washington Bullets.

Ken "The Hawk" Harrelson BASEBALL
Noted for being a snappy dresser, Harrelson would often draw considerable attention when he appeared in public. When not on the GQ circuit, he could put fear into the hearts of pitchers. His best season was in 1968, when he hit 35 home runs for the Red Sox.

Billy Martin BASEBALL
Throughout his stormy managing career—"stormy" as in Hurricane Andrew—this longtime, fired-again-hired-again Yankee skipper was canned six times and suspended on five other occasions. Notorious for getting into fights (his roster of bouts included taking on a traveling marshmallow salesman) Martin, when he piloted the Twins, once refused to permit Senator Hubert Humphrey into his team's locker room after a tough loss.

Eddie "The Eagle" Edwards SKIING
This lovable British plasterer captured the public's eye when he provided a touch of comic relief to the 1988 Winter Olympic Games. Despite not having the opportunity to train using facilities similar to those of his competitors, he showcased his courage in competition. The Eagle competed in the 70-and 90-meter ski jumps. Although he finished last in both events, the Eagle's popularity soared as sports fans admired his effort.

Solly Drake BASEBALL
Drake spent time with three National League teams during the 1956 and 1959 seasons, hitting only two home runs while striking out once per every 5.4 at bats. Take a gander at this: Put Drake together with Lou Hudson, Cortez Kennedy and Dennis Byrd, and you've got the makings of a first-rate All-Explorers Team.

Jose Cardenal BASEBALL
Playing for nine different teams during his 18-year major-league career, Cardenal had 1,913 hits while averaging .275. He played with the Royals when they lost the 1980 World Series to Philly—finally ending the long drought for a baseball championship in that city.

Meadowlark Lemon BASKETBALL
A true showman and leader of the Harlem Globetrotters in their salad days, Lemon was fond of standing at half court and asking for the ball with the clock winding down. Telling the crowd "watch this," he would put up a long hook shot—gleefully strutting his struff when it went in.

Paul Crane FOOTBALL
Crane, who played seven years at linebacker for the New York Jets (including the 1969 Super Bowl Champion team), was a center for Alabama in college. He volunteered for the position when all the other centers on the squad were injured. His coach, Paul "Bear" Bryant, claimed Crane was the best center he ever had.

Ed Kranepool BASEBALL
Kranepool was a member of the original New York Mets, starting his major-league career at age 18 in 1962—straight from high school in The Big Apple. Early on, he was compared to another New Yorker: the

late, great Hank Greenberg. In 18 years, he hit a career .261 and sent 118 balls downtown.

Jeff Parret   BASEBALL

This guy had a great ability to get to the winner's circle, having a winning percentage of over 60 percent. Parret played for four different teams in his first seven years in the major leagues, nearly all of the years spent coming out of the bullpen. He averaged nearly a strikeout per inning pitched.

Pete Falcone   BASEBALL

With the 1983 Braves, Falcone posted the best season of his 10-year career, winning nine games while losing only four— despite walking one more batter than he struck out. It was after Falcone was gone, though, that Ted Turner began putting together in Atlanta one of the best pitching staffs money could buy.

Joe Falcon   TRACK & FIELD

Former Razorback runner Falcon has been among the elite 1500- meter runners in the world during the past few years. He is a legitimate threat to become the first American in over 85 years to win this event at the Atlanta 1996 Olympic Games, but he will have to get past Algeria's Noureddine Morceli—the world record holder—to make that happen.

Harthorne Wingo   BASKETBALL

Wingo, who went directly into the NBA from Friendship Junior College, averaged almost five points per game in four seasons as a forward with New York. When Wingo came along in the '70s, the Knicks—who had just come off a couple of championship seasons—were starting to show signs of wear and tear. DeBusschere and Reed were gone, and it was Turnstile City on the front line.

2 | ALL-OCCUPATIONS TEAM

Eligibility: Each team entry must include a first name, last name, nickname or sports expression that suggests an occupation.

Samples: Earl Weaver
Larry Farmer

And your nominees are ...

_____   _____

_____   _____

_____   _____

_____   _____

_____   _____

_____   _____

_____   _____

_____   _____

_____   _____

Dick's Picks
All-Occupations Team

Earl Weaver *BASEBALL*

Larry Farmer *BASKETBALL*

Miller Barber *GOLF*

Fair Hooker *FOOTBALL*

Mike Marshall *BASEBALL*

Howard Porter *BASKETBALL*

Granville Waiters *BASKETBALL*

Dusty Baker *BASEBALL*

Jim "Catfish" Hunter *BASEBALL*

Billy Gardner *BASEBALL*

Fred Dean *FOOTBALL*

Dean Smith *BASKETBALL*

Woody Fryman *BASEBALL*

Reggie Miller *BASKETBALL*

Grady Alderman *FOOTBALL*

Karl "The Mailman" Malone *BASKETBALL*

Jim Courier *TENNIS*

"The Old Professor," Casey Stengel *BASEBALL*

Jim Brewer *BASEBALL*

Jim Brewer *BASKETBALL*

"The Doctor," Julius Erving *BASKETBALL*

Toi Cook *FOOTBALL*

George Foreman *BOXING*

Willie Shoemaker *HORSE RACING*

Toni Sailer *SKIING*

Sue Barker *TENNIS*

Harold Miner *BASKETBALL*

Brian Teacher *TENNIS*

Pie Traynor *BASEBALL*

Dave Archer *GOLF*

Susan Butcher *SLED DOG RACER*

Mel Sheppard *TRACK & FIELD*

PattiSue Plummer *TRACK & FIELD*

Adolph Plummer *TRACK & FIELD*

Bill Fisher *BASKETBALL*

Anthony Mason *BASKETBALL*

Brett Butler *BASEBALL*

Rob Carpenter *FOOTBALL*

Carl Painter *FOOTBALL*

Paul Butcher *FOOTBALL*

Tom Beier *FOOTBALL*

Bob Usher *BASEBALL*

John Provost *FOOTBALL*

Digger Phelps *BASKETBALL*

Jack Kent Cooke *OWNER*

Trivial Tidbits

Earl Weaver *BASEBALL*

Weaver, who played the ukulele when he wasn't getting his Oriole troops in line, preferred the blockbuster inning more than perhaps anything. He was quick to point out that the winning team usually scored more runs in its big inning than the loser did all game. Weaver ranks 14th on the all-time winningest managers list, with 1,506 wins in 17 seasons.

Larry Farmer *BASKETBALL*

Farmer played for the greatest coach of all, the Wizard of Westwood, John Wooden. He was a forward for the 1971, 1972 and 1973 UCLA National Championship teams, which won the last 60 games of his college career. He also coached the Bruins 1981-1984, and his record for those three seasons was 61-23. He has served as a TV analyst for Pac-10 basketball.

Miller Barber *GOLF*

Despite an unorthodox swing, in which his right elbow seemed to "fly" on the backswing, Barber won 11 PGA tournaments before joining the Seniors Circuit in 1981. There, despite never having won a major tournament when he was at the top of his game, he became more successful, winning the USPGA Seniors his first year and the USGA Senior Open his second. Since 1981 he has won more than two dozen Seniors tournaments, more than anyone else on the tour.

Mike Marshall *BASEBALL*

This 14-year veteran of the majors—who played for about 10 teams altogether—is probably one of the few major-league pitchers to pick off a former student in a World Series game. In the second tilt of the 1974 fall classic, Marshall, pitching in relief for the Dodgers in the top of the ninth inning, erased A's pinch runner Herb Washington. Washington had been a student in a class Marshall taught while the latter was a graduate student at Michigan state. A career pinch

runner, Washington had managed to steal 31 bases and score 33 runs that season, without ever having an at bat for the Oakland A's. Marshall got the save in the game—but the A's won the Series.

Howard Porter *BASKETBALL*

Porter, who played seven years in the NBA, gained national attention during and after the 1971 NCAA Tournament. The "during" part centered around his outstanding play. He was the tourney MVP, leading the Villanova Wildcats into the finals with a double overtime 92-89 victory in the semis over a Jim McDaniels-and Clarence-Glover-led Western Kentucky team. The "after" part was the revelation that he had signed a professional contract earlier in the season. Villanova had to forfeit its second-place trophy and fork over all funds received from its participation in the tournament.

Granville Waiters *BASKETBALL*

During his four seasons in the NBA, the 6-foot-11 Waiters had a field-goal accuracy, 46 percent, that was almost as high as his 56-percent free-throw shooting percentage. His name brings to mind ex-New York Giant, Bobby Gaiters, who could make my All-Cross Country Skiing Apparel Team.

Dusty Baker *BASEBALL*

During the 1977 World Series, this 19-year major-league veteran led the Dodgers by hitting .399 and driving in five runs in a six-game loss to the Yankees. Before the 1993 season, Baker was hired to manage the San Francisco Giants. His rookie year at the helm was the stuff legends are made of—the team won an awesome 103 games. Unfortunately, the Giants didn't even win their division that year, getting edged out by the Braves on the last day of the season.

Jim "Catfish" Hunter *BASEBALL*

One of the best pitchers in the history of baseball, Hunter won 111 games in five consecutive seasons (1971-75). He also became one of baseball's first high-priced free agents. In 1974, when Oakland A's owner Charles Finley allegedly balked at having to pay taxes on a $50,000 insurance annuity provision that the team had agreed to pay Hunter. Catfish wiggled off the hook, into the checkbook-shaped creel of the thankful Yankees, who ponied up to the tune of over $2.5 mil. Hunter has five World Series rings, a perfect game, and a Cy Young Award.

Woody Fryman BASEBALL

Fryman had a 17-year career (1966-83) that was spread over seven major-league teams. Now that's durability from a man whose name suggests that someone on the family tree may have once been employed as a short-order cook.

Reggie Miller BASKETBALL

You talk about Reggie Miller and hoops—he is one of the most underrated superstars in the game. He can flat out knock down the trifecta; he's got the area code J. He showed everyone how great he is when he lit up the Knicks for 25 points in the fourth quarter of a 1994 NBA playoff game. I work with his sister Cheryl, who was women's basketball's predominant superstar during her era at USC, and is now the Trojans' head coach.

Karl "The Mailman" Malone BASKETBALL

Malone has been one of the game's premier power forwards for many years, first at Louisiana Tech, then with the Utah Jazz. He teams with John Stockton to form one of the game's great inside-outside combinations. A perennial All-Star, Malone talks up basketball with his mom, calling her before every game—during which time she advises him as to how many points and rebounds he should get. For faster express deliveries, Malone should feel free to call on either Jim Courier or the 1987 NFL leader in average yards per kickoff return—Mr. Sylvester Stamps.

"The Old Professor," Casey Stengel BASEBALL

As a manager, Stengel experienced in spades both the joy of victory and the agony of defeat. First came the joy. In 1949 he replaced Bucky Harris as skipper for the New York Yankees and immediately led the Bombers to five consecutive World Series Championships. Then came the agony. In 1962 he piloted the New York Mets in their inaugural season to the worst-ever record in modern pro baseball, 40-120. Noted for his "professorial" way of expressing things, Stengel wasn't in top academic form the day he was introduced as the new manager of the expansion Mets and told all "It's great to be back in the Polo Grounds again with the New York Knickerbockers."

Jim Brewer BASEBALL

Brewer lasted 17 seasons in the major leagues, primarily as a relief pitcher with the Cubs and Dodgers. This puts him almost on the level of Tommy John, Jim Kaat, and Hoyt Wilhelm in terms of service. Longevity City. Among Brewer's other impressive statistics are striking out more than twice as many batters as he walked, a 3.07 ERA, and a respectable (for a pitcher) batting average of .150.

Jim Brewer BASKETBALL

Often confused with Randy Breuer—another Minnesota Gopher—Jim Brewer holds the single season rebound record for the Cleveland Cavaliers, pulling down 891 in the 1975-76 season. That was the year the Cavs won the Central Division title. They eventually lost 4-2 in the Eastern Conference finals to the Boston Celtics. Brewer was also a member of the 1972 Olympic team that lost the controversial final game to the Soviet Union.

George Foreman BOXING

Born in 1948, Foreman became Olympic Heavyweight Champion in 1968 and then won his first 40 professional fights. However, heavily favored Foreman lost his heavyweight title to Muhammad Ali in Kenshasa, Zaire in October, 1974. Ali used a punch he dubbed the "ghetto whopper." It was so named by him because the fight occurred at 4 a.m. in Zaire—or 9 p.m. EST—a time he said young people were fighting in U.S. ghettos.

Willie Shoemaker   HORSE RACING
Shoemaker weighed only 2 pounds at birth, and his mother feared that he would not survive infancy. Fortunately for Derby-lovers, her fears were unfounded. In a career that began in 1949 and ended in 1990, Shoemaker rode 40,350 mounts and reached the winner's circle 8833 times. He will also forever be remembered for the race he lost—the 1957 Kentucky Derby. While aboard Gallant Man, Shoemaker mistook the 16th pole on the home stretch for the finish line, stood up too soon in the saddle, and allowed the oncharging Iron Leige to pass his mount and win.

Toni Sailer   SKIING
At the 1956 Winter Olympics in Cortina, Italy, Austrian Sailer won the men's downhill, slalom, and giant slalom races. This triple has only been matched by Jean-Claude Killy. Sailer was so dominant in the giant slalom that his victory margin was an unbelievable 6.2 seconds.

Harold Miner   BASKETBALL
Michael Jordan-wannabe and former USC standout, Miner was the Miami Heat's first round draft pick in 1992. His NBA duties are mostly confined to coming off the bench, but his playing time will increase as he learns the NBA way to shoot the trifecta and he becomes more consistent, especially on the defensive end.

Susan Butcher   SLED DOG RACER
Butcher won Alaska's annual, grueling Iditarod Trail Race on four occasions, 1986-88 and 1990. A Massachussets transplant to the north country, she is the first and only woman to win.

Mel Sheppard   TRACK & FIELD
Sheppard—for whom the mile run at New York's prestigious Millrose Games is named—is the last American to take home the gold in the men's 1500-meter run at the Summer Olympics in 1908. His time was 4:03.4, a crawl by today's standards. Applying his trademark tactic of taking the lead from gun to tape, Sheppard also won the Olympic 800 meters the same year, with a new world record time of 1:52.8. In the 1912 Olympics, his burn-off-the-opposition-early strategy backfired in the 800. He was overhauled at the tape by a 19-year-old high-schooler from Philly, Ted Meredith.

Brett Butler   BASEBALL
A longtime LA Dodger lead off hitter and center fielder, Butler began his career with the Atlanta Braves in 1981. His career is still going strong. When he gets on base, he's ready to steal. Last season he stole base No. 500.

Rob Carpenter   FOOTBALL
A 10-year veteran of the NFL, Carpenter played alongside Earl Campbell with the Houston Oilers, 1978-1980. During those years he averaged almost four yards per carry, while Campbell was running roughshod over defenders to the tune of about 1,650 yards rushing per season.

Digger Phelps   BASKETBALL
Noted for being Threads City by those of us who buy strictly off the rack, Phelps' Fordham University team once beat Notre Dame—a perennial basketball powerhouse back a couple of decades or so ago. The Irish athletic department was so impressed that it hired Digger as soon as the head coaching position became vacant. It was a great move, because Digger was one of the few NCAA coaches able to beat the great UCLA teams. The bottom line is that his players not only performed on the court, but also in the classroom. They walked down the aisle and got their diplomas. He is now my colleague at ESPN.

Will Perdue—a mountain of a man, and I mean mountain—could be reliably counted on to sweep the glass when coming off the pine for the Bulls' championship teams.

3 | ALL-COLLEGES AND UNIVERSITIES TEAM

Eligibility: Each team entry must include a first name, last name, nickname or sports expression that suggests a college or university.

Samples: Yale Lary
Bill Bradley

VU
VITALE UNIVERSITY

And your nominees are ...

_____   _____

_____   _____

_____   _____

_____   _____

_____   _____

_____   _____

_____   _____

_____   _____

_____   _____

Dick's Picks
All-Colleges and Universities Team

Name SPORT	School
Xavier McDaniel BASKETBALL	Xavier University, Cincinnati, OH
Will Perdue BASKETBALL	Purdue University, West Lafayette, IN
Yale Lary FOOTBALL	Yale University, New Haven, CT
Roosevelt Brown FOOTBALL	Brown University, Providence, RI and Roosevelt Univ., Chicago, IL
Cornell Green FOOTBALL	Cornell University, Ithaca, NY
Leon Wagner BASEBALL	Wagner College, Staten Island, NY
Honus Wagner BASEBALL	Wagner College, Staten Island, NY
Elgin Baylor BASKETBALL	Baylor University, Waco, TX
Don Baylor BASEBALL	Baylor University, Waco, TX
John Drew BASKETBALL	Drew University, Madison, NJ
Jamaal (Keith) Wilkes BASKETBALL	Wilkes College, Wilkes-Barre, PA
Sebastian Coe TRACK & FIELD	Coe College, Cedar Rapids, IA
"Tree" Rollins BASKETBALL	Rollins College, Winter Park, FL
Jack Hamilton BASEBALL	Hamilton College, Clinton, NY
Emmitt Smith FOOTBALL	Smith College, Northampton, MA
Johnny Temple BASEBALL	Temple University, Philadelphia, PA
J.R. Rider BASKETBALL	Rider College, Lawrenceville, NJ
Andre Reed FOOTBALL	Reed College, Portland, OR
Seth Morehead BASEBALL	Morehead State Univ., Morehead, KY
Cal Ripken, Jr. BASEBALL	Univ. of California, Berkeley, CA
Leonard Marshall FOOTBALL	Marshall University, Huntington, WV
Cullen Bryant FOOTBALL	Bryant College, Smithfield, RI

Steve Carlton *BASEBALL*	Carleton College, Northfield, MN
Carlton Fisk *BASEBALL*	Carleton College, Northfield, MN and Fisk University, Nashville, TN
Brian Dowling *FOOTBALL*	Dowling College, Oakdale, NY
Frank Howard *BASEBALL*	Howard University, Washington, DC
Bill Bradley *BASKETBALL*	Bradley University, Peoria, IL
Virginia Wade *TENNIS*	Univ. of Virginia, Charlottesville, VA
Kermit Washington *BASKETBALL*	Washington Univ., St. Louis, MO
Billy "The Hill" McGill *BASKETBALL*	McGill University, Montreal (Canada)
David Wheaton *TENNIS*	Wheaton College, Wheaton, IL
Jim Rice *BASEBALL*	Rice University, Houston, TX
Brett Butler *BASEBALL*	Butler University, Indianapolis, IN
Dusty Rhodes *BASEBALL*	Rhodes College, Memphis, TN
Millard Hampton *FOOTBALL*	Hampton University, Hampton, VA
Russell Maryland *FOOTBALL*	Univ. of Maryland, College Park, MD
Minnesota Fats *BILLIARDS*	Univ. of Minnesota, Minneapolis, MN
David Wingate *BASKETBALL*	Wingate College, Wingate, NC
Nate Stephens *BASKETBALL*	Stevens I.T., Hoboken, NJ
Lafayette Lever *BASKETBALL*	Lafayette College, Easton, PA
Bo Lamar *BASKETBALL*	Lamar University, Beaumont, TX
Bobby Jones *BASKETBALL*	Bob Jones University, Greenville, SC
Joe Beaver *RODEO*	Beaver College, Glenside, PA
Darryl Boston *BASEBALL*	Boston University, Boston, MA
Bobby Avila *BASEBALL*	Avila College, Kansas City, MO
Bobby Murcer *BASEBALL*	Mercer University, Macon, GA
Rayfield Wright *FOOTBALL*	Wright State Univ., Dayton, OH

Trivial Tidbits

Will Perdue *BASKETBALL*
He's a great All-Airport selection—he looks super at the airport and gets little PT (playing time). He's your typical role player. Perdue's rebounds-per-minute-played figures are respectable and would work out to about 12-14 boards per game if he played full time.

Yale Lary *FOOTBALL*
Lary was one tough customer and one of the last NFL players to play full time at defensive back and also carry the team's punting chores. A longtime Detroit Lion, his career punting average was more than 44 yards per kick, and in 1963 he averaged 48.9. One of the first two-sport athletes, Lary also played four seasons of minor-league baseball. He was elected to the NFL Hall of Fame in 1979.

Leon Wagner *BASEBALL*
Known as "Daddy Wags," Wagner began his major-league career with the San Francisco Giant team that featured Willie Mays, Orlando Cepeda and Felipe Alou. Willie McCovey joined the team the following season. Wagner averaged about 20 home runs per season for his career.

Honus Wagner *BASEBALL*
Hall of Fame shortstop Wagner—who finished a lengthy career with the Pittsburgh Pirates sporting a .328 batting average—had such long arms and such bowed legs that some joked he was able to tie his shoelaces without bending over. In 21 seasons, he had 3430 hits and won seven National League batting titles.

Elgin Baylor *BASKETBALL*
One of the all-time greats. Holder of the NBA Playoffs one-game scoring record—61 points against the Celtics in 1961. Hey baby, when you looked at Elgin, the scouting report said he could only go to his right.

One night in Madison Square Garden, he put 70 points on the board, and the Knicks played him to the right all night long. Elgin Baylor was a star of stars. He had great agility and mobility.

Don Baylor *BASEBALL*
Colorado Rockies manager Baylor was the American League's MVP in 1979, the first designated hitter to be so honored. He played 19 seasons for eight teams, finishing with 2,135 hits and 338 home runs—placing him 51st on the all-time list of sluggers.

John Drew *BASKETBALL*
Yes, Virginia, there is a Drew University. But John Drew did not go there, opting instead for Gardner-Webb. In 11 seasons with the Atlanta Hawks and Utah Jazz, Drew averaged more than 20 points and nearly seven boards per game, despite averaging only 30 minutes of playing time per game.

Jamaal (Keith) Wilkes *BASKETBALL*
Teammate of Bill Walton on the UCLA team that won the 1972 and 1973 NCAA Championships, smooth-as-silk Wilkes was the 1974-75 NBA Rookie of the Year with the Warriors. He averaged almost 18 points per game in 12 NBA seasons. As far as I know, he's never played any hoops in Wilkes-Barre, Pennsylvania, where Wilkes College is located.

Sebastian Coe *TRACK & FIELD*
One of the finest middle distance runners of all time, this slightly built but gutty Englishman set world records in the 800-meter, 1000-meter, 1500-meter, and mile runs, and he won Olympic Gold in the 1500 meters in both 1980 and 1984. While there is a Coe College, there is no school named Sebastian. There is a Sebastiani Vineyards, however, out on the West Coast, making

this runner an afterthought for my All-Pressed Grapes Team.

"Tree" Rollins   BASKETBALL

Rollins' durability at center is demonstrated by his playing 15-plus NBA seasons, mainly for Atlanta. And he's still around, baby. His field-goal percentage is about 50 percent, while his foul-shooting average is close to 70 percent.

Emmitt Smith   FOOTBALL

The state of Florida's all-time-ground-gaining high school rushing back, Smith broke into the NFL by gaining 937 yards his rookie season with the 7-9 Dallas Cowboys. He raised that total to 1,563 the following year and then became one of the essential cogs in the offense that led the Cowboys to two straight Super Bowls. If you're wondering if he attended Smith College, the answer is no—he was a Florida Gator.

Johnny Temple   BASEBALL

Temple was one of seven Cincinnati Reds selected by fans to start the 1957 All-Star game. In an unprecedented move, Commissioner Ford Frick intervened and replaced two of the Reds—Wally Post and Gus Bell—with future Hall of Famers Mays and Aaron. Not that the change helped. In a wild finish in which both the AL and NL scored three runs in the ninth inning, the junior circuit prevailed, 6-5.

Seth Morehead   BASEBALL

A National Leaguer for all his five-year career, Morehead's lifetime major-league record was 5-19 with a 4.81 ERA. His batting average of .145 was more respectable, considering he was a pitcher. Even if you don't know anything about tiny Morehead State, you've probably heard of its most famous sports alum—longtime N.Y. Giants quarterback Phil Simms.

Cal Ripken, Jr.   BASEBALL

A two-time American League MVP and perennial all-star shortstop, Ripken is less than a season away from breaking one of the most coveted records in baseball—Lou Gehrig's streak of playing in 2130 consecutive games.

Leonard Marshall   FOOTBALL

Now reaching the twilight of his long career, Marshall has played on two Super Bowl champion teams—the 1987 and 1991 New York Giants. He came to the Giants from LSU, home of my friend and world-class motivator, Dale Brown.

Cullen Bryant   FOOTBALL

One of the few NFL running backs to play as long as 13 years, this superstrong Colorado alum was the Rams second-leading rusher during their Super Bowl season of 1979-80. In the championship game, Bryant averaged 5 yards per carry and 7 yards per reception in a losing effort against the powerful Pittsburgh Steelers. The Rams were ahead at the end of three quarters in that one, but Terry Bradshaw and his friends put up 14 unanswered points in the final period to win 31-19.

Steve Carlton   BASEBALL

A very durable pitcher, Carlton holds the major league record for most consecutive starting assignments (544). In 1972 he won an amazing 27 games—pitching for the last-place Phillies, would you believe? The rest of the Phils hurlers won only 34 games that same season. Carlton was not always so fortunate on his pitching outings. Once, he struck out 19 New York Mets in a game, only to lose, 4-3, giving up two long balls to the occasionally irrepressible Ron Swoboda. Carlton, incidentally, is second behind Nolan Ryan on the all-time strikeout list, having fanned 4,136 batters during his career. He was inducted into the Baseball Hall of Fame in 1994.

Carlton Fisk *BASEBALL*
Fisk holds the major league record for number of games caught—2,474. Many fans' most lasting memory of Fisk was the dramatic home run he hit off the foul pole in the 12th inning of the sixth game of the 1975 World Series, giving the Red Sox a dramatic 7-6 victory over the Reds. Unfortunately for the crowd out at Fenway, the Reds won Game 7.

Brian Dowling *FOOTBALL*
Ever hear of Dowling College? Well, no matter; this Ivy Leaguer didn't go there, choosing Yale instead. He quarterbacked the powerful, undefeated Eli team that ended its 1968 8-0-1 season with a 29-29 tie against Harvard. The upset prompted The Harvard Crimson to run the headline "HARVARD BEATS YALE, 29-29." One of Dowling's teammates in New Haven: Calvin Hill. Brian Dowling is not to be confused with Brian Downing, the baseballer, or the Father Dowling mystery series on TV.

Frank Howard *BASEBALL*
At 6-foot-8, this former Ohio State basketball center was one of the tallest players ever to take the field as a professional baseball player. Known as the "Capital Punisher" during the days he meted out justice with the Washington Senators—because of his mammoth home runs—Howard finished his career with 382 dingers, including 44 in both 1968 and 1970.

Virginia Wade *TENNIS*
Not a University of Virginia graduate, Wade is the last British citizen to win a Wimbledon singles title, beating Betty Stove for the women's crown in 1977. Among Wade's other career tournament victories were the 1968 U.S. Open, the 1971 Italian Open, and the 1972 Australian Open. Betty Stove, of course, went bookin' and cookin' her way to even greater glory by snaring a position on my All-Kitchen Team—alongside "The Refrigerator," William Perry, and Oiler DB Chris Dishman.

Kermit Washington *BASKETBALL*
Washington played his college basketball at American University without ever having played in high school. He led the nation in rebounding 1972 and 1973, and became only the seventh college player to average more than 20 points and 20 rebounds in a single season.

Dusty Rhodes *BASEBALL*
Despite a career .186 pinch-hitting average, Rhodes was the batting star for the New York Giants in their 1954 World Series sweep of the Cleveland Indians—a team that won 111 and lost only 43 that season. Rhodes' 10th-inning pinch home run won Game 1. Then his pinch single tied Game 2, and he later hit his second home run of the series in that game to give the Giants an insurance run. His pinch single in Game 3 sparked a three-run rally that led to another Giant victory.

Millard Hampton *FOOTBALL*
Hampton finished second to Don Quarrie in the 200-meter dash at the 1976 Montreal Olympics, with a time of 20.29 seconds. Hampton University is in Virginia.

4 | ALL-TERRAIN TEAM

Eligibility: Each team entry must include a first name, last name, nickname or sports expression that suggests a land feature.

Samples: Calvin Hill
          Rick Mount

And your nominees are ...

_____   _____

_____   _____

_____   _____

_____   _____

_____   _____

_____   _____

_____   _____

_____   _____

_____   _____

Dick's Picks
All-Terrain Team

Kenesaw "Mountain" Landis   *COMMISSIONER*

Rick Mount   *BASKETBALL*

Calvin Hill   *FOOTBALL*

Billy "The Hill" McGill   *BASKETBALL*

Damon Berryhill   *BASEBALL*

Pablo Mesa   *BASEBALL*

Wade Boggs   *BASEBALL*

Henry Marsh   *TRACK & FIELD*

Clarence Peaks   *FOOTBALL*

Chuck Noll   *FOOTBALL*

Darold Knowles   *BASEBALL*

Luis Arroyo   *BASEBALL*

Carroll Dale   *FOOTBALL*

Cliff Levingston   *BASKETBALL*

Houston Ridge   *FOOTBALL*

Pat Beach   *FOOTBALL*

Earle Meadows   *TRACK & FIELD*

Glenn Robinson   *BASKETBALL*

Kenny Fields   *BASKETBALL*

Rueben Sierra   *BASEBALL*

Jose Mesa   *BASEBALL*

Jerry Quarry   *BOXING*

Bill Sodd   *BASEBALL*

Note:
▼ For names that suggest foliage: See All-Foliage Team (page 24)
▼ For names that suggest natural materials: See All-Natural Materials Team (page 142)
▼ For names that suggest water: See All-Water Team (page 204)

Trivial Tidbits

Kenesaw "Mountain" Landis *BASEBALL*

Named the first Commissioner of Baseball after the 1919 Black Sox scandal, Landis was a former federal judge. Landis was strong willed and authoritarian. He once suspended Babe Ruth for a month to demonstrate his power, when the Bambino had defied one of his rules.

Rick Mount *BASKETBALL*

If you wanted the model shooter, you headed out to Purdue, baby, for Rick Mount. The first high school player to appear on the cover of Sports Illustrated, the long-range-shooting Mount led his Purdue team to the NCAA finals against UCLA in 1969. If he had played in the era of the three-point line, the numbers would be astounding. His professional career never approached his college success—where he scored over 32 ppg.

Calvin Hill *FOOTBALL*

The proud papa of Duke All-American and Detroit Piston Grant Hill, Calvin starred at Yale and for the Dallas Cowboys. In a dozen NFL seasons he scored 65 touchdowns rushing and receiving, while gaining 8,964 yards. He averaged 4.2 yards per carry. And, are you ready for this, Calvin's wife is a star as well. She was a roommate of Hillary Clinton at Wellesley.

Damon Berryhill *BASEBALL*

This Red Sox catcher and one-time Brave broke into the majors in 1987 with the Chicago Cubs. His biggest hit ever was a three-run homer in the first game of the 1992 World Series, which Atlanta won over the Jays. 3-1. The Braves went on to lose the series in six games.

Wade Boggs *BASEBALL*

After his first 11 seasons, this perennial all star's lifetime batting average (.338) was higher than anyone since 1960 who had played in the majors for at least a decade.

He won five American League batting titles in his first eight seasons with the Red Sox. Boggs would be a great representative for the chicken industry because he loves chicken as much as he loves fastballs.

Henry Marsh *TRACK & FIELD*

Perennial U.S. steeplechase champion Marsh attributed some of his success to being able to train at high altitude in Utah. This seeming advantage, however, did not help him during the 1983 World Championships. He tripped over the last barrier, thereby costing himself a chance for a medal. Bad luck continued to dog him. Despite being the favorite to win the gold in the 1984 Olympics, he faded and finished well behind the leaders.

Clarence Peaks *FOOTBALL*

Peaks played on the last Philadelphia Eagles team to win the NFL's championship game, defeating the Vince Lombardi-coached Green Bay Packers 17-13 in 1960. That game was also memorable because it was the last NFL game in which a player—Eagle center and linebacker Chuck Bednarik—played the entire contest on both offense and defense. In that championship season, Peaks led his team during the 12-game campaign in rushing, gaining 465 yards while averaging 5.4 yards per carry. For his nine-year career, he scored 24 touchdowns while accounting for almost 5,500 yards rushing and receiving.

Chuck Noll *FOOTBALL*

As in the "grassy knoll," baby. During Noll's first season as head coach of the Pittsburgh Steelers—a team he would eventually lead to four Super Bowl victories—his record was 1-13. The Steelers won their first game, then hit the canvas 13 straight times. That 1969 team featured future stars Joe Greene, L.C. Greenwood, Roy Jefferson, and Ray Mansfield. From 1972 to 1976, his Steelers won 53 regular season games and lost only 14.

Luis Arroyo BASEBALL
Okay, if you're not from the southwest, you may not know what an arroyo is. My deskside Webster's defines it as a small steep-sided gulch with a nearly flat floor. Luis Arroyo, by contrast, was not a gulch but rather a man who drygulched hitters at the plate with a vicious screwball. He pitched eight seasons, primarily as a relief pitcher, often saving the day for Whitey Ford. He was a member of two New York Yankee World Series winners—1961 and 1962.

Cliff Levingston BASKETBALL
In a decade of NBA play, Levingston has served mostly in a reserve capacity—including his stint with the NBA Champion Chicago Bulls in 1991 and 1992. His field-goal accuracy is a little over 50 percent and he averages about seven points and five rebounds when coming off the bench.

Houston Ridge FOOTBALL
I know, the name sounds like a planned community in Upper Saddle River, New Jersey. But it's also the handle of a defensive lineman for the San Diego Chargers circa the late 1960s. While Ridge played for the Chargers, the team gradually improved its record from 7-6-1 to 9-5 (1966-1968). Unfortunately, the club was never able to put away an AFL Western Division championship, due to the presence of the more-powerful Oakland Raiders and Kansas City Chiefs.

Pat Beach FOOTBALL
A tight end during his 10 NFL seasons—spent with the Colts and Jets—Beach was used primarily as a blocker. He did catch 155 passes, however, averaging 9.6 yards per catch. If Beach were to get together with Raiders coach Art Shell and the fictitious Danny Ocean of The Rat Pack film *Ocean's Eleven*, the whole kit and kaboodle would make a good foundation for an All-Seashore Team.

Earle Meadows TRACK & FIELD
At the 1936 Berlin Olympics, Meadows won the pole-vaulting gold medal with a leap of 14 feet, 3 inches, in a competition that lasted over ten hours. Remember, these were metal poles, baby. No give. Competing in the same meet in 1937, he and his USC teammate—Bill Sefton—both cleared a world record height of 14-11. Together, the pair became forever etched in the history of sport as the "The Heavenly Twins."

Glenn Robinson BASKETBALL
"The Big Dog" led the nation in scoring during the 1993-94 college basketball season. Hey—Glenn Robinson to me is the most productive offensive baseline player to come into the game since the days of Larry Bird. The kid is an offensive machine who can put the big numbers on the board immediately in Milwaukee. Hey Glenn, lend me some cash, baby! Are you kidding me—this guy's got so much green he doesn't know what to do with it. But let me tell you, it'll be NBN, nothing but nylon, in Milwaukee. The Big Dog is a bona fide PTPer.

Rueben Sierra BASEBALL
Again I'll send you booking to your Webster's, where you'll discover that a sierra is a chain of mountains that suggests the teeth of a saw. Rueben Sierra, on the other hand, was one of the starting outfielders for the American League in the 1994 All-Star game. He has consistently hit over 20 home runs and driven in over 90 runs a season. The man could also make my All-Cold Cuts Team. Hey, does a Rueben Sierra sound like a fancy sandwich, or what?

Jerry Quarry BOXING
A popular heavyweight boxer, particularly with Irish fans, Quarry fought all of the top contenders of his day. Perhaps his most famous fight was against Muhammad Ali—when Ali returned from the 3½-year layoff caused by his much-publicized dispute with the U.S. Selective Service during the Vietnam War. Despite being rusty, Ali polished off Quarry in the fourth round with a TKO.

5 | ALL-FOLIAGE TEAM

Eligibility: Each team entry must include a first name, last name, nickname or sports expression that suggests some type of flower, shrub, ground cover, tree or term associated with foliage.

Samples: Ickey Woods
            Jacques Plante

And your nominees are ...

_____   _____

_____   _____

_____   _____

_____   _____

_____   _____

_____   _____

_____   _____

_____   _____

Dick's Picks
All-Foliage Team

"Tree" Rollins *BASKETBALL*

"Jungle" Jim Luscatoff *BASKETBALL*

"Jungle" Jim Rivera *BASEBALL*

Cliff Branch *FOOTBALL*

Stirling Moss *AUTO RACING*

Don Mossi *BASEBALL*

Forrest Gregg *FOOTBALL*

Ickey Woods *FOOTBALL*

Lefty Grove *BASEBALL*

Andre Reed *FOOTBALL*

Willis Reed *BASKETBALL*

Graig Nettles *BASEBALL*

Monty Stickles *FOOTBALL*

Cotton Fitzsimmons *BASKETBALL*

Pop Ivy *FOOTBALL*

J.R. Reid *BASKETBALL*

Pete Rose *BASEBALL*

Murray Rose *SWIMMING*

Bob Lilly *FOOTBALL*

Richmond Flowers *FOOTBALL*

Tom Flores *FOOTBALL*

Frank Budd *TRACK & FIELD*

Guy Lafleur *HOCKEY*

Ellsworth Vines *TENNIS*

Jacques Plante *HOCKEY*

Garland Boyette *FOOTBALL*

Trivial Tidbits

"Jungle" Jim Luscatoff   BASKETBALL
Playing nine seasons in the NBA as a reserve with the Boston Celtics, Luscatoff was a member of seven NBA Championship teams. He also came off the bench in the 1959 record-setting game in which the Celtics scored 173 points against the Minneapolis Lakers.

"Jungle" Jim Rivera   BASEBALL
Rivera was a highly regarded center fielder for the Chicago White Sox teams that—save for the pennant-winning team of 1959—consistently finished behind the New York Yankees in the 1950s and 1960s. Unfortunately, when the Chisox finally did get to overhaul the Yanks in 1959 and enter the World Series, Rivera was hitless in 11 at bats. The Series was won by the Los Angeles Dodgers in six games.

Cliff Branch   FOOTBALL
The speedy Branch once ran a 9.2-second 100-yard dash while at CU—the University of Colorado. He scored two touchdowns in the Oakland Raiders 27-10 Super Bowl win over the Philadelphia Eagles in 1981. Three years later, he caught six passes for 94 yards and one touchdown in Oakland's 38-9 Super Bowl triumph over the Redskins—the last time an AFC team has won the January classic.

Stirling Moss   AUTO RACING
Another speedster, Moss won over 40 percent of his races—194 out of 466—including 16 Formula One events, but he never won the world championship for an entire season. He is in the top-10 list of all-time Grand Prix drivers, right up there in the standings with Jackie Stewart, Graham Hill, and Niki Lauda—the latter a member of my All-Ear Splitting Team.

Don Mossi   BASEBALL
Mossi was the star relief pitcher for the 1954 Cleveland Indians team that won 111 of 154 games, posting a 6-1 record with 13 saves and a 1.94 ERA. You baby boomers from the Motor City will probably also remember him as part of the Tiger rotation that featured Jim Bunning, Frank Lary and Paul Foytack. Mossi lasted 12 years in the bigs, winning slightly over 100 games.

Forrest Gregg   FOOTBALL
Hey, if you look up the definition of an All-Rolls Royce lineman, you'll find Forrest Gregg's name. Elected to the NFL Hall of Fame in 1977, Gregg was an offensive leader on the great Green Bay Packer teams coached by Vince Lombardi and lasted over 16 seasons as a player. One of the great rushing clubs of all time, the Packers dominated other teams by controlling the ball. Later, Gregg became a head coach, first with Cincinnati and then with Green Bay.

Ickey Woods   FOOTBALL
Famous for his post-touchdown dance—the "Ickey Shuffle", a thing I remember looking like a cross between the foot movement a tennis player uses waiting on serve and a clip from *Night of the Living Dead*—Woods led the Bengals to the AFC title in 1989 by rushing for over 100 yards against the Bills and scoring two touchdowns. In Super Bowl XXIII, he was the leading rusher in the game with 79 yards on 20 carries.

Lefty Grove   BASEBALL
Between 1927 and 1933, Grove averaged over 24 wins per season for the Philadelphia Athletics, compiling a 31-4 record in 1931 and winning the first official MVP Award given by baseball writers. On one occasion he came on in relief against the Yankees and struck out Babe Ruth, Lou

Gehrig and Tony Lazzeri on just 10 pitches. Heat City it had to be, baby, to get it past those guys. Despite often losing his temper and subsequently throwing objects and punching lockers, he always was careful not to injure his famed left arm and hand.

Andre Reed FOOTBALL
This 10-year NFL veteran wide receiver has been a member of four Buffalo Bill Super Bowl teams—all of them coming up on the short end of that stick known as the scoreboard, I probably don't need to add. Reed's best season was 1989, when he caught 88 passes for 1312 yards for an average of almost 15 yards per catch. He is one of the few players from tiny Kutztown State to make an NFL roster.

Willis Reed BASKETBALL
Reed led his Grambling team to an NAIA title and then later captained the New York Knicks to two NBA titles (1969 and 1973). He also earned NBA Rookie of the Year honors in 1965 and was a member of the NBA All-Star team in each of his first seven seasons. In the final game of the 1969 NBA Championships against the Los Angeles Lakers, Reed took the floor hardly able to walk. He hit the first two shots from the field and used his defensive skills to slow down Wilt Chamberlain in a 113-99 New York victory. Many players should try to emulate this guy. He had courage, heart and spirit and was the backbone of Red Holzman's Knicks.

Graig Nettles BASEBALL
Here, we've got one of the all-time great keepers of the hot corner—a man whose outstanding defensive plays were largely responsible for the Yankees' 1978 World Series victory over the Los Angeles Dodgers. Nettles eventually broke Brooks Robinson's career American League home run record for a third baseman—finishing with 390 round trippers.

Monty Stickles FOOTBALL
Stickles, who played tight end for about eight or nine NFL seasons, kicked the extra point in Notre Dame's 7-0 win over Oklahoma in 1957, ending the Sooners NCAA-record 47-game winning streak. He played his pro ball out in the Bay Area with the 49ers.

Cotton Fitzsimmons BASKETBALL
Before becoming an NBA skipper, Fitzsimmons coached teams that won the National Junior College tournament on two occasions. In 1970—right about the time Lon Kruger was learning to shoot the rock in Manhattan, Kansas—Fitzsimmons led K-State to the Big Eight basketball title.

Pete Rose BASEBALL
Charlie Hustle—given the name by Whitey Ford—was one of the greatest ever. So great, in fact, that he appeared in the All-Star game (to which he was elected regularly) at five different positions over the years. His many records include being the major-league career leader for games played (3562), hits (4256), singles (3215), and at bats (14053). Pete Rose was born to play baseball. This guy, despite his off-the-field problems, belongs in the Hall of Fame for his many achievements.

Murray Rose SWIMMING
An Australian who competed in the 1956 and 1960 Summer Olympics, Rose twice won the 400-meter freestyle—just barely before Don Schollander came along to break all of his records. During Rose's grand career, he also won a gold and silver medal in the 1500-meter freestyle, and a gold in the 4x200-meter freestyle relay. One of the best ever in the water.

Bob Lilly FOOTBALL
An NFL legend, defensive lineman Lilly starred first for Texas Christian University in 1959 and helped it win a share of the Southwest Conference Championship. As a pro

on Dallas' Doomsday Defense, he was regularly double-teamed, but he still finished among league leaders in quarterback sacks. Down in Big D, he was Mr. First—the Cowboys' first draft choice, their first Pro Bowl selection, their first All-Pro, and their first Hall of Famer. He made the Pro Bowl eleven times and was All-Pro six straight years. In a word, a star.

Richmond Flowers *FOOTBALL*

Flowers, whose father was in the Alabama State Legislature, caused an uproar in his home state by choosing to attend the University of Tennessee. Would you believe, it's all depicted on celluloid in a made-for-TV movie? At the UT, Flowers excelled as a wide receiver and as both a sprinter and a hurdler on the track team. He played defensive back and wide receiver during his NFL career, shared with the Dallas Cowboys and New York Giants. By the way, I've just tossed you an easy layup for my All-U.S. Cities Team, which you'll be getting to in a few pages down the road.

Tom Flores *FOOTBALL*

Flores—Spanish for flowers—is one of the select group of NFLers to have been both a successful player and coach. He quarterbacked for about 10 years in the pros and coached for about 10 years—most of the time with the Raiders. Flores was among the league leaders in yards per attempt for 1960s quarterbacks. As the skipper of the Raiders, he led the team to two Super Bowls. He's now the head coach and GM of the Seattle Seahawks.

Frank Budd *TRACK & FIELD*

Budd copped the world record in the 100-yard dash in 1961 by running 9.2 seconds—shattering a standard that had stood since 1948. He finished fifth in the 100-meter event at the 1960 Rome Olympic Games, won by Armin Hary of Germany. Budd also had a brief career as an NFL wide receiver.

Guy Lafleur *HOCKEY*

As a junior-league hockey player, Lafleur once scored 144 goals in a season (including playoffs) for the Quebec Ramparts. As a pro in the '70s and '80s, he was a long-time star for the perennial NHL-power Montreal Canadiens. He also won the Hart Memorial Trophy, given to the NHL's MVP, in both 1977 and 1978. He holds the Canadiens career record for assists (728) and points (1,246).

Jacques Plante *HOCKEY*

The first NHL goalie to use a face mask, Plante played for almost 20 years—and holds the Montreal Canadiens record for most games by a goaltender (556). Plante got the idea of the mask from a fan who sent him a welder's mask to wear after he had his nose broken by a flying puck.

Mr. Earl "The Pearl" Monroe's patented shake-and-bake magic act, finished off with a velvet touch, dazzled fans and players alike for a dozen NBA seasons.

6 | ALL-PRESIDENTS TEAM

Eligibility: Each team entry must include a first name, last name, nickname or sports expression that is the same as or similar to a president of the United States.

Samples: Claudell Washington
Michael Adams

And your nominees are ...

_____   _____

_____   _____

_____   _____

_____   _____

_____   _____

_____   _____

_____   _____

_____   _____

Dick's Picks
All-Presidents Team*

Name SPORT	President (number)
Claudell Washington BASEBALL	George Washington (1)
Michael Adams BASKETBALL	John Adams (2) John Quincy Adams (6)
John Jefferson FOOTBALL	Thomas Jefferson (3)
Scotti Madison BASEBALL	James Madison (4)
Earl Monroe BASKETBALL	James Monroe (5)
Stu Jackson BASKETBALL	Andrew Jackson (7)
Steve Van Buren FOOTBALL	Martin Van Buren (8)
Harrison Dillard TRACK & FIELD	William Henry Harrison (9) Benjamin Harrison (23)
Wendell Tyler FOOTBALL	John Tyler (10)
Robert Taylor TRACK & FIELD	Zachary Taylor (12)
Greg Fillmore BASKETBALL	Millard Fillmore (13)
Billy Pierce BASEBALL	Franklin Pierce (14)
Buck Buchanan FOOTBALL	James Buchanan (15)
Lincoln Kennedy FOOTBALL	Abraham Lincoln (16)
Jimmy Johnson FOOTBALL	Andrew Johnson (17) Lyndon B. Johnson (36)
Travis Grant BASKETBALL	Ulysses S. Grant (18)
Hayes Jones TRACK & FIELD	Rutherford B. Hayes (19)
Garfield Heard BASKETBALL	James A. Garfield (20)

Arthur Ashe *TENNIS*	Chester A. Arthur (21)
Reggie Cleveland *BASEBALL*	Grover Cleveland (22, 24)
McKinley Boston *FOOTBALL*	William McKinley (25)
Roosevelt Brown *FOOTBALL*	Theodore Roosevelt (26) Franklin D. Roosevelt (32)
Morris Taft *BASKETBALL*	William H. Taft (27)
George Wilson *FOOTBALL*	Woodrow Wilson (28)
Tonya Harding *SKATING*	Warren G. Harding (29)
Calvin Hill *FOOTBALL*	Calvin Coolidge (30)
Melvin Hoover *FOOTBALL*	Herbert Hoover (31)
Truman Clevenger *BASEBALL*	Harry S. Truman (33)
Larry Eisenhauer *FOOTBALL*	Dwight D. Eisenhower (34)
Theodore Kennedy *HOCKEY*	John F. Kennedy (35)
Norm Nixon *BASKETBALL*	Richard M. Nixon (37)
Chris Ford *BASKETBALL*	Gerald R. Ford (38)
Joe Carter *BASEBALL*	Jimmy Carter (39)
Phil Regan *BASEBALL*	Ronald Reagan (40)
George Bush *BASEBALL*	George Bush (41)
Curtis McClinton *FOOTBALL*	Bill Clinton (42)

* Because of the prodding of my publisher, Masters Press, to keep this book under 10,000 pages, I've supplied the name of only one athlete for each presidental surname. You know, I'll bet you could probably come up with enough Jacksons and Johnsons to staff an All-Jackson Team or an All-Johnson Team. Hmmm, let's see ... Magic Johnson, Gus Johnson, Walter "The Big Train" Johnson, Howard Johnson, Davey Johnson, Randy Johnson, Avery Johnson, Billy "White Shoes" Johnson, John Henry Johnson, ...

Trivial Tidbits

Claudell Washington *BASEBALL*
Claudell Washington spent 16 years in baseball, his best years coming with the A's in the early 70s. For his career, he finished with a .279 batting average—not bad.

Michael Adams *BASKETBALL*
In his seven-year NBA career, spent among several clubs, Adams put up over 2300 three-point field-goal attempts and was successful about a third of the time. He holds the NBA record for most consecutive games making a three-point shot.

John Jefferson *FOOTBALL*
Jefferson, who averaged more than 16 yards per NFL reception, once made such a spectacular grab against college rival Arizona that Arizona State fans still refer to it as "The Catch" (not to be confused with the famous Dwight Clark reception of the same name).

Scotti Madison *BASEBALL*
Madison played from 1985-1989 with the Tigers, Royals, and Reds, batting .163 in 71 games with one home run.

Earl Monroe *BASKETBALL*
Earl "The Pearl" Monroe was the master of the spin move. When you talk about Earl, you talk about spin, whirl, go to the glass with the rock, baby! When he was a guard at Winston-Salem College, he put up 1,329 points (averaging 41.5 points per game) during the 1966-67 season. They said he wouldn't be able to hook up with Walt Frazier, the Clyde, that they needed two basketballs. But forget it. The two came together and they made music. They were absolutely sensational together. "The Pearl" is one of the most special personalities ever to lace them up in the big leagues.

Stu Jackson *BASKETBALL*
Stu Jackson has both NBA and college experience. He coached the Knicks prior to the Pat Riley era and almost took the team to the NBA finals. He then went to coach at the University of Wisonsin and built up the Badger program before returning to the NBA with the new Vancouver team in 1994. He is looking forward to the challenge of leading his new team to the winner's circle.

Steve Van Buren *FOOTBALL*
Van Buren led the NFL in rushing twice during the 1940s and coached the Philadelphia Eagles to the 1948 and 1949 NFL titles. He is credited with leading LSU over Texas A&M in the 1944 Orange Bowl, scoring two touchdowns—one of them 63 yards.

Harrison Dillard *TRACK & FIELD*
Let me tell you what a hero can mean to a kid. The 1948 London Olympics gold medal winner in the 100-meter dash, Dillard was inspired by the great Jesse Owens, who gave him a pair of his running shoes when Dillard was 13 years old.

Wendell Tyler *FOOTBALL*
A former UCLA running back who starred in the 23-10 1976 Rose Bowl upset over Ohio State, Tyler averaged 4.7 yards per carry for his decade or so in the NFL, playing with the Rams and 49ers.

Robert Taylor *TRACK & FIELD*
Taylor was the 100-meter dash Olympic silver medalist in 1972. The race was marred by the disqualification of two U.S. world record holders—Rey Robinson and Eddie Hart—who missed the semifinal heat when their coach misunderstood the starting time. It was listed as 14:30 under the international time system, and the coach assumed 1430 meant 4:30 p.m.—not the correct 2:30 p.m.

Greg Fillmore *BASKETBALL*

The 7-foot-1 Greg Fillmore lasted only two seasons with the New York Knicks, averaging only 2.4 points per game as Willis Reed's backup.

Billy Pierce *BASEBALL*

During his 13-year career pitching for the Chicago White Sox, Pierce hit only 30 batters. His 18-year career record was 211 wins and 169 losses, with only 1178 bases on balls in 3305 innings. He was named to the major league All-Star team in 1956 and 1957, having won 20 games each of those seasons. In 1953 he pitched seven shutouts.

Buck Buchanan *FOOTBALL*

An outstanding defensive lineman and a member of the Kansas City Chiefs Super Bowl IV championship team, his stellar career lasted 13 NFL seasons.

Lincoln Kennedy *FOOTBALL*

Able to qualify for the All-Presidents Team with either his first or last name, this 325-pound offensive lineman may have weighed almost as much as Abraham Lincoln and JFK collectively did when they were U.S. presidents. But Kennedy can protect QB Rick Mirer in Seattle and create daylight for his running backs.

Jimmy Johnson *FOOTBALL*

It is said that Johnson is able to so thoroughly prepare his teams for a game because he combines a strong work ethic with an IQ of over 150. Jimmy led the Dallas Cowboys to victories in Super Bowl XXVII and Super Bowl XXVIII. He's now working for FOX, making big cash. He'll be on the most wanted list by every NFL team seeking to make a change and soon should be back on the sidelines.

Travis Grant *BASKETBALL*

Known as "The Machine" for his scoring regularity while at Kentucky State, where he averaged 39 points per game his senior year. Talk about creating offense, he once lit up the board for 75 points. Grant went on to play three NBA seasons.

Hayes Jones *TRACK & FIELD*

Winner of the 110-meter high hurdles in the 1964 Olympic Games at Tokyo, Hayes nipped U.S. teammate Blaine Lindgren at the tape in a close finish. The U.S. was expected to sweep this race, but the great Willie Davenport—winner in 1968 and member of my All-Furniture Team—was victimized by a leg injury and was eliminated in the semis.

Garfield Heard *BASKETBALL*

This 10-year NBA veteran may best be remembered for the buzzer-beating prayer he hit in the fifth game of the 1976 Celts-Suns matchup for the NBA championship—sending the game into triple overtime. Heard's Suns eventually lost, 128-126, in one of the most exciting games ever played. Heard's Hail Mary is forever immortalized as "the Heard shot around the world."

Arthur Ashe *TENNIS*

Talk about class, this guy was a terrific role model. He was an All-American at UCLA 1963-1965 and won the 1965 NCAA singles championship. Ashe was U.S. Clay Court Champion in 1967 and 1970, U.S. Open Champion (1968) and Australian Open winner (1970). He always handled himself in a class manner and consistently stressed the importance of education to young people, telling them, "When you have knowledge, you have options." Among other achievements during his exemplary career, Ashe was responsible for tennis' first code of conduct. Arthur Ashe lost his life in a battle with AIDS on February 6, 1993.

Reggie Cleveland *BASEBALL*
Reggie Cleveland's 13-year career was spent with the Cardinals, Red Sox, Rangers and Brewers. He compiled 105 wins with 106 losses, with a 4.01 ERA. His batting average was respectable for a pitcher—.211. Cleveland is one of only a relative handful of Canadians to play in the major leagues. He may be the only player ever from the town of Swift Current, Saskatchewan. This man also does double duty as a member of my All-U.S. Cities Team.

McKinley Boston *FOOTBALL*
Eligible also for the All-U.S. Cities Team, Boston played defensive end and linebacker for the 1968 and 1969 New York Giants.

Roosevelt Brown *FOOTBALL*
Hall of Fame offensive lineman for the outstanding New York Giants teams of the mid-1950s and 1960s, Brown was noted for his ability to throw downfield blocks for Giant running backs—one of them being Frank Gifford, now starring in broadcasting at ABC.

Morris Taft *BASKETBALL*
Taft played alongside future NBA star Willie Naulls on the 1955-56 UCLA team that was the 53rd consecutive victim of Bill Russell's San Francisco Dons. The Bruins lost to the Dons 72-61 in the opening round of the 1956 NCAA Tournament, despite 16 points each from Taft and Naulls.

George Wilson *FOOTBALL*
Longtime holder of the NFL record for the longest return with a recovered fumble, Wilson can thank the legendary Jim Thorpe for his limelight. Thorpe coughed the pigskin up at the 2-yard line, then chased Wilson, in vain, for 98 yards.

Tonya Harding *SKATING*
Harding was suspended for life by the U.S. Olympic Commitee and stripped of her 1993 U.S. Figure Skating Championship because of her involvement in the deliberate injury to skater Nancy Kerrigan. For this Teapot Dome of the sports world, she also makes my All-Scandals Team.

Melvin Hoover *FOOTBALL*
Former Arizona State wide receiver Hoover played three years with the Philadelphia Eagles and one with the Detroit Lions. He finished his career with 16 receptions and an astounding 22.8 yards per catch.

Truman Clevenger *BASEBALL*
Clevenger was fortunate to be a member of two World Series Championship teams— the 1961 and 1962 New York Yankees. Game 7 of the 1962 series had a great ending. San Francisco slugger and Hall of Famer Willie McCovey was batting with two outs and the bases loaded with his team trailing 1-0. He hit the ball hard, but Yankee second baseman Bobby Richardson snared the line drive and the Bronx Bombers had another World Series victory.

Larry Eisenhauer *FOOTBALL*
Boston College alumnus Eisenhauer played nine seasons with the Boston Patriots as a defensive end. When I was considering who to pencil in here, it was neck-and-neck between Eisenhauer and former baseballer Ike Delock.

Theodore Kennedy *HOCKEY*
This Ted is a Hall of Fame forward who won the Hart MVP Trophy in 1955, playing his last full season in the NHL. His entire 15-year career was with the Toronto Maple Leafs.

Norm Nixon *BASKETBALL*
Nixon arrived on the Laker scene after a scintillating career at Duquesne University. A clutch shooter and longtime Laker, Nixon averaged almost 18 points per game in almost 60 NBA playoff games. He was replaced in the Laker lineup by Byron Scott, a

shoo-in for my All-Poets Team. And, hey, get a load of this—there was a guy who played baseball in the early part of the century named Sam Agnew. Do we have the makings of an All-Watergate Team here or what?

Chris Ford *BASKETBALL*
Ford was a Villanova guard who had a brilliant career under Jack Kraft with the Wildcats. His NBA playing career lasted about seven years, and he went on to even greater prominence as an NBA coach. I had the pleasure of coaching Chris with the Pistons before he was traded to the Boston Celtics. This was a monumental mistake as we traded Chris for Earl Tatum. Chris played a major role with the Celtics as a player, which led to his present position as their head coach.

Joe Carter *BASEBALL*
Carter became the second player to hit a home run that ended a World Series, taking Mitch Williams downtown in Game 6 of the 1993 fall classic. Bill Mazeroski of the 1960 Pittsburgh Pirates was the other player.

In 1991 Carter became the first major leaguer to knock in 100 RBIs in three consecutive seasons with three different teams.

Phil Regan *BASEBALL*
I really am tempted to stick the former President on this list, but the closest he ever came to sports legend was playing George Gipp on the screen. Phil Regan, known as "The Vulture," spent most of his career in Detroit. Then he was traded to the Dodgers and had his best year ever. In 1966 he was 14-1, with a sparkling 1.62 ERA.

George Bush *BASEBALL*
This actual U.S. President captained the 1948 Yale baseball team, which finished second in the NCAA tournament that year. George Bush Jr.—his son—is part owner of the Texas Rangers.

Curtis McClinton *FOOTBALL*
A former Kansas Jayhawk who played fullback and tight end for eight years in the NFL, McClinton averaged 4.1 yards per carry.

When coach Red Auerbach lit up his trademark victory cigar on the Celtic bench, fans knew that the fat lady had begun to sing.

7 | ALL-COLORS TEAM

Eligibility: Each team entry must include a first name, last name, nickname or sports expression that suggests a color.

Samples: Vida Blue
Jim Brown

And your nominees are ...

_____   _____

_____   _____

_____   _____

_____   _____

_____   _____

_____   _____

_____   _____

_____   _____

Dick's Picks
All-Colors Team

Jim Brown *FOOTBALL*	Ed Pinckney *BASKETBALL*
Paul Brown *FOOTBALL*	Bill Sorrell *BASEBALL*
Roosevelt Brown *FOOTBALL*	Joe Lavender *FOOTBALL*
Bill White *BASEBALL*	Golden Richards *FOOTBALL*
Ted Green *HOCKEY*	Carmine Salvino *BOWLING*
Mel Gray *FOOTBALL*	Bobby Wine *BASEBALL*
Red Auerbach *BASKETBALL*	Chet Lemon *BASEBALL*
Harold "Red" Grange *FOOTBALL*	The Purple People Eaters *FOOTBALL*
Red Schoendinst *BASEBALL*	Orange Crush *FOOTBALL*
Larry Black *TRACK & FIELD*	Earlene Brown *TRACK & FIELD*
Joe Black *BASEBALL*	Sherman White *FOOTBALL*
Bob "Hurricane" Hazle *BASEBALL*	Sihugo Green *BASKETBALL*
Vida Blue *BASEBALL*	Hubert Green *GOLF*
"Le Grande Orange," Rusty Staub *BASEBALL*	Johnny Gray *TRACK & FIELD*
Pete Rose *BASEBALL*	John "Blue Moon" Odom *BASEBALL*
Jalen Rose *BASKETBALL*	Meadowlark Lemon *BASKETBALL*
Rosie Ruiz *MARATHON*	

Trivial Tidbits

Jim Brown FOOTBALL
When he had the pigskin in his hands, he was unbelievable, baby. He ran for 12,312 yards and scored 756 points in only nine pro seasons. His other career totals included a superb 5.2 yards per carry average, 262 pass receptions for almost 10 yards per catch. Ask Sam Huff about him. Huff, the big linebacker who played for the Giants, used to get on Brown all the time. Huff's favorite story involves one game where he yelled out, "You stink Brown. You stink." Well, Brown broke loose and Huff chased him down the field. As they got into the end zone, Brown turned around and said, "How do I smell now, Sam?" Brown was elected to the Hall of Fame in 1971.

Paul Brown FOOTBALL
One the most successful head coaches in the history of pro football, Brown is the only coach to have a team named after him. If you guessed "the Browns," you're right. He caoched Cleveland from 1950-1962, then led the Bengals from 1968-1975. He was called the "coach of the '50s," because he led the Browns to three NFL titles and four second place finishes. He was elected to the Hall of Fame in 1967. Of course, football isn't the only sport with famous head coaches named Brown. Take basketball and my good friends Dale Brown (LSU Tigers), Larry Brown (Indiana Pacers), and Hubie Brown (onetime Knick coach).

Bill White BASEBALL
Currently National League President, White was an outstanding fielder and a good hitter, finishing his career with a .286 batting average. He was in one World Series—1964—which his St. Louis Cards bested the Yanks, four games to three. Bob Gibson shut the Bombers down off the mound in that Series, while Tim McCarver wielded the heavy lumber from the plate. White batted .303 that season.

Mel Gray FOOTBALL
A swift and feared wide receiver, Gray played a dozen NFL seasons with the mavens of mediocrity, the St. Louis Cardinals. Always a deep threat, Gray averaged 18.9 yards per reception.

Red Auerbach BASKETBALL
If anyone is Mr. Boston Celtic, it's Red Auerbach. In his 16 NBA seasons as the Beantowner's coach, Auerbach's teams won nine NBA titles. He delighted in lighting up a cigar during a game, when he believed a Celtic victory was inevitable. Legend has it that forward-center Mel Counts sat near Auerbach on the bench so much one season that he practically developed a smoker's hack.

Harold "Red" Grange FOOTBALL
Grange was *the* running back in college and professional football in the 1920s and 1930s. His achievements are legendary. In one college game, he scored four touchdowns and rushed for 265 yards—and that's only in the first 12 minutes, baby! During his senior year at Illinois he was persuaded to leave and help the struggling professional football league become established. Traveling the country for two months, his appeal was such that fans by the thousands came to see him play, and the new league gained financial stability. When asked to recall his fondest memory on the gridiron Grange modestly told of the time he held the ball for a teammate who kicked a 55-yard field goal. Yes, Red Grange was first class all the way.

Red Schoendienst BASEBALL
There were many highlights in Schoendienst's 19-year career. In addition to being second in the National League in hitting in 1953—.342 to Dodger Carl Furillo's .344—and appearing in three World Series, he won the 1950 All-Star Game for the National League by sending

one into the seats in the top of the 14th inning. He was such a good fielder that his teammates referred to him as "The Glove"—and deservedly so, as he set a National League fielding record for second basemen in 1956 by making only two errors while playing almost 100 games. One of baseball's best pinch hitters, he had a career .303 average and led the league in 1962 with 22 pinch hits in 72 attempts.

Larry Black TRACK & FIELD

Black won two medals in the 1972 Olympics—a silver medal in the 200-meter dash and a gold medal in the 4x100-meter relay. In the latter event, the team tied the then world record of 38.19 seconds.

Joe Black BASEBALL

Black's best season in the major leagues was his first. He compiled a 15-4 record with 15 saves, most of the wins coming out of the bullpen. His versatility and strength led to his being chosen to start three games for the Brooklyn Dodgers in the 1952 World Series against the Yankees. The Yanks won in seven, and Brooklyn fans would have to wait until 1955 for their own World Series celebration.

Bob "Hurricane" Hazle BASEBALL

Hazle was brought up to the majors by the Milwaukee Braves at the end of the 1958 season. In 41 games he was a sensation. He hit .403 with seven home runs and 27 RBIs, while scoring 26 runs. Hazle played two more seasons in the big leagues.

Vida Blue BASEBALL

Blue won both the American League MVP and the Cy Young Awards in 1971. A few years later, following a contract dispute with Oakland A's owner Charles Finley, Blue stated he would rather take a job with a plumbing-fixtures company than accept Finley's offer. He was promptly traded to the Giants. Blue went 18-10 his first year with his new team. For his career, Blue won

209 games and had 2,175 strikeouts in 3,344 innings. He pitched a no hitter in 1970.

"Le Grande Orange," Rusty Staub BASEBALL

Noted for being a gourmet cook, Staub acquired his nickname in Montreal. One of his most important years was 1973, when he led the weak-hitting Mets with 76 RBIs. The team took the powerful Oakland A's to seven games in the World Series before losing, with Staub driving in six of the 24 runs the Mets scored, while batting .423 for the Series. He lasted 23 years in the bigs, hitting .279 lifetime. Not bad for a guy who not only knows what "escargot" means but knows what to do with them in the kitchen.

Jalen Rose BASKETBALL

A tallish guard at Michigan who played in two NCAA Final Fours, Rose was one of Steve Fisher's Fab Five freshmen who reached the NCAA Championship game in 1992 and 1993. He had the ability to play three positions. He's now headed for the NBA with the Denver Nuggets.

Rosie Ruiz MARATHON

Perhaps inspired by the old Duke Ellington tune, Ruiz literally took the A train en route to qualifying for the 1980 Boston Marathon and "winning" it. In the New York Marathon held the previous October, a qualifying race for the 26-miler at Beantown, she "posted" a time of 2:56:29. Then came Boston. Two Harvard students claimed they eyeballed Ruiz coming out of the crowd and entering the marathon about a half mile from the tape, where her "time" of 2:31:56 would have made Ruiz the third-fastest woman finisher ever. When questioned by the press, Ruiz knew neither her split times or, for that matter, what "split times" meant. Then came an investigation into the qualifying time in New York. A photographer in the Big Apple said that she had seen Ruiz take a subway shortcut during the race, and a videotape check revealed she had never crossed the finish line. She was disqualified from both races.

Ed Pinckney   *BASKETBALL*

A little bit of a stretch for the color pink, but that's OK. Hey, it's my book, baby. Pinckney won the MVP Award in the 1985 NCAA tournament. His Villanova team (19-10 before the tournament and unranked) upset highly favored Georgetown (30-2 before, and rated No. 1) 66-64. Pinckney was flat out unbelievable in this game; he took it to the rim against Patrick Ewing. That's jamming with the best of them.

Vic Sorrell   *BASEBALL*

Sorrell played three big league seasons. He pitched only for the Detroit Tigers, 1928-1937, winning 92 games and losing 101 with 10 saves. Of the 216 games he started, Sorrell completed 95. Sorrell is both a color and a type of horse, so Mr. Sorrell is also a candidate for my All-Equestrian Team.

Joe Lavender   *FOOTBALL*

Nicknamed "Big Bird," the 6-foot-4 Lavender played ten years in the NFL as defensive back—with the Eagles and Redskins—and was one of the tallest players at his position during his career.

Golden Richards   *FOOTBALL*

This wide receiver out of the Lance Alworth mold, who did his college ball at Hawaii, played for the Cowboys and Bears in the 1970s. He scored 108 points in his pro career. One of his more memorable catches was in Super Bowl XII, when Dallas beat the Broncos—the first of Denver's four Super Bowl losses. In the fourth quarter, Richards caught a spectacular 27-yard pass from Robert Newhouse, who was on an option rolling left. It was the only score of the period. When the final whistle had blown, the Cowboys were on top, 27-10.

Carmine Salvino   *BOWLING*

Salvino was one of the all-time prime-timers out at the lanes. He holds the PBA tour record for highest score in 16 consecutive games, 4,015 pins, set in 1980. Now that's rolling—close to a 251-pin-per-game average.

Bobby Wine   *BASEBALL*

Wine was an excellent infielder who could throw out runners from deep in the hole. He batted .215 for his 12-year career with 682 hits. He played with the Phillies and the Expos and began managing in the big leagues in 1985 with the Atlanta Braves. His son, Robbie Wine, also played in the big leagues.

Sihugo Green   *BASKETBALL*

Green was a former Duquesne All-American—one of America's blue chippers. He was way ahead of his time, a slasher who was poetry in motion. He was graceful as could be. I used to love watching him floating in the air—he had hang time and could flat out shoot the J.

The Purple People Eaters   *FOOTBALL*

The Minnesota Vikings defensive line of Jim Marshall, Carl Eller, Alan Page and Gary Larsen, they were. This beefsteak quartet terrorized opposing quarterbacks while leading the Vikes into several Super Bowls in the 1970s. The team came away empty handed each time.

Orange Crush   *FOOTBALL*

In 1977, the Broncos experienced a surprisingly wonderful season under coach Red Miller, going 12-2 and turning a regular AFC cupcake into a perennial winner. Dallas castoff Craig Morton—NFL Comeback Player of the Year—had his best season ever, and the Denver defense—called Orange Crush by fans—had a banner year. Some of the more memorable members of that defensive squad were Randy Gradishar, Lyle Alzado and Louis Wright, all of whom went on to Accolade City. Despite that terrific turnaround season, the Orange were crushed by Dallas in the Super Bowl.

Mr. Marvelous Marv Throneberry graciously shouldered much more than his share of ribbing as the poster boy for the early Amazing Mets teams.

8 | ALL-FRUITS, VEGGIES, AND GRAINS TEAM

Eligibility: Each team entry must include a first name, last name, nickname or sports expression that suggests a fruit, vegetable, grain or seed.

Samples: Darryl Strawberry
Zack Wheat

And your nominees are ...

_____   _____

_____   _____

_____   _____

_____   _____

_____   _____

_____   _____

_____   _____

_____   _____

Dick's Picks
All-Fruits, Veggies, and Grains Team

Milt Plum *FOOTBALL*

Darryl Strawberry *BASEBALL*

Ray Berry *FOOTBALL*

Marv Throneberry *BASEBALL*

Bob Lemon *BASEBALL*

Chet Lemon *BASEBALL*

"Le Grande Orange," Rusty Staub *BASEBALL*

Peaches Graham *BASEBALL*

Deron Cherry *FOOTBALL*

Dave Bing *BASKETBALL*

Elijah Pitts *FOOTBALL*

Spud Webb *BASKETBALL*

Andy Bean *GOLF*

Bob "Butterbean" Love *BASKETBALL*

Cale Yarborough *AUTO RACING*

Zack Wheat *BASEBALL*

Johnny Oates *BASEBALL*

John Olive *BASKETBALL*

Rich Dill *BASKETBALL*

Jim Korn *HOCKEY*

Willy Mays *BASEBALL*

Pernell "Sweetpea" Whitaker *BOXING*

Trivial Tidbits

Milt Plum *FOOTBALL*

After a tough 9-7 loss to the Green Bay Packers in 1962, in which Plum's ill-advised, late-fourth-quarter pass was intercepted and returned 40 yards to the Lion 18-yard line—leading to the winning field goal—Plum went to the locker room with his Detroit Lion teammates. There, defensive tackle Alex Karras flung his helmet at Plum for costing the team the victory. And that wasn't the worst of it: the loss also meant the season. The Lions finished 11-3 to the Packers 13-1.

Darryl Strawberry *BASEBALL*

Did you hear about this? Darryl demonstrated his jump shot form for me in the clubhouse last summer. He said, "Dickie, check it out. I can stroke the J, baby. I played for Crenshaw High School." That super high school in Los Angeles produced so many outstanding guys, like Marques Johnson. Not only can Darryl stroke the J, he also knows how to really swing the lumber. Darryl was National League Rookie of the Year 1983 and led the league in slugging percentage with .545 in 1988. From 1983 through 1990, he averaged over 30 home runs per season and his 39 was best in the National League in 1988. A good clutch hitter, he has batted .333 in six All-Star game appearances.

Ray Berry *FOOTBALL*

Baltimore Colts wide receiver Berry caught 12 passes in the 1958 NFL title game with the New York Giants, helping the Colts to a 23-17 overtime win in what many people call the greatest football game ever played. Berry reportedly wrote to his mother every evening during the football season.

Marv Throneberry *BASEBALL*

Throneberry was one of the most memorable members of the original New York Mets. In one game, Marvelous Marv drove a ball deep between the outfielders with runners on base, hustling all the way to third—an apparent triple. The Chicago Cubs appealed by throwing the ball to first, and the umpire called Throneberry out for not touching the base. When manager Casey Stengel came out to contest the call, the ump told him not to bother—Throneberry had also missed touching second.

Bob Lemon *BASEBALL*

Winner of 207 games during his 15-year major league career with the Cleveland Indians, Lemon managed the 1978 New York Yankees team that won the American League pennant in a one-game playoff with Boston. The Yanks trailed the Sox by 14 games at one point in the season under Billy Martin. Following a falling-out with George Steinbrenner, Martin was let go, and Lemon was brought in. From there, it's straight up. Bucky Dent hits a three-run homer in the playoff game to win the AL East for the Yanks, and, after the Bombers drop KC in the ALCS, Dent becomes the World Series MVP as the Dodgers become the next victim. Yes, 1978 was quite a Cinderella for the Yankees and Bob Lemon deserves a lot of the credit.

Deron Cherry *FOOTBALL*

Much of the success of the 1986 Kansas City Chiefs, who finished 10-6 and made the AFC playoffs for the first time in many years, can be attributed to Cherry and his defensive backfield mates. Their blocked kicks and returns of interceptions for touchdowns won many games for the Chiefs.

Dave Bing *BASKETBALL*

A two-time All-American at Syracuse, where he teamed in the backcourt with current Orangeman coach, Jimmy Boeheim, Bing became an instant NBA success. A quick player, he was Rookie of the Year for the

Pistons in 1967, and, in the next season he became the first guard in 20 years to lead the NBA in scoring—averaging over 27 ppg. Bing was also the MVP of the 1976 All-Star game and finished his 12-year career with a 20.3 ppg scoring average. He still holds the Detroit Pistons single season scoring record with 2,123 points.

Spud Webb *BASKETBALL*

Despite measuring in at 5 feet 7 inches, Spud Webb was a star at N.C. State. As a pro, Webb has averaged five assists per game playing mostly in a reserve role and shoots about 50 percent from the floor. Webb has such great leaping ability that one year he won the NBA's Slam Dunk Contest.

Bob "Butterbean" Love *BASKETBALL*

After not being very successful with either the Cincinnati Royals or Milwaukee Bucks, Love rather surprisingly became an NBA star and the go-to guy for the Chicago Bulls under Coach Dick Motta. For his 11 NBA seasons, he averaged over 17 ppg—and over 25 ppg in both 1971 and 1972. As a child growing up in Los Angeles, Love practiced hoops by trying to throw an old stuffed sock through a barrel rim nailed to a tree.

Cale Yarborough *AUTO RACING*

As in the cabbagelike plant, kale, baby. Of all the competitors in the history of NASCAR, only Yarborough has won three consecutive overall titles (1976-78). He took the prestigious Daytona 500 four times.

Zack Wheat *BASEBALL*

Wheat was the first Brooklyn Dodger elected to the Hall of Fame. He was a lifetime .317 hitter over 19 seasons and was considered by Casey Stengel to be one of the best National League fielders ever.

John Olive *BASKETBALL*

A former Villanova Wildcat, Olive has something in common with Bill Walton—they both missed nearly all of the 1979-80 season with the San Diego Clippers due to injuries. While Walton would make a comeback, the same was not true for Olive, whose NBA career ended after just two seasons.

Rich Dill *BASKETBALL*

Dill played only one season of professional basketball with the Pittsburgh Pipers of the old ABA, on a team that sported Trooper Washington, Chico Vaughn and Steve Vacendak.

Willy Mays *BASEBALL*

As in "maize." One of the greats of all time, Mays is a man who needs no introduction. For his career he had 3,283 hits, 660 home runs (the third highest ever), scored 2,062 runs, and played in a record 24 consecutive All-Star games. He also holds the major-league career record for putouts by an outfielder—7,095. Who can ever forget the incredible, back-to-the-plate catch he made of Vic Wertz's fly ball in the ninth inning of the first game of the 1954 World Series? When asked to rate that particular defensive heroic, Mays replied that he merely caught fly balls and did not bother to rate his catches. Say hey?

9 | ALL-BEVERAGES TEAM

Eligibility: Each team entry must include a first name, last name, nickname or sports expression that suggests a type of beverage, a brand of beverage or a company that makes beverages (a brewery, say).

Samples: Charlie Waters (type of beverage)
Mike Schmidt (brand of beer)

And your nominees are ...

_____   _____

_____   _____

_____   _____

_____   _____

_____   _____

_____   _____

_____   _____

_____   _____

Dick's Picks
All-Beverages Team

Beverages:

Bobby Wine *BASEBALL*

Jarvis Redwine *FOOTBALL*

Larry Sherry *BASEBALL*

Norm Sherry *BASEBALL*

Anicet Lavodrama *BASKETBALL*

Howard Porter *BASKETBALL*

Pedro Borbon *BASEBALL*

Ricky Watters *FOOTBALL*

Charlie Waters *FOOTBALL*

Junior Coffey *FOOTBALL*

Ken Coffey *FOOTBALL*

Wes Stock *BASEBALL*

O.J. Simpson ("Juice") *FOOTBALL*

Tom Beer *FOOTBALL*

Bill Laimbeer *BASKETBALL*

Mickey Finn *BASEBALL*

Coco Laboy *BASEBALL*

Midori Ito *SKATING*

Theopolis ("T.") Bell *FOOTBALL*

Brands of Beverages and Beverage Companies:

Mike Schmidt *BASEBALL*

Stu Miller *BASEBALL*

Bud Harrelson *BASEBALL*

George Foster *BASEBALL*

Ernie Beck *BASKETBALL*

Bill Knickerbocker *BASEBALL*

Gussie Busch *BASEBALL*

Randy Bush *BASEBALL*

Sam Adams *FOOTBALL*

Jack Ham *FOOTBALL*

Bob Schafer *BASKETBALL*

Jacob Schaefer *BILLIARDS*

John Walker *TRACK & FIELD*

Carling Bassett *TENNIS*

Trivial Tidbits

Beverages:

Jarvis Redwine *FOOTBALL*
Redwine started his football career at Oregon State. When he signed a letter of intent, head coach Craig Fertig—a former USC quarterback great—remarked that while the Trojans once had "The Juice," the Beavers now had "The Wine." It was not for very long. Redwine transferred to Nebraska, where he was a standout.

Larry Sherry *BASEBALL*
This 11-year veteran of the majors won a total of 53 games. He was the MVP of the 1959 World Series, where the Dodgers polished off the White Sox in six games. Sherry was 2-0, with a 0.71 ERA and two saves. He was the Series MVP.

Anicet Lavodrama *BASKETBALL*
One of my all-time favorite names. It makes me think of bathroom adventure as theatre—like the anguish that might take place if your hotel ran out of hair conditioner, and you were at risk for split ends. Now if that's not lavodrama, what is? Anyway, before I get too far afield here, I should mention that Anicet was on the only Houston Baptist team to compete in the NCAA tournament. Anisette, incidentally, is a liqueur.

Junior Coffey *FOOTBALL*
Coffey's promising NFL career was cut short by injuries. He led the Atlanta Falcons two consecutive years (1966 and 1967), with exactly 722 yards rushing both seasons. For his career—in which he played about four full seasons—he accounted for over 2500 yards rushing and receiving and scored 15 touchdowns.

Ken Coffey *FOOTBALL*
Defensive back for the Washington Redskins 1983-86, Coffey has been one of only a handful of Southwest Texas State University players to make the NFL. While not noted for producing pro athletes, the Division II school once rescheduled final exams so that students could travel to watch their team compete in the NCAA Division II championship game. Coffey's rookie year was memorable—not only for his four interceptions but also for his playing on the winning team in Super Bowl XVIII.

O.J. Simpson ("Juice") *FOOTBALL*
The first NFL running back to rush for over 2000 yards in a season, the Bills' O.J. Simpson also possessed world-class speed. He once was a member of USC's world-record-setting 4x100-meter relay team. Running one of the legs was Earl McCullough, NCAA 110-meter high hurdle champion and former Detroit Lions wide receiver. O.J. rushed for 11,236 yards in his 11 NFL seasons, averaging 4.7 yards per carry. He scored 75 touchdowns, 61 by rushing. In June 1994, he was charged with the murder of his ex-wife Nicole and Ronald Goldman.

Bill Laimbeer *BASKETBALL*
Bill Laimbeer was one of the premier rebounders in the NBA during his tenure. He was also one of the biggest crybabies ever to wear a uniform. In fact, he made my All-Crybaby team. But let me tell you, he could also make the perimeter jump shot in the clutch and could do the little things that got his team to the winner's circle. He graduated from Notre Dame where he played under Digger Phelps before moving on to the NBA. There he played an integral part in the Detroit Pistons' NBA Championships in 1989 and 1990.

Mickey Finn *BASEBALL*
You think I'm making that one up, I'll bet. Finn played in the bigs in the 1930s—with the Dodgers and Phils—and had over a thousand at bats. A career .262 hitter.

Midori Ito SKATING
Spelling her name just like the liqueur—Midori—Japan's Midori Ito was a silver-medal winner in figure skating behind the U.S.'s Kristi Yamaguchi, in the 1992 Winter Olympic games at Albertville.

Theopolis ("T.") Bell FOOTBALL
"T" as in tea, in case you need a hint on this one. Bell spent 10 years in the NFL as a backup receiver, finishing with 136 receptions and a 17.5 yards-per-reception average. He was a member of the only two Tampa Bay Buccaneer teams to make the NFC playoffs (1981 and 1983).

Brands of Beverages and Beverage Companies:

Mike Schmidt BASEBALL
Schmidt is one of only three National League players to win the MVP award three times. The slugging Philly third baseman completed his career with 548 home runs, seventh on the all-time list. He holds the major-league record for most home runs in a season by a third baseman (48 in 1980).

Stu Miller BASEBALL
A noted junkball pitcher who relied on finesse rather than speed, Miller was one of baseball's top stoppers from 1952 to 1968—mostly with the Giants and O's—earning 154 saves. Two of his most infamous moments were serving up the pitch that Mickey Mantle hit for his 500th home run and getting blown off the pitcher's mound by a stiff wind during the 1961 All-Star game. Miller was, however, the winning pitcher in that latter contest.

Bud Harrelson BASEBALL
Harrelson was a relatively small shortstop who possessed a great throwing arm. He was instrumental in leading the New York Mets into the 1969 and 1973 World Series.

Harrelson was on Army Reserve duty during one of the most memorable of all Met games. His close friend—Hall of Famer Tom Seaver—pitched a one-hitter against the Chicago Cubs in 1969, a game in which Tom Terrific had his perfect game broken up by a single in the ninth inning. Harrelson could only watch on TV and cheer his friend on.

George Foster BASEBALL
Foster was the leading slugger on the Cincinnati "Big Red Machine" juggernaut of the 1970s. From 1976 to 1978 he averaged 40 home runs and 130 RBIs a season. In the sixth game of the 1975 World Series between the Reds and the Boston Red Sox at Fenway Park, Foster threw out Sox runner Denny Doyle in the bottom of the ninth inning to preserve a 6-6 tie. Boston eventually won the game in 12 innings, 7-6, but the Reds went on to win the Series in Game 7.

Ernie Beck BASKETBALL
Though only 6-foot-4, Beck led the NCAA in rebounding with over 20 boards per game in the 1951-52 season, playing for Pennsylvania. He played six years with the Philadelphia Warriors, but averaged only 3.2 boards per game.

Bill Knickerbocker BASEBALL
In his 10-year major-league career, Knickerbocker batted .276. His best season was in 1934, when he hit .317 for the Cleveland Indians.

Gussie Busch BASEBALL
Gussie Busch once owned both a sports franchise and a brewery. Busch, who died in 1989 at the age of 90, was the longtime owner of the St. Louis Cardinals and the Anheuser-Busch brewery. He often hit the highways in a 33-foot-long, Pullmanlike motor coach called "The Adolophus." The

coach also doubled as a floating gin-rummy game. When any stranger on board asked for a "beer" instead of a "Bud," Busch would say "You want a what?" The offending party was then asked to conform to one of Busch's rules: Pony up two bucks to the kitty.

Sam Adams   FOOTBALL

Sam Adams was a fine offensive guard for the New England Patriots from 1972-80. He teamed with John Hannah, forming one of the best offensive guard tandems in the NFL. His son, Sam Adams Jr., was an All-American defensive lineman at Texas A&M and was selected by the Seahawks in the first round of the 1994 NFL draft.

Jack Ham   FOOTBALL

Named like the celebrated beer from the land of 10,000 lakes, Ham was one of the great outside linebackers in pro football history. He played his entire college and pro football careers in the state of Pennsylvania—first for Joe Paterno's Nittany Lions and then for Chuck Noll's Pittsburgh Steelers. As a pro, he had 32 career interceptions and was present on four Super Bowl Championship teams with the Steelers.

Jacob Schaefer   BILLIARDS

During the late 19th century, well before Minnesota Fats and Willie Mosconi—Schaefer was largely responsible for the development of modern billiards tactics.

Superfamous now as the coach of the Bulls, Phil Jackson once played great "D" coming off the pine for the Knicks, grabbing and swatting away the rock with his Godzillalike reach.

10 | ALL-U.S. CITIES TEAM

Eligibility: Each team entry must include a first name, last name, nickname or sports expression that suggests a city in the United States. (Note: You may wish to limit your list to cities of a certain size or to include towns of any size in your home state.)

Samples: Tracy Austin (as in Austin, Texas)
Francisco Cabrera (close enough
for the city by the bay)

And your nominees are ...

_____   _____

_____   _____

_____   _____

_____   _____

_____   _____

_____   _____

_____   _____

_____   _____

Dick's Picks
All-U.S. Cities Team

Name *SPORT*	City/State
Dallas Green *BASEBALL*	Dallas, TX
Ralph Boston *TRACK & FIELD*	Boston, MA
Phil Jackson *BASKETBALL*	Jackson, MI
Chico Carrasquel *BASEBALL*	Chico, CA
Dwight "Bo Peep" Lamar *BASKETBALL*	Lamar, TX
Trenton Jackson *FOOTBALL*	Trenton, NJ
	Jackson, MI
Byron Houston *BASKETBALL*	Houston, TX
Wilbert Montgomery *FOOTBALL*	Montgomery, AL
Orlando Woolridge *BASKETBALL*	Orlando, FL
Tom "Hollywood" Henderson *FOOTBALL*	Hollywood, CA
Reno Bertoia *BASEBALL*	Reno, NV
Reggie Cleveland *BASEBALL*	Cleveland, OH
Earl Monroe *BASKETBALL*	Monroe, LA
Mark Macon *BASKETBALL*	Macon, GA
Raymond Chester *FOOTBALL*	Chester, PA
Alton Lister *BASKETBALL*	Alton, IL
Diego Segui *BASEBALL*	San Diego, CA
Dave Philley *BASEBALL*	Philadelphia, PA
Chuck Muncie *FOOTBALL*	Muncie, IN
John Stockton *BASKETBALL*	Stockton, CA
Cincy Powell *BASKETBALL*	Cincinnati, OH
	Powell, WY
Floyd Patterson *BOXING*	Paterson, NJ
Billy Casper *GOLF*	Casper, WY
Pat Sheridan *BASEBALL*	Sheridan, WY
Tracy Austin *TENNIS*	Austin, TX
Len Dawson *FOOTBALL*	Dawson, AK
Kellen Winslow *FOOTBALL*	Winslow, AZ
Tim Richmond *AUTO RACING*	Richmond, VA
Johnny Rutherford *AUTO RACING*	Rutherford, NJ
Troy Aikman *FOOTBALL*	Troy, NY

Eugene "Mercury" Morris	*FOOTBALL*	Eugene, OR
Lynn Shackleford	*BASKETBALL*	Lynn, MA
Lafayette Lever	*BASKETBALL*	Lafayette, IN
Greg Norman	*GOLF*	Norman, OK
Jim Everett	*FOOTBALL*	Everett, WA
Elgin Baylor	*BASKETBALL*	Elgin, IL
Gary Player	*GOLF*	Gary, IN
Gwen Torrence	*TRACK & FIELD*	Torrance, CA
Boog Powell	*BASEBALL*	Powell, WY
Vegas Ferguson	*FOOTBALL*	Las Vegas, NV
Kent Lawrence	*FOOTBALL*	Kent, CT
		Lawrence, KS
Caldwell Jones	*BASKETBALL*	Caldwell, NJ
Francisco Cabrera	*BASEBALL*	San Francisco, CA
Orlando Merced	*BASEBALL*	Orlando, FL
		Merced, CA
Dick Selma	*BASEBALL*	Selma, AL
Rudy York	*BASEBALL*	York, PA
Dave Hampton	*FOOTBALL*	Hampton, VA
Hiawatha Francisco	*FOOTBALL*	San Francisco, CA
Seth Morehead	*BASEBALL*	Moorhead, MN
Dave Logan	*FOOTBALL*	Logan, UT
Cortez Kennedy	*FOOTBALL*	Cortez, CO
Warren Jabali	*BASKETBALL*	Warren, OH
Nate Newton	*FOOTBALL*	Newton, MA
Quincy Watts	*TRACK & FIELD*	Quincy, MA
Wendell Tyler	*FOOTBALL*	Tyler, TX
Willie Davenport	*TRACK & FIELD*	Davenport, IA
Sterling Sharpe	*FOOTBALL*	Sterling, CO
Harry Carson	*FOOTBALL*	Carson, CA
Alan Page	*FOOTBALL*	Page, AZ
Kevin Mitchell	*BASEBALL*	Mitchell, SD
Walker Gillette	*FOOTBALL*	Gillette, WY
Carl Warwick	*BASEBALL*	Warwick, RI
Duke Carmel	*BASEBALL*	Carmel, CA
Frank Ramsey	*BASKETBALL*	Ramsey, NJ

Trivial Tidbits

Ralph Boston *TRACK & FIELD*
One of the great track and field competitors, Boston was the first long jumper to exceed 27 feet. He is one of two long jumpers—the other is Carl Lewis—to win three medals in consecutive Olympic games. He won the gold medal in the 1960 Rome Olympics, the silver four years later in Tokyo, and the bronze medal in Mexico City in 1968—finishing over 2 feet behind Bob Beamon's incredible jump of 29 feet 2½ inches jump. Beamon's leap broke the existing world record by almost 2 feet and stood for about a quarter of a century.

Chico Carrasquel *BASEBALL*
Having excellent range in the field, Carrasquel was one of the premier major-league shortstops in the 1950s—defensively at least—teaming with my All-Mammal Team guy, Nellie Fox, to form a superior double-play combination for the Chicago White Sox. Carrasquel played in the American League for 10 years with the White Sox, Indians, Royals and Orioles. For his career he had a .258 batting average with 474 RBIs and 1199 hits in 1325 games.

Trenton Jackson *FOOTBALL*
This ex-New York Giant and former track star is a double hit. In other words, he represents two cities—Trenton, New Jersey and Jackson, Mississippi. Other double hits on this list are Cincy Powell and Orlando Merced. If you're doing this book as a game, allow yourself double points on such names.

Raymond Chester *FOOTBALL*
As in Chester, Pa., baby—just a forward pass away from Philly. A dependable tight end who was able to go deep, Raymond Chester caught over 350 passes in his 12-year NFL career, for 48 touchdowns. He went out at the top, retiring just after his Raider team won Super Bowl XV.

Alton Lister *BASKETBALL*
Space-eater Lister—named like the city of Alton, Illinois—shot 52 percent from the field and averaged seven ppg and seven rebounds throughout his 1982-1992 NBA career. He was a shot blocker deluxe. Lister played his college hoops on a fine Arizona State squad that sported Byron Scott at guard.

John Stockton *BASKETBALL*
Hey—where were all the experts when John Stockton was being recruited out of high school? They said he wasn't good enough. He went on to Gonzaga. That's right. Everybody recruiting him said he was too small, too slow. Are you serious? Check it out. He has made it! One of the all-time greats. He is a 3D man. He drives, draws the defense and dishes off with the best of them.

Chuck Muncie *FOOTBALL*
Muncie's best and probably most exciting NFL years were those he spent with the San Diego Chargers, 1980 through 1984. As the main groundhog in the Air Coryell offense, opposing defenses had to respect the team's passing threat. In 1981, Muncie helped lead the team into the AFC Championship game by rushing for 1,144 yards. A prolific scorer, he finished his career with 71 touchdowns.

Cincy Powell *BASKETBALL*
This man gets double points for his name—Powell is in Wyoming, and we all know where Cincinnati is. Cincy Powell played professional basketball in the ABA for eight seasons with four different teams. He was a consistent scorer—in the 16 ppg range for both the regular season and playoffs.

Floyd Patterson *BOXING*
At age 17, Patterson took the gold medal at the 1952 Helsinki Summer Olympics in the

middleweight division. He won the World Heavyweight title in 1956, later lost it to Ingemar Johansson, and then became the first person to regain the title by beating Johansson in a rematch. After defending the title a few more times, he twice was knocked out by Sonny Liston, each time in less than 2½ minutes of Round One.

Tracy Austin *TENNIS*
Entering the professional tennis circuit at age 14, Austin became the youngest player ever to win the U.S. Open by defeating Chris Evert in 1979 at the age of 16. She won the Italian Open that year also and was the No. 1 ranked USA tennis player in 1980. In 1981 she won the U.S. Open again, this time besting Martina Navratilova. Unfortunately, after being named Associated Press Female Athlete of the Year while she was still a teenager, Austin had to retire from the sport at age 21, due to injuries. She is on her way to becoming the Bud Collins of the tennis-analyst world.

Troy Aikman *FOOTBALL*
The 1993 Super Bowl MVP, Aikman led his team to two consecutive Super Bowls. He is presently the 15th highest ranked quarterback in NFL history based upon his 1,191 completions in 1,920 attempts for 68 touchdowns. After the Cowboys won the Super Bowl for the second consecutive time in 1994, some practical jokester skulking around the town of Troy, Texas, changed the name of one of the town's road signs— visible from Interstate 35—to read "Troy Aikman."

Lynn Shackleford *BASKETBALL*
There is no city that I know of named Shakleford but their certainly is a Lynn, Mass. At UCLA, this 6-foot-5 forward played with Kareem Abdul-Jabbar on three consecutive NCAA Tournament-winning teams. He played just one year of professional basketball, though—with the Miami Floridians of the old ABA. He appeared in 22 games and averaged only 2.6 points per game.

Greg Norman *GOLF*
Norman has been one of the PGA Tour's leading golfers for almost a decade. He has won the prestigious Vardon Trophy more than once for his consistently low scores and is usually right near the top of the leader board. However, he has yet to win a major tournament. One of his most bitter losses came in the 1987 Masters, when, in a playoff with Larry Mize, he watched as the latter pitched a shot into the hole from over 60 feet away for a birdie. Norman missed his own 20-foot birdie putt, and is still waiting to earn his first green jacket—traditionally given to the Masters winner.

Gary Player *GOLF*
Winner of more than 100 tournaments worldwide, and the first foreigner to win the Masters, Player is one of golf's all-time PTPers. He brought home the bacon in nine majors—three Masters, one U.S. Open, three British Opens and two PGAs. He was easy to spot on the golf course, for he always wore black, saying it made him feel strong.

Rudy York *BASEBALL*
A strong first baseman for the Detroit Tigers who had over 100 RBIs six times, York set a record that many sluggers have tried unsuccessfully to surpass. In a single month—August 1937—he hit 18 home runs. Babe Ruth, with 17 in September of 1927, had the old record.

Fantastic. Unbelievable squared. Maybe the best ever. I'll never be able to say enough great things about Mr. Michael Jordan.

11 | ALL-COUNTRIES AND NATIONALITIES TEAM

Eligibility: Each team entry must include a first name, last name, nickname or sports expression that suggests a foreign country or nationality.

Samples: Michael Jordan (country)
Alex English (nationality)

And your nominees are ...

_____   _____

_____   _____

_____   _____

_____   _____

_____   _____

_____   _____

_____   _____

_____   _____

Dick's Picks
All-Countries and Nationalities Team

Countries:

Ken Spain   *BASKETBALL*

Mark Portugal   *BASEBALL*

Mel Israel   *BASEBALL*

Terry Holland   *BASKETBALL*

George Ireland   *BASKETBALL*

Doug France   *FOOTBALL*

Michael Jordan   *BASKETBALL/BASEBALL*

Larry Canada   *FOOTBALL*

Wilbur Holland   *BASKETBALL*

Nationalities:

"The Yankee Clipper,"
Joe DiMaggio   *BASEBALL*

Ned Irish   *BASKETBALL*

Francie Larrieu   *TRACK & FIELD*

Jap Trimble   *BASKETBALL*

Frenchy Fuqua   *FOOTBALL*

Alex English   *BASKETBALL*

Jake Scott   *FOOTBALL*

Dane Iorg   *BASEBALL*

Dutch Dotterer   *BASEBALL*

"The Dutchman," Norm Van
Brocklin   *FOOTBALL*

"The Flying Dutchwoman," Fannie
Blankers-Koen   *TRACK & FIELD*

Cornelius "Dutch"
Warmerdam   *TRACK & FIELD*

Turk Lown   *BASEBALL*

"The Mad Hungarian,"
Al Hrabosky   *BASEBALL*

"The Polish Rifle," Ron Jaworski   *FOOTBALL*

Jimmy "The Greek" Snyder   *VARIOUS*

"The Throwin' Samoan,"
Jack Thompson   *FOOTBALL*

Mike Brittain   *BASKETBALL*

Swede Halbrook   *BASKETBALL*

"The Italian Stallion,"
Johnny Musso   *FOOTBALL*

"The Flying Finn,"
Paavo Nurmi   *TRACK & FIELD*

"The Flying Czech,"
Emil Zatopek   *TRACK & FIELD*

Trivial Tidbits

Countries:

Ken Spain *BASKETBALL*

Spain was the starting center on the 1968 Houston team that upset UCLA 71-69 during the regular season. Spain averaged over 14 ppg in that terrific Cougar year, second behind The Big "E", Mr. Elvin Hayes himself. Sadly, Spain died of cancer at age 44.

Mark Portugal *BASEBALL*

As a free agent, Portugal signed a lucrative contract with the Giants last year. To split a geographical hair even further, the twosome of Mark Portugal and Ken Spain make my All-Iberian Team.

Mel Israel *BASEBALL*

Longtime Yankee announcer Israel was known to the radio public as Mel Allen. When excited about a play by one of the Yankees, Allen would often resort to his signature expression—"How about that?!!!" He's one of the rare sportscasters to have had his own day—Mel Allen Day was celebrated at Yankee Stadium.

Terry Holland *BASKETBALL*

Currently the Davidson College athletic director, Holland has also played and coached there. As a college senior in 1964, he was deadly accurate with his J's—his 63.1 field-goal percentage led the nation. He starred for Lefty Driesell and helped lead Davidson to a national ranking. Between his playing and coaching stints at Davidson, Holland piloted Virginia to an NIT title and to two NCAA Final Fours. As a coach, Holland was one of the classiest guys to work the sidelines.

George Ireland *BASKETBALL*

Ireland was a college star at Notre Dame, where he was a two-time All-American. Mr. Consistency, he never missed a practice or a game in college. He took his love for basketball into coaching and led Loyola of Chicago to the NCAA title in 1963, defeating—in overtime on a hoop by Vic Rouse—a Cincinnati team that had won the two previous NCAA championships.

Michael Jordan *BASKETBALL*

America's premier athlete, this acrobatic superstar dazzled them in the NBA when he led the Chicago Bulls to three consecutive championships before retiring. He also was a diaper dandy. He led the North Carolina Tar Heels as a freshman in 1982, hitting the jump shot to beat the Georgetown Hoyas in the NCAA final. He is currently chasing a dream and attempting to play major-league baseball as he works diligently to learn his outfield position and improve his hitting skills with the Chicago White Sox AA Birmingham team.

Nationalities:

"The Yankee Clipper," Joe DiMaggio *BASEBALL*

I remember watching this guy play. He was smooth as can be. He played so effortlessly that he made all the tough plays look easy. DiMaggio is holder of what may be the most difficult record for any major-league hitter to break. No, it's not Most Consecutive Years Pushing Mr. Coffee. It's that impossible 56-game hitting streak. DiMaggio was a great base runner, as well, and could go from first to third on a hit as fast as anyone who ever played the game in his day. He attributed his base speed between the corners to never looking at second base while he ran. When asked how he could pull this off without peeking, he responded that he knew before a game started where second base was and that, to his knowledge, it had never been moved. For his 13 seasons, he had 2,214 hits, was named American League MVP three times and won three batting championships.

Ned Irish BASKETBALL
A member of basketball's Hall of Fame, Irish founded the New York Knickerbockers in 1946. He was also president of the Madison Square Garden Corporation that promoted such events as the rodeo, the circus, track & field, and concerts in addition to basketball.

Frenchy Fuqua FOOTBALL
A Steeler running back circa 1969-76, Fuqua led the Steelers in rushing in 1971—just before the arrival of Franco Harris—and finished his career with 4,278 yards rushing and receiving. He was notorious for his outrageous attire. In fact, he may have been the guy that put the "O" in outrageous. One of his more memorable outfits sported high-heeled shoes with clear heels. In each heel he had a goldfish and water that was color coordinated with the rest of his ensemble.

Alex English BASKETBALL
Alex English was a scoring wiz. A 14-year NBA star, English averaged 21.5 points per game while scoring over 25,000 points for his career. From 1982 through 1989, he was elected to play in the All-Star game each year. Because he played on NBA also-rans, he only appeared in 10 playoff games, but he made the most of it by averaging 24.4 ppg. English still holds the Denver Nuggets' career scoring record (21,645 points), career assist record (3,679), and season scoring record (2,414 points).

Jake Scott FOOTBALL
Scott finished his NFL career (1970-1978) with 49 interceptions. Two of them came in Super Bowl VII and helped the Miami Dolphins to a 14-7 victory over the Washington Redskins. For his efforts, Scott won Super Bowl MVP. He was also on the 1972 Dolphin team that became the only NFL team to finish the entire season undefeated (17-0).

Dane Iorg BASEBALL
A utility player most of his career, Iorg averaged 45 hits per year. He played about half as much as his brother Garth, but had a higher batting average—.270 for Dane versus Garth's .258.

Dutch Dotterer BASEBALL
Dotterer played 107 games in five seasons as a backup catcher for the Reds, just prior to the arrival of Johnny Bench— a favorite on my All-Things You Find In A Park Team. For his career, Dotterer had only 74 hits.

"The Dutchman," Norm Van Brocklin FOOTBALL
Van Brocklin, one of the blue-ribbon quarterbacks of the '50s and '60s, led the Eagles to the 1960 NFL title. That year, he was the second-ranked passer in the league. He also punted 60 times for the club for an average of 43.1 yards. When Van Brocklin retired in the '60s he left the team in the capable hands of Sonny Jurgenson.

Cornelius "Dutch" Warmerdam TRACK & FIELD
Warmerdam set his first world record in the pole vault in 1940 and held it for the next 17 years. His best leap was 15 feet 7 3/4 inches—outstanding considering he used a metal pole. Despite retiring with a best leap that was 9 inches higher than the next best pole vaulter, he never competed in the Olympics. Not surprising considering there were no Olympic games in 1940 and 1944.

Turk Lown BASEBALL
Lown's 11-year career was mainly as a middle reliever. He compiled a lifetime 55-61 record and a 4.12 ERA, with more walks (590) than strikeouts (574). Although some consider his major-league record less than stellar, Lown did well in the White Sox's losing 1959 World Series effort, pitching a little over three innings and not giving up any runs.

"The Mad Hungarian," Al Hrabosky *BASEBALL*

Hrabosky pitched relief through most of the 1970s and early 80s, his glory years coming as a St. Louis Cardinal at the front end of his career—when he was one of the premier stoppers in the game. The way he visibly psyched himself up on the mound before and after each of his trademark blazing fastballs made him a fan favorite and always added drama to any contest in which he was summoned. Once, in a nationally televised game, he walked the bases loaded against the powerful Cincinnati Reds, then fanned the next three batters—including George Foster.

"The Polish Rifle," Ron Jaworski *FOOTBALL*

Jaworski—also known as "Jaws"—was a good quarterback, participating in 16 NFL campaigns and three Super Bowls. The Rifle finished his career with over 28,000 yards passing and 179 touchdown passes.

The Flying Finn," Paavo Nurmi *TRACK & FIELD*

Perhaps the greatest distance runner of all time, Nurmi competed in three Summer Olympic games (1920, 1924, and 1928), raking in a total of seven golds. His Olympic events included the 1500-meter and 5000-meter runs, the 10,000-meter cross-country run, and the 4x3000-meter relay. For his career, Nurmi set 20 world records in distances ranging from 1,500 to 20,000 meters. He also set a record in the one-hour run. In the Paris 1924 Olympics he won the 5000-meter run just one hour after winning the 1500.

"The Flying Czech," Emil Zatopek *TRACK & FIELD*

Zatopek dominated world distance running from 1948 to 1960. He was the only runner ever to win the 5000-meter run, the 10,000-meter run, and the marathon in the same Olympic games—a feat he achieved at the 1952 Helsinki Olympics. His times for the 5000-meter and 10,000-meter races set Olympic records, while his marathon time of 2:23:03.2 was a new world record. His training regime included running through the snow with heavy shoes or army boots.

Mr. Wally Moon swung a respectable stick in the nifty '50s, racking up a career 142 home runs and a sparkling .289 batting average.

12 | ALL-EXTRATERRESTRIAL TEAM

Eligibility: Each team entry must include a first name, last name, nickname or sports expression that suggests flight or something found beyond the earth's surface.

Samples: Bart Starr
John "Blue Moon" Odom

And your nominees are ...

_____   _____

_____   _____

_____   _____

_____   _____

_____   _____

_____   _____

_____   _____

_____   _____

Dick's Picks
All-Extraterrestrial Team

"E.T.," Willie McGee *BASEBALL*

"The Spaceman," Bill Lee *BASEBALL*

Don "Air" Coryell *FOOTBALL*

Wally Moon *BASEBALL*

John "Blue Moon" Odom *BASEBALL*

Sonny Jurgenson *FOOTBALL*

Buck Rodgers *BASEBALL*

Eugene "Mercury" Morris *FOOTBALL*

Bart Starr *FOOTBALL*

Raghib "The Rocket" Ismail *FOOTBALL*

Tom Kite *GOLF*

Greg Kite *BASKETBALL*

"The Flying Dutchwoman," Fannie Blankers-Koen *TRACK & FIELD*

Angel Cordero *HORSE RACING*

"The Avenging Angel," Bjorn Borg *TENNIS*

Len Gabrielson *BASEBALL*

Roman Gabriel *FOOTBALL*

Cosmo Iacovazzi *FOOTBALL*

Mars "The Planet" Evans *BASKETBALL*

James Jett *FOOTBALL*

Chet "The Jet" Walker *BASKETBALL*

Norm Van Lier *BASKETBALL*

"The Glider," Ed Charles *BASEBALL*

Danny "Lightning T" Buggs *FOOTBALL*

"Chocolate Thunder," Darryl Dawkins *BASKETBALL*

Trivial Tidbits

"E.T.," Willie McGee   *BASEBALL*

Nicknamed because of his uncanny resemblance to the not-of-this-world character in the Steven Spielberg move, E.T., McGee has been a steady and reliable player through the years. A fleet and dependable outfielder, he has batted almost .300 lifetime, with over 1,800 hits.

Don "Air" Coryell   *FOOTBALL*

Coryell took over as head coach of the San Diego Chargers in 1978 and was an instant success. His 1979 team set an NFL record for yards gained passing, and his 1980 and 1981 teams won the AFC Western Division title. Unfortunately, the high-powered "Air Coryell" offense was not complemented by a championship defense. So despite having one of the most aerially successful offenses ever seen in the history of the universe, the Chargers never made it beyond the AFC title game.

Wally Moon   *BASEBALL*

A fortunate turning point in Wally Moon's 12-year career came in 1959, when he was traded by the Cards to the Los Angeles Dodgers for Gino Cimoli. Although he would finish his career with only 142 home runs, Moon became an instant threat in the Los Angeles Coliseum, where the Dodgers were then playing their home games. Helped by a short left field—it was only 250 feet down the foul line—Moon hit three home runs in one game and 19 for the 1959 campaign.

John "Blue Moon" Odom   *BASEBALL*

Despite getting plenty of offensive support—he played on the 1972-73 Oakland A's World Series champion teams—Odom finished his 13-year stint in the majors almost even in the won-loss column, 84-85. He played part of his career before the designated hitter was introduced and hit 12 home runs.

Buck Rodgers   *BASEBALL*

Piloting the Milwaukee Brewers into the 1982 World Series, Rodgers has been far more successful as a manager than as a player—where he batted .232 lifetime and averaged about one home run per every 100 times at bat. The Brew Crew came close to beating the Cards in '82. They were up 3-1 in the sixth inning of the seventh game, but St. Louis lit up the scoreboard for another five runs and the World Series title.

Eugene "Mercury" Morris   *FOOTBALL*

Morris played alongside Jim Kiick and Larry Csonka on the 1969-76 Miami Dolphins clubs that won two consecutive Super Bowls (1973 and 1974). In 1972, he and Csonka set NFL history when they became the first two players in a single backfield to rush for over 1,000 yards in a season. Morris finished his career with an excellent 5.1 yards per carry average.

Bart Starr   *FOOTBALL*

Starr quarterbacked the great Vince Lombardi Green Bay Packer teams of the 1960s which won the first two Super Bowls. The team featured such NFL greats as Paul Hornung, Jim Taylor, Forrest Gregg, Willie Davis, Ray Nitschke and Herb Adderley. Starr was one of the last at his position to call his own plays. He wound up completing 57 percent of his passes and threw for 152 touchdowns in a 16-year career—playing on teams that relied heavily on the running game. His most famous play was sneaking into the end zone at the end of the 1967 NFL title game, in which the Pack beat the Cowboys, 17-14. Quarterback for the 'pokes that year—Dandy Don Meredith.

Raghib "The Rocket" Ismail   *FOOTBALL*

This wide receiver and kick returner is best remembered for his electrifying runs when playing for Notre Dame. In his last college game, he returned a punt that seemingly put Notre Dame ahead of Colorado in the 1991 Orange Bowl in the last minute of play. It was a spectacular run—almost the entire length of the field—with Ismail faking out defenders left and right and bouncing off of them. Thrill City, squared. Unfortunately, Notre Dame was penalized for clipping and the storybook finish was erased.

Tom Kite   GOLF
Kite was the first professional golfer to reach $5 million in tournament earnings. He long had a reputation for near misses in big tournaments but finally put all the nattering nabobs of negativism in their place when he won the 1992 U.S. Open. Over his career, he has been extremely consistent and has finished among the top 10 players about 20 times.

"The Flying Dutchwoman," Fannie Blankers-Koen   TRACK & FIELD
This Dutch Olympian competed in the 1948 and 1952 Summer Olympics. Her four gold medals in the 1948 Games were the most of any track and field athlete competing in London. She won the 100-meter dash, 80-meter hurdles and 200-meter dash, and she anchored the winning 4x100-meter relay team.

Angel Cordero   HORSE RACING
One of the all-time great jockeys, Cordero was involved in a controversial Preakness race in 1980 that provoked a storm of protest. Employing his aggressive riding style while aboard a horse named Codex, Cordeo appeared to guide his mount into the path of onrushing Genuine Risk. Some claim he even hit the opposing animal. Cordero's horse held on to win the race and he withstood the protest.

"The Avenging Angel," Bjorn Borg   TENNIS
Borg, a great baseline player, dominated men's tennis from 1974 to the early 1980s. He won five consecutive Wimbledon singles titles—a record—and the French Open six times—another record. Borg was Mr. Calm under pressure.

Len Gabrielson   BASEBALL
A utility player, Gabrielson was mostly used for defensive purposes. In his last season, 1970, he tied a major-league record for best season fielding average for someone who played in at least 40 games, 1.000. However, he didn't miss the cutoff by much—he was in 43 games.

Cosmo Iacovazzi   FOOTBALL
One of the rare Ivy Leaguers to make the NFL, this Princeton running back played only one season with the New York Jets, 1965. He was a role player, while most of the rushing real estate on the team was gobbled up by Matt Snell, Bill Mathis and Mark Smolinski.

Mars "The Planet" Evans   BASKETBALL
The 6-foot-10 Evans landed on the Houston campus before the astronauts made it to the moon. Unfortunately for Evans, it was just after Elvin Hayes had departed for the NBA and the team had lost its magic. The Cougars would still manage to post good records, but they did not become a threat in the NCAA tournament again until Hakeem and Clyde Drexler started to jam in the early 1980s.

13 | ALL-RELIGIOUS TEAM

Eligibility: Each team entry must include a first name, last name, nickname or sports expression that suggests a religious figure or term.

Samples: Edwin Moses
Lance Parrish

And your nominees are ...

_____

_____

_____

_____

_____

_____

_____

_____

Dick's Picks
All-Religious Team

Jesus Alou *BASEBALL*	Jose Pagan *SASEBALL*
Ivan DeJesus *BASEBALL*	Irv Cross *FOOTBALL*
Moses Malone *BASKETBALL*	Johnny Podres *BASEBALL*
Edwin Moses *TRACK & FIELD*	Bubba Church *BASEBALL*
Muhammad Ali *BOXING*	Dave Pope *BASEBALL*
Calvin Schiraldi *BASEBALL*	Jethro Pugh *FOOTBALL*
Alaa Abdelnaby *BASKETBALL*	Bucky Pope *FOOTBALL*
Harold Solomon *TENNIS*	Dave Concepcion *BASEBALL*
Dana X. Bible *FOOTBALL*	Kirk Baptiste *TRACK & FIELD*
Harold Abrahams *TRACK & FIELD*	Ron Rector *FOOTBALL*
J.V. Cain *FOOTBALL*	"Preacher" Rowe *BASEBALL*
Sid Abel *HOCKEY*	Ralph Bishop *BASKETBALL*
Yannick Noah *TENNIS*	Christian Laettner *BASKETBALL*
Isiah Thomas *BASKETBALL*	Evander Holyfield *BOXING*
Van Joshua *BASEBALL*	Luther Rackley *BASKETBALL*
Ralph Sampson *BASKETBALL*	Sonny Bishop *FOOTBALL*
Goliath Yeggins *BASKETBALL*	Mark Grace *BASEBALL*
Deacon Jones *FOOTBALL*	Howie Nunn *BASEBALL*
Art Monk *FOOTBALL*	Len Chappell *BASKETBALL*
Johnny Temple *BASEBALL*	Jim Abbott *BASEBALL*
Robert Parish *BASKETBALL*	Bob St. Clair *FOOTBALL*
Lance Parrish *BASEBALL*	The Immaculate Reception *FOOTBALL*

Trivial Tidbits

Jesus Alou   *BASEBALL*

Alou, one of three outstanding brothers to play in the major leagues, had one of the lowest walk percentages of all time. In 1968 he accepted passes to first base only seven times in 419 at bats. Now that's what I call conservative. You know—protect the plate and avoid having the ump point to the dugout with the lumber still on your shoulder. You couldn't fault Alou for his hitting, though—.280 lifetime. One of the highlights of his 17-year career came in September of 1963—his rookie season—when he started in the outfield for the San Francisco Giants with his older brothers Felipe and Manny. Collectively, the Alous racked up 47 years in the bigs.

Moses Malone   *BASKETBALL*

Malone was the most highly recruited high-school player in the country 20 years ago. He signed a letter of intent to play for Maryland, then changed his mind and entered the ABA. Once known as The Chairman of the Boards for his excellence at glass sweeping, he led the NBA in rebounds in 1982 and 1983. He was prolific at putting the ball in the hoop, as well. In 1983, when the '76ers whitewashed the Lakers 4-0 in the NBA finals, Malone was the MVP—an accolade that complemented nicely his second-straight regular-season MVP. One more amazing stat from his illustrious 20-year pro career: he fouled out only five times, yet he plays with big time tenacity.

Edwin Moses   *TRACK & FIELD*

One of the all-time great track stars, Moses dominated the 400-meter hurdles from 1976 until the 1988 Seoul Olympics, where he finished a suprising third. During his reign, he lowered the world record a number of times and won 122 races consecutively between 1977 and 1988. Interestingly, he was the only American male to win an individual running event at the 1976 Summer Olympic Games in Montreal.

Muhammad Ali   *BOXING*

Maybe the greatest fighter in the history of the sport, Ali's charge to immortality began with a gold medal in the light heavyweight division at the 1960 Rome Olympics. Then, in 1964, during his fly-like-a-butterfly-and-sting-like-a-bee period, he TKOed Sonny Liston and won both the World Heavyweight title and a solid place on my All-Poets Team. Three years later, when Ali was still the reigning world champion, he showed a heavyweight strength of conviction by standing up for his pacifist beliefs and stiffing Uncle Sam's military draft. He was stripped of his crown and declared ineligible to fight for over three years. Eventually, through a Supreme Court ruling, he was allowed in the ring again, where he hardly lost a stride, winning the World Heavyweight title twice more. In his prime Ali was Mr. Boxing—he is special, one of the greatest sports personalities of all time.

Calvin Schiraldi   *BASEBALL*

Schiraldi may be best known as the pitcher who was on the mound for the Red Sox in the sixth game of the 1986 World Series when the Red Sox fans' dreams of a championship were shot. It was the bottom of the 10th, two outs, and nobody on base for the Mets. The Sox, who had already won three games, were two runs up—a thin out away from winning their first World Series since 1918. But the true Red Sox fan knows better—defeat is always there waiting in the weeds and will defy all laws of probability. So then the Mets get three singles in a row. Schiraldi leaves and a wild pitch by Bob Stanley quickly ties the game. Mookie Wilson comes to the plate, hits a slow roller into the Twilight Zone between Bill Buckner's legs, and the rest is history. The Sox go on to lose in Game 7, and Schiraldi finishes the Series 0-2 and with a 13.50 ERA.

Harold Abrahams   TRACK & FIELD
Winner of the 100-meter dash in the 1924 Paris Olympics, Abrahams feats and motivations were distorted in the movie *Chariots of Fire*. But even Abrahams, if he were alive, would tell you that he never raced around the courtyard at Cambridge's Trinity College—that was Lord Burghley, a member of the 1932 British Olympic team and the winner of the 400-meter Olympic hurdles in 1928.

Sid Abel   HOCKEY
Abel spent 15 years in the NHL, with the Detroit Red Wings and Chicago Black Hawks. In Chicago, he was named player-coach. After more than 10 NHL seasons as a skipper, he became the St. Louis Blues general manager and quickly built the team into the best of the six expansion franchises that entered the NHL in the early 1970s.

Yannick Noah   TENNIS
In 1983, benefitting from years of coaching and encouragement from Arthur Ashe, Noah became the first French male to win the French Open in more than three decades. He ranks about 20th on the list of all-time tournament wins.

Isiah Thomas   BASKETBALL
Thomas had the ability to do it all from the perimeter. He was instant offense who could also create havoc defensively. Thomas showed he could play with the big boys early on in his life. In fourth grade, he was already the star of the eighth-grade team. After leading Bob Knight and the Indiana Hoosiers to the 1981 NCAA title, he left early to join the Detroit Pistons, where he played until 1994. There, he directed his team to back-to-back NBA titles (1989 and 1990). Thomas is the Pistons career leader in points (17,966) and assists (8,662), and he also holds the single-season record for assists (1,123). He is now serving as part owner and head of operations for the new Toronto Raptors.

Von Joshua   BASEBALL
During his 10-year career in the 1970s, in which he batted a respectable .273, Joshua played mostly for the Dodgers. One unusual aspect of his career numbers is that he hit more triples (31) than home runs (30).

Ralph Sampson   BASKETBALL
While he was at the University of Virginia, Ralph Sampson's teams won more games than any other major college power. Yet, they were victorious in only one major postseason tournament—the NIT. After Virginia, Sampson went on to Houston, where he and Akeem (now Hakeem) Olajuwon formed the mighty "Twin Towers" that led the Rockets into the playoffs in 1986 and 1987. Sampson played little thereafter. Due to his weak knees, his promising NBA career—which began with his being named Rookie of the Year—was cut short after eight years.

Deacon Jones   FOOTBALL
Jones was one of the "Fearsome Foursome" linemen that spearheaded the Rams defensive attack in the 1960s. A 14-year veteran who is said to have coined the term "sack"—to describe his plopping of quarterbacks—Jones was able to outrun many running backs. He was elected to the Hall of Fame in Canton in 1980.

Art Monk   FOOTBALL
Monk is the leading active NFL receiver, accounting for more than 10,000 yards in receptions. Always in top physical condition, he set an NFL record in 1984 with 106 catches, and in 1992, he set the all-time reception record at 847. Along with Steve Largent, Charlie Taylor, and James Lofton, Monk is widely considered as one of the top wide receivers in NFL history.

Lance Parrish   BASEBALL
No relation to Larry Parrish, whose career numbers as a major-leaguer are slightly better, Lance Parrish played 13 years in the

majors, mostly for the Detroit Tigers. In 1,523 games, he had 5,596 at bats and a .256 batting average.

Irv Cross *FOOTBALL*

Now a popular TV commentator, Irv Cross spent nine years in the NFL as a defensive back—mostly with the Eagles. He joined the team right after their championship season in 1960 and also ran back punts.

Dave Concepcion *BASEBALL*

Longtime shortstop for Cincinnati during their Big-Red-Machine period. Once—during a nationally televised game—Concepcion stepped into the batters box, blessing himself with the sign of the cross. Announcer Tony Kubek asked partner Joe Garagiola if he thought that making the sign of the cross helped. Garagiola allowed that it helped batters an awful lot, but only if they knew how to hit.

"Preacher" Rowe *BASEBALL*

One of the mainstays of the great Brooklyn teams of the early '50s, Roe won 78 games and lost only 25 from 1949 through 1953, going 22-3 in 1951. Careerwise, he was 127-84 with a 3.43 ERA. When asked how he pitched the great Stan Musial, Roe said that he liked to walk Musial and then try to pick him off first base.

Len Chappell *BASKETBALL*

This guy was a big time power forward who could clean the glass and shoot the J. He and teammate Billy Packer were on Bones McKinney's 1962 Wake Forest team, which lost the NCAA tournament semi-final game to Ohio State, 86-68.

Christian Laettner *BASKETBALL*

Laettner was the star of the Duke Blue Devils' NCAA championship season in 1992.

He made one of the most famous shots in the history of college basketball—a near-impossible buzzer-beater against Kentucky in the NCAA Regional finals. A picture-perfect pass combined with almost unconscious shotmaking by Laettner sent Rick Pitino's Wildcats packing back to Lexington. Then there was the buzzer-beater against Connecticut the year before ... Mr. Clutch, if ever any collegian deserved the title after Jerry West left the Lakers. As a rookie with the Minnesota Timberwolves in 1992-93, Laettner set a team record with 708 rebounds.

The Immaculate Reception *FOOTBALL*

One of the most bizarre plays in the history of pro football, it advanced the Steelers into the next round of the AFC playoffs in 1972 against the Dolphins. The play happened toward the end of Pittsburgh-Raiders play-off game when quarterback Terry Bradshaw threw a desperate downfield pass to one of his wide receivers. Both the ball and defender Jack Tatum got to the receiver at the same time. The ball then ricocheted into the waiting arms of Franco Harris, who caught it on a dead run and scooted it into the end zone. Extra point, Pittsburgh. Final score: Steelers, 13-7. Postscript: It was never determined whether the offensive or defensive player first touched the ball. If the offensive player touched it, the play would have been declared void back then. Some Raiders supporters claim that the referee ruling on the play first checked to see how many security people were on duty that day in Pittsburgh's Three Rivers Stadium. When he found there were not enough, they say, he ruled for the Steelers.

Mark Price was great at Georgia Tech but has been even better as a pro, thrilling fans and impressing yours truly with his hustle and his ability to bury the trey.

14 | ALL-MONEY AND BANKING TEAM

Eligibility: Each team entry must include a first name, last name, nickname or sports expression that suggests money, banking, income or wealth.

Samples: Dave Cash
Curt Schilling

And your nominees are ...

_____   _____

_____   _____

_____   _____

_____   _____

_____   _____

_____   _____

_____   _____

_____   _____

_____   _____

Dick's Picks
All-Money and Banking Team

Don Money *BASEBALL*

Eric Money *BASKETBALL*

Norm Cash *BASEBALL*

Dave Cash *BASEBALL*

Wayne Cashman *HOCKEY*

Ernie Banks *BASEBALL*

Carl Banks *FOOTBALL*

Willie Banks *TRACK & FIELD*

"Dollar Bill" Bradley *BASKETBALL*

Cameron Dollar *BASKETBALL*

Ken Singleton *BASEBALL*

Buck Rodgers *BASEBALL*

Buck Buchanon *FOOTBALL*

Anfernee "Penny" Hardaway *BASKETBALL*

The Nickel-Package Defense *FOOTBALL*

The Dime-Package Defense *FOOTBALL*

Curt Schilling *BASEBALL*

Mark Price *BASKETBALL*

Sterling Sharpe *FOOTBALL*

Julie Krone *HORSE RACING*

Franco Harris *FOOTBALL*

Cliff Richey *TENNIS*

Nancy Richey *TENNIS*

Hosea Fortune *FOOTBALL*

Fortune Gordien *TRACK & FIELD*

Andy Mill *SKIING*

Bobby Bonds *BASEBALL*

Leroy Hoard *FOOTBALL*

Chuck Knox *FOOTBALL*

Eugene Profit *FOOTBALL*

Lute Olson *BASKETBALL*

Trivial Tidbits

Don Money BASEBALL

After being traded from Philadelphia, where he began his time in the major leagues, Money had a steady career. His batting average, which had been in the .220s in his last two seasons with the Phils, consistently stayed about 50 to 70 percentage points higher for the next several years, which he spent with the Milwaukee Brewers.

Eric Money BASKETBALL

In his four NBA seasons with three different teams, Money averaged over 12 points and four assists per game. He had superb quickness and penetration ability, which made him extremely dangerous at the offensive end. In the mid '70s Money came off the bench for the Pistons when Bob Lanier—a man with two of the biggest feet in the history of the world and the captain of my All-Huge Shoes Team—was at center.

Norm Cash BASEBALL

A man born to hit, Cash hit 377 home runs throughout his career. However, this popular Detroit Tiger never finished first in the American League in home runs. Mantle, Maris and Killebrew were around in those years to pick up the home run title. Cash had a great season in 1961, leading the league with his batting average of .361. No relation to Johnny or Rosanne Cash.

Dave Cash BASEBALL

Dave Cash had a steady career of 12 years, batting a lifetime .283 during the regular season and .288 over the four National League Championships in which he participated. In the Pirates' 1971 World Series victory over the O's of Baltimore, Cash batted only .133, but—along with most of the team—was carried by Roberto Clemente and Manny Sanguillen, who between them had exactly half of the Pirates' 66 hits.

Wayne Cashman HOCKEY

A teammate of Hall of Famer Bobby Orr in the Canadian juniors and on the Boston Bruins, Cashman scored 28 points in 48 playoff games and was named to the Team Canada squad that defeated the Soviet Union team in an eight-game series (4-3-1) in 1972.

Ernie Banks BASEBALL

"Mr. Cub," whose on-field demeanor was so first class that he was never ejected from a game, did what no other shortstop has ever accomplished—he won consecutive MVP awards (1958 and 1959). In 1958 he hit 47 home runs with 129 RBIs, while the following year his numbers were 45 round trippers and 143 ribbies. He finished his career with 512 home runs—making him the greatest power-hitting shortstop of all time, and, for that matter, one of the best baseball players ever.

Carl Banks FOOTBALL

A solid-gold linebacker who played alongside one of the greatest linebackers of all time, Lawrence Taylor. Banks was one of the key defensive players on the New York Giants' 1987 and 1991 Super Bowl Champion teams. In Super Bowl XXI he made 10 solo tackles to lead the Giants over the Denver Broncos, 39-20.

Ken Singleton BASEBALL

After the New York Mets gave up on him in his second major-league season, Singleton went on to have an excellent career, most of it with the Baltimore Orioles. His best season was 1979, playing for the O's team that made it into the World Series—getting beaten there by the Willie Stargell-led Pittsburgh Pirates in seven games. That year, Singleton hit 35 home runs, drove in 111 runs, and hit .295. For his career, he had 2,029 hits and 246 home runs, and he batted .282.

Curt Schilling *BASEBALL*

Schilling, 1993 MVP in the National League Championships with the Phils and one of only a few professional athletes from Alaska, began his major-league career in 1988. Although he was only 18-22 in his first four pro seasons—playing for teams with losing records—he allowed only seven hits per nine innings and struck out twice as many batters as he walked.

Mark Price *BASKETBALL*

Price, star point guard for the Cleveland Cavaliers, helped Bobby Cremins establish Georgia Tech as a perennial top-20 collegiate power. As a pro, Price has habitually led the Cavs into the playoffs, where, unfortunately, they have been habitually dumped on their ears by the Chicago Bulls. He is the career assist leader for Cleveland and the single-season record holder for free throw percentage—94.8 percent.

Sterling Sharpe *FOOTBALL*

One of the leading wide receivers in the NFL today, Sharpe could make anyone's All-Grit Team. Playing the entire 1993 season with an injured foot which prevented him from practicing effectively, he led the NFL in receptions. With an average of about 70 catches a year for his first four years, Sharpe seems to be getting better and better with time.

Franco Harris *FOOTBALL*

One of the most durable running backs in NFL history, Harris led the Pittsburgh Steelers to four Super Bowl victories. His career totals include 12,120 yards rushing—a mark exceeded only by Walter Payton, Tony Dorsett, Eric Dickerson and Jim Brown—and a total of 91 touchdowns.

Hosea Fortune *FOOTBALL*

This wide receiver from Rice played only year in the NFL, for the 1983 San Diego Chargers. This was a Coryell-and-Fouts-era pass-oriented team that had 369 total aerial receptions, many of them caught by such greats as Kellen Winslow, Charlie Joiner, and Wes Chandler.

Fortune Gordien *TRACK & FIELD*

Three-time Olympian in the discus throw, Gordien won the silver medal in 1956 and the bronze in 1948. He set and then broke the world record on two other occasions. His best throw of 194 feet, 6 inches was the world record for 10 years.

Andy Mill *SKIING*

Although widely known today for being married to one of the all-time great tennis players, Chris Evert, Mill was America's best downhill skier for many years. At the 1976 Winter Olympics, he finished sixth in the downhill, 1.23 seconds behind the winner of that memorable race—Franz Klammer.

Bobby Bonds *BASEBALL*

Father of Barry Bonds—a member of my All-Jewelry Team—Bobby Bonds was a more than respectable hitter in his day (1968-1981), with 332 career home runs. He hit at least 30 home runs and stole 30 or more bases in the same season five times, a feat never before accomplished. He also won three Golden Glove awards during his 14-year career and had 1,886.

Chuck Knox *FOOTBALL*

Often a winner during regular-season play, this longtime NFL head coach is named like the fort where they store gold. At the beginning of 1994 he ranked sixth on the all-time list of winningest coaches in NFL history. His record for regular season and postseason games is 189-146 with one tie.

15 | ALL-MAMMALS TEAM

Eligibility: Each team entry must include a first name, last name, nickname or sports expression that suggests a mammal—including man.

Samples: Rob Deer
Stan "The Man" Musial

And your nominees are ...

_____   _____

_____   _____

_____   _____

_____   _____

_____   _____

_____   _____

_____   _____

_____   _____

Dick's Picks
All-Mammals Team

Ronnie Bull *FOOTBALL*

"The Baby Bull," Greg Luzinski *BASEBALL*

Bill "Moose" Skowron *BASEBALL*

Bob Moose *BASEBALL*

Ed "Moose" Krause *BASKETBALL*

Jim "Kitty" Kaat *BASEBALL*

Harry "The Cat" Brecheen *BASEBALL*

"The Kitten," Harvey Haddix *BASEBALL*

Joe Wolf *BASKETBALL*

Jimmy Foxx *BASEBALL*

Rick Fox *BASKETBALL*

Walter "Rabbit" Maranville *BASEBALL*

Rob Deer *BASEBALL*

Buck Williams *BASKETBALL*

Buck Buchanan *FOOTBALL*

Dick Tiger *BOXING*

The Hamill Camel *SKATING*

Clyde "Bulldog" Turner *FOOTBALL*

"The Big Dog," Glenn Robinson *BASKETBALL*

Carling Bassett *TENNIS*

Bill "Poodles" Willoughby *BASKETBALL*

Fred "Mad Dog" Carter *BASKETBALL*

Tim Bassett *BASKETBALL*

The Dawg Pound *FOOTBALL*

Ed Badger *BASKETBALL*

Bruce Seals *BASKETBALL*

"The Walrus," Craig Stadler *GOLF*

Allan "The Horse" Ameche *FOOTBALL-*

"The Italian Stallion," Johnny Musso *FOOTBALL*

Joe Morgan *BASEBALL*

Dave Philley *BASEBALL*

Gerela's Gorillas *FOOTBALL*

Joe Beaver *RODEO*

Paul "Bear" Bryant *FOOTBALL*

Harry "The Horse" Gallatin *BASKETBALL*

Bronko Nagurski *FOOTBALL*

Amos Alonzo Stagg *FOOTBALL*

Charles Mann *FOOTBALL*

Stan "The Man" Musial *BASEBALL*

Chuck Person *BASKETBALL*

Woody Peoples *FOOTBALL*

"The Human Eraser," Marvin Webster *BASKETBALL*

Ivo Van Damme *TRACK & FIELD*

Trivial Tidbits

Ronnie Bull *FOOTBALL*

What a great name for a running back! After leaving Baylor, Bull played nine NFL seasons with the Chicago Bears and one with the Philadelphia Eagles. For his career, he gained 4,701 yards rushing and receiving. In the 1963 NFL title game—a 14-10 win over the New York Giants—he was the Bears leading rusher with 42 yards.

"The Baby Bull," Greg Luzinski *BASEBALL*

In 15 years in the major leagues, Luzinski hit 307 home runs and batted .276. He led the National League with 120 RBIs in 1975, and was the league leader in strikeouts in 1977 with 140. In the 1978 National League Championship Series with the Los Angeles Dodgers, Luzinski brashly predicted that his team, the Phils, would win. Unfortunately, he misplayed a fly ball in the ninth inning of Game 3—with the series tied 1-1 and the Phillies ahead 5-3—which led to a three-run Dodger rally and a 6-5 victory. The Phillies went on to lose the series.

Bill "Moose" Skowron *BASEBALL*

The best years of Skowron's 14-year career were his eight seasons with the New York Yankees—seven of which the team played in the World Series. In the unforgettable 1960 fall classic against the Pittsburgh Pirates—the one in which Bill Mazeroski hit his famous homer—Skowron led his team by batting .375 and getting a dozen hits, the latter a feat that tied the Series record.

Bob Moose *BASEBALL*

Moose completed his 10-year career with a 76-71 record and a not-so-bad 3.70 ERA, all of it with the Pirates. His high point was a 14-3 record and 2.91 ERA in 1969; his low point was the 1972 National League Championship Series. The Pirates were tied in the bottom of the ninth inning of the fifth and deciding game against the Reds when Moose uncorked a wild pitch, allowing George Foster to score the Series-winning run.

Ed "Moose" Krause *BASKETBALL*

A great all-around athlete, some insiders claim Moose was the greatest Notre Dame athlete of all time. Krause won All-American honors in both basketball and football between 1931 and 1933. He coached basketball and football in college, compiling a 92-45 record at Notre Dame over six years before becoming athletic director. Krause started at tackle for the College All-Star team that tied the NFL-champion Chicago Bears 0-0 in the first such game in 1934. Krause recovered a fumble inside his team's 20-yard line to stave off a Bear scoring drive.

Jim "Kitty" Kaat *BASEBALL*

One of the most durable pitchers of all time, this likeable player turned television broadcaster pitched for 25 years in the major leagues. He finished his career with a 283-232 won-loss record and a 3.45 ERA, with three seasons winning 20 or more games. He is one of three pitchers ever to win 25 games in a single season and not get the Cy Young Award. (Juan Marichal and Mickey Lolich are the other two.) Kaat is also in the top 10 on the all-time list for number of games appeared in by a pitcher (898).

"The Kitten," Harvey Haddix *BASEBALL*

Haddix's 14-year career is footnoted by one of the weirdest happenings in the history of baseball. On May 26, 1959, he pitched 12 perfect innings of baseball for the Pittsburgh Pirates—only to lose the game in the 13th inning after an error, a walk, and a three-run home run by Joe Adcock of the Braves. But every cloud has its silver lining. While the pitcher may have cursed his luck for losing the game, the final result assured Haddix a lifetime of name recognition for an awesome pitching performance.

Jimmy Foxx *BASEBALL*

One of baseball's finest, Hall of Famer Foxx finished his 20-year career—virtually all of it spent with the Philadelphia Athletics and Boston Braves—with a total of 534 homers and 1,922 RBIs. He was consistently excellent throughout his pro lifetime, compiling a .325 average in the bigs and setting major league records for most consecutive seasons with 30 or more home runs (12) and most consecutive seasons with over 100 RBIs (13). In 1932 he hit 58 home runs, the strongest challenge to Babe Ruth's record prior to Roger Maris.

Walter "Rabbit" Maranville *BASEBALL*

Maranville played 23 years in the major leagues, 1912 to 1935, mostly with the Braves and Pirates. At one time he held either the National or major league records for number of seasons played, number of seasons played at shortstop, most chances by a fielder, most assists at shortstop, and putouts. His .258 batting average is lower than any other hitter in the Baseball Hall of Fame.

Buck Williams *BASKETBALL*

Williams has been a superior performer during his NBA career, which has lasted more than a dozen years. Not only has he averaged about 11 rebounds per game, but also his shooting accuracy exceeds 56 percent. He is one of the few players to hold career records for two different NBA teams—the New Jersey Nets (points and rebounds) and the Portland Trail Blazers (field goal percentage).

The Hamill Camel *SKATING*

This move was patented by figure skater Dorothy Hamill, on her way to an Olympics gold medal in the 1976 Games in Innsbruck, Austria. Don't press me for the technical details of how it's done or ask me to show it to you. All I can remember is that it involved some sort of spinning—double twists, double axles, and stuff like that. It reminded me of something that Earl Monroe might come up with down in the paint. Like the Pearl, Dorothy was grace personified.

Clyde "Bulldog" Turner *FOOTBALL*

In 13 years with the "Monsters of the Midway," mostly in the 1940s, Turner played five different positions for the Chicago Bears: center, offensive guard, offensive tackle, linebacker and halfback. He is a member of football's Hall of Fame and was selected a member of the All-NFL Team for the decade of the 1940s.

Bill "Poodles" Willoughby *BASKETBALL*

Willoughby is one of only a few athletes to go directly from high school into the NBA. He was so dominant as a high school player in Englewood, New Jersey, that he scored 46 of his team's 54 points in the state's Group III state championship game—despite being double- and triple-teamed.

Fred "Mad Dog" Carter *BASKETBALL*

One of the few professional athletes ever to attend Mount St. Mary's College, Carter averaged over 15 points per game during his eight-year (1970-77) NBA career. He was a tenacious defender on the court. Carter served as coach of the Philadelphia 76ers until recently being replaced by John Lucas.

Allan "The Horse" Ameche *FOOTBALL*

Ameche's six years in the NFL with the powerful Baltimore Colts were impressive: 44 touchdowns and an average 800 yards gained per season rushing and passing. Keep in mind that Ameche was around when the regular season was only 12 games. He will be forever remembered for scoring the touchdown in overtime in the Colts 23-17 triumph over the New York Giants in the 1958 NFL Championship. It was the first overtime game ever played and a contest that many call the greatest football game of all time.

Joe Morgan *BASEBALL*

A PTPer with power and grace, Joe Morgan was Mr. Electricity. A 22-year veteran (1963-84) and a key member of Cincinnati's Big Red Machine of the 1970s, Morgan finished his career third on the all-time list for bases on balls and seventh in stolen bases. He was one of the most powerful-hitting second basemen of all time, finishing with 268 home runs and having led the National League in 1976 with a slugging percentage of .576. He won five Gold Glove Awards, the NL MVP Award in 1975 and 1976, and was elected into Baseball's Hall of Fame in 1990. He is now an outstanding commentator for ESPN.

Paul "Bear" Bryant *FOOTBALL*

When you talk about Rolls Royce coaches, you talk about "Bear" Bryant. Bryant finished his coaching career with 323 wins, the most in NCAA college football history. Six times his Alabama team won or shared the national championship. They were always prepared to play the tough D—in 1966 they held opponents to 37 points for the entire season.

Harry "The Horse" Gallatin *BASKETBALL*

Between 1948 and 1958, Gallatin played 10 seasons with the New York Knicks and one with the Detroit Pistons. On that 1948 Knicks team was Butch van Breda Kolff, Bill Bradley's coach at Princeton, as well as Ray Lumpp—a guy who makes my All-Contours Team along with Slick Watts and Fuzzy Zoeller. At 6 feet 6 inches, Gallatin led the NBA in rebounding in 1954, averaging 15.3 per game. On two occasions he made the All-NBA second team.

Bronko Nagurski *FOOTBALL*

One of the most versatile and durable players ever in college, Nagurski was named to the All-American team as a fullback and defensive tackle. He led the Chicago Bears to consecutive NFL championships in 1932 and 1933 and became a charter member of the NFL Hall of Fame. One legendary tale about him is that he was asked to play at Minnesota after the coach, on a recruiting tour, saw him plowing a field without a horse. Another concerns a comment he made when returning to the huddle, just after bouncing off a number of would-be tacklers and crashing into a brick wall behind the end zone. Nagurski allegedly said, "That last guy hit me awfully hard."

Amos Alonzo Stagg *FOOTBALL*

Teammate of the father of basketball, Dr. James Naismith, Stagg himself introduced basketball to the University of Chicago. He also coached college football for 56 years at Springfield, Chicago and Pacific. A firm believer in physical conditioning, he never drank coffee or hard liquor, and he never smoked. He finally stopped coaching at the age of 98. Stagg was credited by the great Knute Rockne as developing all of "modern" (1920s) football's innovations. These innovations include the diagrammed playbook, the huddle, the man in motion, the onside kick, and the reverse. Teams Stagg coached won over 60 percent of the time, and he completed his career with 314 victories—a total surpassed only by Paul "Bear" Bryant. Stagg is a member of the National Football Foundation Hall of Fame.

Stan "The Man" Musial *BASEBALL*

One of the game's greats, Musial won the National League batting crown seven times in his 22-year career and had a .331 lifetime average. His best season was in 1948, when he hit .376. Among his other accomplishments were playing 3,026 games (5th all time), having 3,630 hits (4th all time), and driving in 1951 runs (5th all time).

Ivo Van Damme *TRACK & FIELD*

A little bit of a stretch, but "Damme" can be read as "dame," which counts in the mammal category. A Belgian middle distance runner, Van Damme won a silver medal in both the 800-meter and 1500-meter runs at the 1976 Montreal Olympics. He died not long thereafter in an automobile accident. In his memory there is an annual Ivo Van Damme Invitational Track Meet in Europe.

How can anyone ever forget Sid Bream, the former Pittsburgh Pirate, pushing the envelope with his tired legs in his pennant-winning run and slide to lead Atlanta past his former teammates in the 1992 NLCS? Talk about taking one for the team!

16 | ALL-FISH TEAM

Eligibility: Each team entry must include a first name, last name, nickname or sports expression that suggests a fish, crustacean, mollusk, any other type of sea creature or part of one, or anything related to fishing.

Samples: Kevin Bass (fish)
Kendall Gill (fish part)
Rich Caster (something
related to fishing)

And your nominees are ...

_____   _____

_____   _____

_____   _____

_____   _____

_____   _____

_____   _____

_____   _____

_____   _____

Dick's Picks
All-Fish Team

Sea Creatures:

Matt Fish *BASKETBALL*

Gus Fish *BASKETBALL*

Dick Bass *FOOTBALL*

Kevin Bass *BASEBALL*

Jerry "Tark the Shark" Tarkanian *BASKETBALL*

Jack Sharkey *BOXING*

Dizzy Trout *BASEBALL*

Tim Salmon *BASEBALL*

Chico Salmon *BASEBALL*

Jim "Catfish" Hunter *BASEBALL*

Clifford Ray *BASKETBALL*

Sid Bream *BASEBALL*

Wahoo McDaniel *FOOTBALL*

Galen Cisco *BASEBALL*

Shad Barry *BASEBALL*

Jack Chesbro *BASEBALL*

Gar Heard *BASKETBALL*

Ralph Garr *BASEBALL*

Sam Pollack *HOCKEY*

Mac Haik *FOOTBALL*

Jess Pike *BASEBALL*

Al Pike *HOCKEY*

Lip Pike *BASEBALL*

Bobby Sturgeon *BASEBALL*

Marlon Redmond *BASKETBALL*

Sterling Marlin *AUTO RACING*

Buster Crabbe *SWIMMING*

Katrin Krabbe *TRACK & FIELD*

Parts of a Fish:

DeWayne Scales *BASKETBALL*

Mohander Gill *TRACK & FIELD*

Kendall Gill *BASKETBALL*

"The Flying Finn,"
Paavo Nurmi *TRACK & FIELD*

Curtis Rowe *BASKETBALL*

Preacher Roe *BASEBALL*

Bob Kipper *BASEBALL*

Fishing Terms and Equipment:

Jack Fisher *BASEBALL*

Jay Hook *BASEBALL*

Valerie Brisco-Hooks *TRACK & FIELD*

Rod Kanehl *BASEBALL*

Rich Caster *FOOTBALL*

John Riggins *FOOTBALL*

Tug McGraw *BASEBALL*

Dock Ellis *BASEBALL*

Matt Snell *FOOTBALL*

Peter Snell *TRACK & FIELD*

Fly Williams *BASKETBALL*

Trivial Tidbits

Sea Creatures:

Gus Fish BASKETBALL

Fish was a catch of the day as a coach. In 25 years at the helm of Emporia State, his teams were 334-287. He was elected to the NAIA Hall of Fame. No relation to Hamilton Fish, U.S. Secretary of State in the 1800s and a guy who has one of the most protein-loaded names I've ever seen. If you can top Ham Fish, drop me a card.

Dick Bass FOOTBALL

In 1958, Bass, playing for the University of Pacific, scored 38 points against San Diego State. That's not a bad afternoon's haul for a guy that was destined to become one of the more respectable pro backs of the '60s. In 10 years with the Los Angeles Rams—back in the Roman Gabriel era of Tinseltown for those of you who are too young to worry about cholesterol—Bass gained 5,417 rushing yards, averaging 4.1 yards per carry. He scored 41 touchdowns rushing and receiving.

Jerry "Tark the Shark" Tarkanian BASKETBALL

Tarkanian was the longtime coach at Nevada-Las Vegas and before that, the coach at Long Beach State in LA. He had the unique ability to win with an up tempo style at UNLV, and he also won big at Long Beach State, where his teams played zone defense and ball control offense. In 1991, his UNLV Running Rebels took apart virtually everything that moved en route to an NCAA Tournament championship and a 103-73 shellacking of Duke in the final game.

Jack Sharkey BOXING

Sharkey fought three times for the heavyweight championship. He lost on a foul in 1930 to Max Schmeling, won the rematch two years later, and then lost in his first title defense to Primo Carnera in 1933.

Dizzy Trout BASEBALL

In a 15-year career, almost all of it with the Tigers, Trout compiled a 170-161 record with a 3.23 ERA. His best two seasons were 1943 and 1944, when the major leagues were depleted of talent by World War II. He led the American League with 20 W's in 1943 and, in 1944, in games started (40) and complete games (33). He had 27 victories in 1944, but teammate Hal Newhouser upstaged him with 29.

Tim Salmon BASEBALL

Salmon has been one of few players to be Rookie of the Year two years in a row. In 1992 he was rookie of the year in the minor leagues. That bought him a trip to the bigs, where he was American League Rookie of the Year in 1993. In 1993 he led the California Angels in home runs (31) and doubles (35).

Clifford Ray BASKETBALL

Led by small forward Rick Barry, Ray's San Francisco Warrior team won the NBA title in the 1974-75 season, shocking the highly favored Bullets in four straight. Ray (as in Manta Ray) was the starting center on the team. Just a couple of years earlier, he was the backup center to Tom Boerwinkle—on a tenacious but ill-fated Chicago Bulls team that you could bet your bottom dollar would lose in the playoffs.

Sid Bream BASEBALL

A longtime National Leaguer and respectable batter. Bream's crowning moment came in the 1992 National League Championship Series, where he scored the winning run for the Braves with two out in the bottom of the ninth in the seventh and final game. Talk about dramatics, Bream—who has had several leg operations and isn't exactly speedy—lumbered it in from second on a pinch-hit single by Francisco

Cabrera, sliding in a gnat's hair under the glove of Pirate catcher Mike LaValliere. That's what can make sports so exciting and so exasperating. Both teams had played roughly 1,500 innings to get to that point and the whole shooting match comes down to a split second.

Wahoo McDaniel FOOTBALL

In addition to playing linebacker for four American Football League teams during the 1960s, McDaniel also performed in the ring as a professional wrestler. A wahoo, incidentally, is a large, ocean-going game fish.

Galen Cisco BASEBALL

Joining the New York Mets in their second year of existence, Cisco compiled a 17-42 record over the next three seasons. He had little offensive or defensive support, as evidenced by his having a 3.62 ERA for 1964 but a 6-19 won-lost record. A cisco is in the whitefish family and is found in the Great Lakes and other parts of eastern North America.

Jack Chesbro BASEBALL

No jack mackerel, this Hall of Famer won 199 games in the early part of this century. His big statistic is winning 41 games in 1904, when he was with the Yankees. Nobody has won 40 since.

Sam Pollack HOCKEY

As director of the Montreal Canadiens farm system for 10 years before becoming general manager in 1964, Pollack helped build the powerful Montreal teams that won 15 NHL championships between 1954 and 1979—finishing runner-up three times during that period. No relation to another famous director, Sidney Pollack.

Al Pike HOCKEY

Pike played six NHL seasons in the 1940s, finishing his career with 42 goals and 77 assists.

Lip Pike BASEBALL

Although his nickname was "The Iron Batter," Pike hit only five home runs in a five-year career played between 1876 and 1887. He did, however, have a .304 batting average.

Parts of a Fish:

DeWayne Scales BASKETBALL

At Louisiana State, Scales was very versatile, playing three positions: small forward, power forward and guard. He had an excellent vertical leap and stroked the J in a very unique style, making it almost impossible to block. He was in the NBA for only three years, however, averaging 4.6 points per game while shooting only 42 percent from the field.

Curtis Rowe BASKETBALL

Between the dynasties of Alcindor and Walton, there was the Curtis Rowe-Sidney Wicks "mini-era" of UCLA basketball. In the NBA, the Celts teamed up Rowe and Wicks again, but the pair of forwards were not able to even remotely reproduce their championship college form. Ironically, by landing in Boston, Rowe and Wicks were sandwiched between two other historical dynasties: the John Havlicek era and the Larry Bird era.

Fishing Terms and Equipment:

Jay Hook BASEBALL

One of the original New York Mets, Hook struggled for three seasons with the team. For the 1962 and 1963 seasons he finished a combined 12-33 with an ERA above 5.00. For his eight-year career, he lost a little over twice as many games as he won.

Valerie Brisco-Hooks TRACK & FIELD

Brisco-Hooks turned in one of the great track performances in Olympic history at the 1984 Summer Games in Los Angeles. She won a gold medal each in the 200-meter dash, 400-meter dash, and 4x400-meter relay—setting an Olympic record in each event.

John Riggins FOOTBALL

John Riggins' long career as a running back for the New York Jets and the Washington Redskins finished with his having gained 11,352 yards rushing and scoring 116 touchdowns. He was the outstanding player in Super Bowl XVII, gaining 166 yards on 38 carries, as the Redskins beat the Miami Dolphins 27-17. The key play came in the fourth quarter on a fourth-down-and-inches play at the Miami 43-yard line. With his team losing 17-13, Riggins broke through the line and ran untouched into the end zone to turn the game in Washington's favor. At the height of his career, which was during the presidency of the guy who starred in *Bedtime for Bonzo* and has a wife named Nancy, the Redskins' strategy of letting Riggins carry the ball on big plays was referred to as Rigginomics.

Tug McGraw BASEBALL

If you've ever been fishing for any length of time, you've probably gotten a tug from a fish. This Tug may best be remembered for the "you gotta believe" phrase he popularized during the 1969 New York Mets' pennant drive. He finished a 19-year career 96-92—with a 3.13 ERA in 824 games—but he was even better in postseason play. McGraw had a 2-1 World Series record with a 2.11 ERA, along with three saves in nine Series games, helping both the Phils and Mets to a World Series championship.

Matt Snell FOOTBALL

Ever use a snelled hook? New York Jets running back Matt Snell gaffed the heavily favored Baltimore Colts in Super Bowl III, a 16-7 Jet triumph. He carried the ball 30 times for 121 yards, and caught four passes for 40 more. He scored the only Jet touchdown.

Peter Snell TRACK & FIELD

Peter Snell burst onto the world track scene when, as an unknown, he won the 800-meter run at the 1960 Rome Olympics in a time of 1 minute, 46.3 seconds—a full 2 seconds faster than the existing Olympics record. He was even better four years later in Tokyo, winning both the 800- and 1500-meter runs—the first runner to do so in 44 years.

Mr. David Cone—the man who inspired Coneheadmania—is presently finding everything up to date in Kansas City after brilliant stints in New York and Toronto.

17 | ALL-FOOD TEAM

Eligibility: Each team entry must include a first name, last name, nickname or sports expression that suggests a dinner entree, condiment or spice, dessert or snack.

Samples: Jack Ham
Dell Curry

And your nominees are ...

_____   _____

_____   _____

_____   _____

_____   _____

_____   _____

_____   _____

_____   _____

_____   _____

Dick's Picks
All-Food Team

Main Courses and Side Dishes:

Chili Davis *BASEBALL*

Stew Johnson *BASKETBALL*

Stu Miller *BASEBALL*

Jack Ham *FOOTBALL*

Johnny "Ham" Jones *FOOTBALL*

"Hambone" Williams *BASKETBALL*

Coot Veal *BASEBALL*

Joe "Turkey" Jones *FOOTBALL*

Bob Veale *BASEBALL*

Bernie Fryer *BASKETBALL*

Irving Fryar *FOOTBALL*

Coy Bacon *FOOTBALL*

Ray Lamb *BASEBALL*

Johnny "Lam" Jones *FOOTBALL*

Chris Hanburger *FOOTBALL*

Gerhard Berger *FOOTBALL*

"The Whopper," Billy Paultz *BASKETBALL*

Chico Salmon *BASEBALL*

Tim Salmon *BASEBALL*

Jerry Rice *FOOTBALL*

Grantland Rice *SPORTSWRITER*

Cedric "Cornbread" Maxwell *BASKETBALL*

Cheese Johnson *BASKETBALL*

Johnny Romano *BASEBALL*

Spices and Condiments:

Herb Elliot *TRACK & FIELD*

Pepper Martin *BASEBALL*

Benedict Cayenne *TRACK & FIELD*

Salty Parker *BASEBALL*

Bill Curry *FOOTBALL*

Dell Curry *BASKETBALL*

Aparicio Curry *BASKETBALL*

Sugar Ray Leonard *BOXING*

Sugar Ray Robinson *BOXING*

Wilmer "Vinegar Bend" Mizell *BASEBALL*

Scott Dill *FOOTBALL*

Pickles Kennedy *BASKETBALL*

Johnny "Jam" Jones *FOOTBALL*

Snacks and Desserts:

Peanuts Lowery *BASEBALL*

Pretzels Pezzullo *BASEBALL*

Cookie Rojas *BASEBALL*

Cookie Lavagetto *BASEBALL*

Cookie Gilchrist *FOOTBALL*

Pie Traynor *BASEBALL*

Willie "Puddin' Head" Jones *BASEBALL*

David Cone *BASEBALL*

Bob Moose *BASEBALL*

Levern Tart *BASKETBALL*

Candy Maldonado *BASEBALL*

"The Candy Man," John Candelaria *BASEBALL*

"Chocolate Thunder," Darryl Dawkins *BASKETBALL*

Duke Carmel *BASEBALL*

Trivial Tidbits

Main Courses and Side Dishes:

Joe "Turkey" Jones *FOOTBALL*

Jones played defensive end throughout the 1970s, mostly for the Cleveland Browns. In one game he picked up Terry Bradshaw and dumped him on his head. Bradshaw had to leave the game, the Browns won, and this and similar incidents eventually led to the "in the grasp" rule designed to protect NFL quarterbacks.

Bob Veale *BASEBALL*

Veale had an outstanding fastball. In his 13 major-league seasons he finished with an ERA of 3.08, once leading the National League in strikeouts. However, his career mark was only 120-95. The book on him was that if your team could stay close, he would make mistakes in the late innings and cost himself the W.

Johnny "Lam" Jones *FOOTBALL*

"Lam" Jones played with the New York Jets for five years, being the second player chosen in the 1980 NFL draft. His career numbers were respectable—138 catches for 2,322 yards, with an average of almost 17 yards per reception. During the late 1970s, the Texas Longhorn team featured Johnny "Lam" Jones, Johnny "Ham" Jones, and Johnny "Jam" Jones, as well as Earl Campbell (like the soup)—although not all at the same time. A smorgasbord of talent, you might say.

Jerry Rice *FOOTBALL*

Rice, a 10-year NFL veteran from Mississippi Valley State, has averaged over 17 yards per reception for the 49ers. Some of his more memorable plays occurred in the 1989 and 1990 Super Bowls. For the two games combined, Rice caught 18 passes for 363 yards and four touchdowns. When he leaves the game, people will long remember him as one of the one of the greatest impact players ever. He recently broke Jim Brown's NFL record for touchdowns in a career, scoring his 127th touchdown in his team's first game of the 1994 NFL season.

Grantland Rice *VARIOUS*

It was Rice—one of America's greatest sportswriters—who made the famous quote, "When the last Great Scorer comes to mark against your name, he'll write not 'won' or 'lost,' but how you played the game." Rice would be doing reverse Hamill Camels in his grave if he could see what money has done to sports today. He also is often given credit for popularizing the name "Four Horsemen"—the 1924 Notre Dame backfield.

Cedric "Cornbread" Maxwell *BASKETBALL*

Maxwell starred for North Carolina-Charlotte, leading them to the NCAA finals in 1977, where they lost to Al McGuire's Marquette squad. He was drafted by the Boston Celtics in 1977 and played about seven seasons with them. He still holds the Celtic single-season and career record for field-goal percentage, finishing his career with a 55.9 percent scoring average.

Spices and Condiments:

Herb Elliot *TRACK & FIELD*

Elliot once held the world record for both the 1500-meter and mile runs. A convincing winner of the 1500-meter run at the

1960 Rome Olympics, setting a world record there, Elliott did not lose a race against international competitors between 1957 and 1960. He retired at age 22—undefeated in both the 1500-meter and mile runs. His success was attributed to demanding training schedules that were largely devised by his coach, Percy Cerutty. Elliot's routine consisted of running up and down sand dunes and consuming a vegetarian diet that included seaweed—cooked to perfection, as he claimed, by his mother.

Pepper Martin BASEBALL

Johnny "Pepper" Martin was a member of the famed St. Louis Cardinals' "Gashouse Gang" of the 1930s. A center fielder, he starred in the 1931 Cards' World Series triumph over the Philadelphia Athletics. His batting average was .500 for the series, and he drove in five runs. He also stole five bases and fielded superbly. For his 13-year career, Martin's batting average was .298. He holds the World Series record for highest batting average, .418, for players with at least 50 World Series at bats.

Sugar Ray Robinson BOXING

On five occasions Robinson—born Walker Smith—was world champion in the welterweight or middleweight division. Some rate him as the greatest boxer of all time, because he was an athlete who could masterfully outpoint his opponents rather than just pummel them into submission. Even Muhammad Ali paid great tribute, telling Robinson he was his, Ali's, idol. A flashy dresser and one who enjoyed *la dolce vita*, Robinson spent many years living in Europe. His European entourage included a valet, a barber, his trainer, and some family members. When he did it, baby, it was first class all the way.

Wilmer "Vinegar Bend" Mizell BASEBALL

Mizell, whose career pitching record was 90-88 with a 3.85 ERA, learned to pitch as a kid by throwing a ball through a hole in a barn wall.

Snacks and Desserts:

Cookie Lavagetto BASEBALL

Lavagetto spent five years managing two American League clubs in the '50s and '60s, but he also had some unforgettable games during his 10-year playing career, all of it spent in the National League. In the fourth game of the 1947 World Series, despite having only 18 hits all season, he was inserted as a pinch hitter in the bottom of the ninth inning and doubled. It was the Brooklyn Dodgers' first hit, and it won the game.

Cookie Gilchrist FOOTBALL

One of the iron men for the Buffalo Bills between 1962 and 1964—the pre-Juice era if you're checking the calendar—Gilchrist gained over 4 yards per carry and 10 yards per reception, a difficult feat for a man who weighed over 240 pounds. At one time he held the AFL single-game rushing record (243 yards) and the AFL career rushing record. He led the Bills to the 1964 AFL title game, going 122 yards in only 16 carries.

Pie Traynor BASEBALL

An early Hall of Famer, Traynor had a lifetime batting average of .320 over 18 seasons—most of which was played at the hot corner for the Pittsburgh Pirates. He struck out only 278 times in 7,559 at bats—a figure Bobby Bonds (Barry's pop) could maybe reach in about two seasons when he was with the Giants.

Willie "Puddin' Head" Jones *BASEBALL*

A prototype of the durable, hard-hitting third baseman that was to later be refined by Mike Schmidt, Brooks Robinson, Graig Nettles, and Ron Cey, Jones was a veteran of 15 National League seasons, 1947-61, most of them with the Phils. He hit for a career .258 with 190 homers.

David Cone *BASEBALL*

Having a superior command of many pitches, Cone has the potential to be one of baseball's greats. In the Mets' most recent division-winning year (1988), his record was 20-3 with a 2.22 ERA. He led the major leagues in strikeouts from 1990 through 1992 and never missed his turn in the pitching rotation during that period. In the middle of the 1992 season, he departed New York for the Toronto Blue Jays. In Canada, he retained his winning form and pitched for the American League in the 1994 All-Star game. Cone now anchors the rotation for the Kansas City Royals.

Levern Tart *BASKETBALL*

In Tart's four years in the ABA, he averaged over 19 points per game during the regular season and over 23 in playoff action. He was, however, only a 25 percent three-point shooter. He played his college ball at Bradley. When Tart was a sophomore there, he was the best player on his team, and his coach could not decide whether to use him at guard or forward and just "wished he were twins."

A steady performer with a long shelf life, Bob Walk is one of the few active pitchers I know of to post big W's 12 years apart in the postseason (1980 and 1992).

18 | ALL-FOOT TEAM

Eligibility: Each team entry must include a first name, last name, nickname or sports expression that suggests something having to do with feet or footwear or with an activity done with feet.

Samples: Billy "White Shoes" Johnson
Bob Walk

And your nominees are ...

_____   _____

_____   _____

_____   _____

_____   _____

_____   _____

_____   _____

_____   _____

_____   _____

Dick's Picks
All-Foot Team

John Walker *TRACK & FIELD*

Boots Day *BASEBALL*

"Shoeless" Joe Jackson *BASEBALL*

Billy "White Shoes" Johnson *FOOTBALL*

Clete Boyer *BASEBALL*

Lou "The Toe" Groza *FOOTBALL*

Jeff Kinney *FOOTBALL*

Gene Shue *BASKETBALL*

Ken Barefoot *FOOTBALL*

Bob Walk *BASEBALL*

Neal Walk *BASKETBALL*

Davey Lopes *BASEBALL*

Howard "Hopalong" Cassady *FOOTBALL*

Jim Kiick *FOOTBALL*

Lindy McDaniel *BASEBALL*

John Salley *BASKETBALL*

Skip Lockwood *BASEBALL*

Franklin Stubbs *BASEBALL*

Brian Trottier *HOCKEY*

Stanley Dancer *HORSE RACING*

Joe Pace *BASKETBALL*

Johnny Hopp *TRACK & FIELD*

The Ickey Shuffle (Ickey Woods) *FOOTBALL*

Trivial Tidbits

John Walker TRACK & FIELD
Walker was one of the best milers in the world during the 1970s and the winner of the 1500-meter run at the 1976 Montreal Olympics. At one point in his career he held the world record in the mile—being the first man to break 3 minutes, 50 seconds. The record was broken several times thereafter, with the current mark being Steve Cram's 3:46.32, set in 1985.

Boots Day BASEBALL
A six-year veteran of the bigs, Day came to the bat a little over a thousand times and lightly stroked his stick for a lifetime .256. He was a productive pinch hitter on the 1973 Montreal Expos team that finished only 3 1/2 games out of first place, despite having a 79-83 record. In 1970, Day was traded from Chicago to Montreal—the team he spent most of his time with—for Jack Hiatt, a pillar of my All-Hotels Team.

"Shoeless" Joe Jackson BASEBALL
Jackson allegedly only played without shoes once—due to sore feet—but an opposition fan mocked him for being shoeless and the name stuck. Ending his career with the second-best batting average in American League history—.356—Jackson was one of the principals in the 1919 "Black Sox" scandal, in which he and seven other players on the Chicago White Sox were banned for life from baseball for conspiring with gamblers in fixing games. While Jackson and his colleagues were not entirely blameless, there is widespread feeling that they were treated less than fairly by the baseball owners, who had just appointed a Commissioner—Kenesaw "Mountain" Landis—to "clean up the sport" before the government stepped in to do it for them. Jackson has been recently lionized in the movie Field of Dreams.

Billy "White Shoes" Johnson FOOTBALL
A product of Widener College, Johnson thrilled NFL audiences for 15 years with his white shoes and with his play at wide receiver and at returning kicks for the Oilers. He is the all-time NFL leader in total punt returns (282) and total yards returning punts. But that's only half of the story. Johnson was most exciting after he scored a touchdown. He would hold the ball over his head and do a wobbly legged dance that resembled the "mashed potatoes" of the 1960s, only keeping his feet in place.

Clete Boyer BASEBALL
While considered a great fielder, longtime New York Yankee Clete Boyer was sometimes regarded as a liability in the hitting department. In one World Series game, he was pinch hit for in the second inning. Clete Boyer is the brother of Ken Boyer, National League MVP in 1964, who led the Senior Circuit in RBIs with 119 in that championship year for the St. Louis Cardinals. The Boyer brothers had a combined 31 years in the majors.

Lou "The Toe" Groza FOOTBALL
Groza's career spanned the period 1946-1967. He played all of those years with the same team, which became the Cleveland Browns in the 1950s. A Hall of Famer, he was both a placekicker and an offensive tackle. Back in Groza's day, teams were limited to 33 players, and most clubs couldn't afford the luxury of having a guy on the roster who could only kick. Most of the placekickers of that era were Beefcake City. The Toe finished his NFL career second in number of extra points converted and fourth in field goals made. He was an All-Pro six times and the NFL's MVP in 1954.

Gene Shue BASKETBALL

Shue was a basketball star as a collegian and did well at the professional level as a player and coach. A guard at Maryland, he set scoring records and was an All-American in 1954. In over 700 NBA games he averaged more than 14 ppg, relying on his jump shot. He played in five NBA All-Star games and was All-NBA first team one season and second team another season. He was an NBA coach for 23 seasons. Perhaps his best coaching performance was when he took the injury-riddled Baltimore Bullets (with Wes Unseld, Gus Johnson and Earl Monroe) to the 1971 Eastern Division Championships—defeating the heavily favored Knicks in seven games.

Bob Walk BASEBALL

Although Bob Walk is not exactly a household name, he has played in the majors since 1980 and his career is dotted with some memorable moments. In his rookie year, he was 11-7 for the World Champion Philadelphia Phillies, and was undefeated in both the National League Championship Series and World Series. In the memorable 1992 NLCS, pitching with the Pirates, Walk threw a brilliant 3-hit complete game against the Braves in Game 5. Unfortunately, the gem was almost an afterthought after Game 7, which the Braves won on the dramatic run by Sid Bream in the bottom of the ninth.

Neal Walk BASKETBALL

A former Florida Gator, Walk has the distinction of being the second player picked in the 1971 NBA draft. He was selected by the Phoenix Suns right after Kareem Abdul-Jabbar was grabbed by the Bucks. Although he did not come close to rivaling Jabbar in either longevity or point production, Walk could clean the glass and was a steady, if not sometimes spectacular, performer.

Howard "Hopalong" Cassady FOOTBALL

Contrary to what you might be thinking, this Hoppy had nothing to do with either Gabby Hayes or a horse. The 1955 Heisman Trophy winner while a running back at Ohio State, Cassady had more success coming out of the backfield for passes than he did as a runner. For his career he totaled 1,229 yards from scrimmage and six touchdowns, but as a receiver he had 1,601 yards and 18 TDs. His glory years were spent with the Detroit Lions.

Jim Kiick FOOTBALL

Miami's version of Butch Cassidy and a PTPer for Coach Don Shula. In addition to thrilling Miami Dolphin fans for many seasons as a running back, Kiick delighted the Wyoming University Cowboy faithful when he led the team into the 1968 Sugar Bowl. About 15,000 Wyoming wellwishers attended the game. Hey, in a sparsely peopled state like Wyoming, that's about five percent of the entire population.

Lindy McDaniel BASEBALL

McDaniel had a 21-year career as a pitcher—a tenure in the bigs that was no doubt elongated when he went to the bullpen after having been a starter his first few years. At his retirement, he was third on the all-time major-league list for number of games appeared in by a pitcher (987) and second in wins by a reliever (119).

John Salley BASKETBALL

Drafted by the Pistons in 1986—along with "The Worm," Dennis Rodman, a member of my All-Nematode Team—Salley was used mostly as a substitute forward by Detroit. He earned two NBA Championship rings with the team—1989 and 1990. He is no longer with the Pistons but still in the NBA, mostly coming in off the bench for the Miami Heat. His forte is playing defense, rebounding and blocking shots.

19 | ALL-ANATOMY TEAM

Eligibility: Each team entry must include a first name, last name, nickname or sports expression that suggests a part of the human body.

Samples: Maurice Cheeks
Roy Face

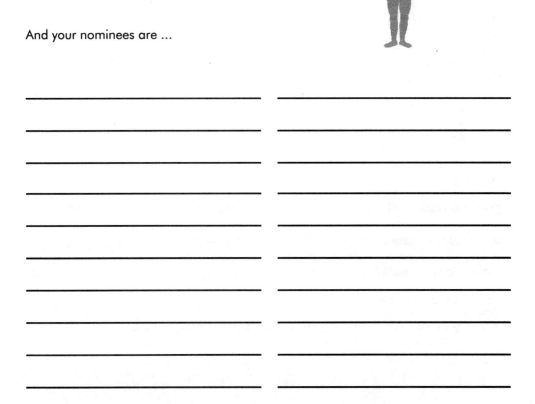

And your nominees are ...

_____   _____

_____   _____

_____   _____

_____   _____

_____   _____

_____   _____

_____   _____

_____   _____

Dick's Picks
All-Anatomy Team

Happy Hairston *BASKETBALL*

Carl Hairston *FOOTBALL*

Roy Face *BASEBALL*

Maurice Cheeks *BASKETBALL*

George Shinn *BASKETBALL*

Louis Lipps *FOOTBALL*

Deon Figures *FOOTBALL*

Bones Ely *BASEBALL*

Elroy "Crazylegs" Hirsch *FOOTBALL*

Rollie Fingers *BASEBALL*

Don Gullet *BASEBALL*

Bones McKinney *BASKETBALL*

Jim Shoulders *RODEO*

I.M. Hipp *FOOTBALL*

Walt "No Neck" Williams *BASEBALL*

Butch Beard *BASKETBALL*

Johnny Temple *BASEBALL*

Ron Jaworski ("Jaws") *FOOTBALL*

Jim Hart *FOOTBALL*

Jim Ray Hart *BASEBALL*

Eddie Hart *TRACK & FIELD*

Doris Hart *TENNIS*

Willie T. Ribbs *AUTO RACING*

David Brain *BASEBALL*

Charles Pores *TRACK & FIELD*

Phil Shinnick *TRACK & FIELD*

Paul LaPalme *BASEBALL*

Bill Hands *BASEBALL*

Ed Eyestone *TRACK & FIELD*

Marion Butts *FOOTBALL*

Frank "Heinie" Manush *BASEBALL*

Fanny Blankers-Koen *TRACK & FIELD*

Ricky Bones *BASEBALL*

Note:
▼ For names dealing with the foot: See All-Foot Team (page 102)

Trivial Tidbits

Roy Face *BASEBALL*
During his 16 major-league years, nearly all them with the Pittsburgh Pirates, Face was one of the great relief pitchers. He led the league in games appeared in 1956 (60), and in 1959, he compiled a record of 18-1. He is sixth on the all-time list in wins by a reliever (96) and 10th in saves (193). Face played alongside Vernon Law, a member of my All-Legal Team along with Bob Rule and Willie Miranda.

Maurice Cheeks *BASKETBALL*
Cheeks holds the NBA Championship Finals series record for most steals in a game—six—set against the Los Angeles Lakers in 1980 when he was with the Philadelphia 76ers. The Lakers won that series, 4-2. Three years later, it was a different story—Cheeks' 76ers rolled through the season with a 65-17 record and won it all while losing only one game in the playoffs. That single loss was not to the Lakers, who they whitewashed in the finals. Cheeks liked to pass the rock and is the career and single-season record holder in assists for the 76ers.

Rollie Fingers *BASEBALL*
When you think of big-time bullpen stoppers, you think of this guy. With the Milwaukee Brewers in 1981, Fingers went on to win the American League MVP Award and—this is extremely rare for a reliever—the Cy Young Award.

Bones McKinney *BASKETBALL*
A wearer of many basketball hats, McKinney was a player, coach, announcer and promoter of his sport. He played in an NCAA final game (with North Carolina), played six NBA seasons (once making the All-Star first team), coached briefly in the NBA, and then began a long college coaching career at Wake Forest. It was McKinney who told his players that the only reason you played the first half was so that you could get to the second half—where he believed all games were won. Let me tell you, Bones McKinney flat out was a winner.

Walt "No Neck" Williams *BASEBALL*
With a 5-foot-6 height and an appearance that suggested he may have undergone a neck-bypass operation early in life, Williams looked more like a wrestler than a baseball player. In 12 seasons in the bigs, primarily as a reserve, he batted a respectable .270. He also played in Japan and Mexico for a few years. Unfortunately, he was not popular in Japan, and pitchers were not averse to throwing at him. This led to a new name tag: "No Neck, the Nippon Ham Fighter."

Butch Beard *BASKETBALL*
A former Louisville Cardinal, Beard was a nine-year veteran and 49 percent shooter who averaged almost 10 ppg in the pre-three-point shot days. He was one of the young players who complemented Rick Barry in leading the San Francisco Warriors to the 1975 NBA Championship over the Baltimore Bullets in four games. He coached at Howard University and is making the transition to the NBA, having recently been named head coach of the New Jersey Nets by his former teammate, Willis Reed, who heads basketball operations for the Nets.

Jim Hart *FOOTBALL*
Hart's NFL career spanned 19 seasons, almost all of them with the St. Louis (football) Cardinals. Among the all-time statistical leaders in the NFL, Hart finished sixth in passes attempted, seventh in passing yardage, and eighth in completions. He was the beneficiary of a strong offensive line championed by the controversial Conrad Dobler. Dobler was effective in protecting Hart. During one three-season period, the star quarterback was sacked only 41 times.

David Brain   BASEBALL

I like this name. It sounds like the guy went the Ivy League route or that he pulls down a buck as a plutonium scientist at the Los Alamos Labs. David Brain—IQ unknown to me—had a pro baseball career that lasted seven years, 1901-1908. He led the National League in home runs in 1907 with 10.

Charles Pores   TRACK & FIELD

This athlete was the AAU champion in the 5-mile run for three consecutive years, 1917-1919, and in 1918, the AAU champion in the 10-mile run.

Phil Shinnick   TRACK & FIELD

Shinnick once soared past the then-existing world record in the long jump with a leap of 27 feet, 4 inches. Unfortunatley for him, the official responsible for watching the wind gauge failed to do so, later allegedly claiming that he only looked at the gauge when a jumper he believed was capable of breaking the world record was competing. The jump could not be considered for a world record. So it goes.

Bill Hands   BASEBALL

A New Jersey native out of Rutherford, Hands began his career with the Chicago Cubs in 1965 and was a respectable starting pitcher. In 1969, he was 20-14 with a sparkling 2.49 ERA. He had a career ERA of 3.35, and those numbers would make him a multimillionaire in the big leagues today.

Frank "Heinie" Manush   BASEBALL

One of the old time greats, Manush had a lifetime .330 batting average with 2524 hits in 17 big-league seasons. With the Tigers in 1926, he led the American League with a .378 batting average. He was also the AL's leader with 241 hits in 1928, playing with the St. Louis Browns. Manush struck out less than once in every 20 at bats.

20 | ALL-DOCTORS TEAM

Eligibility: Each team entry must include either (1) someone who has earned the title of doctor or (2) a first name, last name, nickname or sports expression that suggests a doctor.

Samples: Doc Rivers
Dr. Tom Osborne

And your nominees are ...

_____   _____

_____   _____

_____   _____

_____   _____

_____   _____

_____   _____

_____   _____

_____   _____

Dick's Picks
All-Doctors Team

"The Doctor," Julius Erving   *BASKETBALL*

"Doctor Strangeglove," Dick
Stuart   *BASEBALL*

Elmore "Doc" Hayes   *BASKETBALL*

Doc Rivers   *BASKETBALL*

Doc Medich   *BASEBALL*

Doc Gooden   *BASEBALL*

Dr. Frank Ryan   *FOOTBALL*

Dr. Cary Middlecoff   *GOLF*

James "Doc" Counsilman   *SWIMMING*

Felix "Doc" Blanchard   *FOOTBALL*

Dr. Delano Meriweather   *TRACK & FIELD*

Dr. Tom Osborne   *FOOTBALL*

Dr. Tom Davis   *BASKETBALL*

Dr. Gil Morgan   *GOLF*

Dr. Bobby Brown   *BASEBALL*

Dr. Sammy Lee   *SWIMMING*

The Docter sisters, Mary & Judy   *SKATING*

"Doctor Death," Oscar Edwards   *FOOTBALL*

The Doctors of Dunk   *BASKETBALL*

"Doctor Dunkenstein," Darryl
Griffith   *BASKETBALL*

"The Fight Doctor," Ferdie Pacheco   *BOXING*

Trivial Tidbits

"The Doctor," Julius Erving *BASKETBALL*

Agility and acrobatics personified, The Doctor is named for the surgical precision of his moves. He was electricity when he stepped on the floor—a real crowd favorite as he was an entertainer who also knew how to win. He was one of the best ever to wear a basketball uniform. Dr. J was voted five times to the All-NBA first team. His moves were sensational, super and scintillating. He could fly, then throw down a major league high riser.

Elmore "Doc" Hayes *BASKETBALL*

This flamboyant college coach, claimed some, was as good a show as any game itself. His Southern Methodist teams won eight Southwest Conference championships during his 1948-1967 coaching tenure at the school. In 1956, his SMU team finished fourth in the NCAA tournament, led by future NBA star center Jim Krebs.

Doc Rivers *BASKETBALL*

On my All-Water team as well, Rivers is a steady floor leader and scorer (almost 13 points per game) who likes to pass the rock. He is the Hawks' career and single season assist leader.

Doc Medich *BASEBALL*

The Doc pitched for seven teams in 11 years, including three in 1977. He was very durable in his early years, and in 1974 he won 19 games, completing 17 of his 38 starts.

Doc Gooden *BASEBALL*

The Mets' PTPer—the man they look to as their stopper. Gooden's first six years in the major leagues were sensational. He won 100 games and lost only 39. During that time he led the National League in wins (24, in 1985), ERA (1.53, in 1985), and strikeouts (276 and 268 in 1984 and 1985, respectively).

Dr. Frank Ryan *FOOTBALL*

A real physician who knew how to operate against a defense, Ryan ranks about 50th on the all-time list of NFL quarterbacks for touchdown passes. He teamed with Jim Brown to lead the Cleveland Browns in the 1960s. The Ryan-piloted Browns beat the favored Baltimore Colts in the NFL title game in 1964, 27-0, and lost 23-12 to the powerful Green Bay Packers the following year.

Dr. Cary Middlecoff *GOLF*

U.S. PGA Hall of Famer Middlecoff won 37 tour events, including the 1955 Masters—sinking an 80-foot putt along the way—and the 1949 U.S. Open. He tied for the Open lead the next year, but lost in a playoff.

James "Doc" Counsilman *SWIMMING*

This swimmer extraordinaire coached the Indiana University swimming team to six NCAA championships and led two U.S. Olympic swimming teams to a combined 21 out of 24 gold medals. And as if that weren't enough, in 1979—at age 59—he became the oldest person ever to swim the English Channel. Are you kidding me? This last feat gets him on my All-George Blanda Team.

Felix "Doc" Blanchard *FOOTBALL*

This three-time All-American and winner of the Heisman Trophy and Sullivan Award in 1945 led Army to national titles in 1944 and 1945. In these consecutive years, Army crushed Notre Dame 59-0 and 48-0, respectively, the first victories over the Irish since 1931 in what was an annual game.

Dr. Delano Meriweather TRACK & FIELD

Talk about a guy with both education and confidence, Meriweather began his career as a sprinter at the age of 28—very late in the afternoon for someone who has to burst out of starting blocks. While watching a race on television, he told his wife that he could beat "those guys." He did. In his first year of competition, he won the 100-yard dash at an AAU-sanctioned championship meet. Meriweather was a consummate showboat, and he occasionally competed wearing getups composed of a combination of shades, suspenders, bathing suit, and hospital smock. He once ran a wind-aided 9.0 seconds for the 100 dressed in such attire.

Dr. Tom Osborne FOOTBALL

Let me tell you about a guy who knows how to coach his team into the winner's circle. Tom Osborne is one of the most successful college coaches of all time. His Nebraska teams have won over 80 percent of their games since he became head coach in 1973. They have played in a bowl game every year since, and only once failed to win at least nine games in a season. Twice they have come within inches or seconds of a national championship. An innovative play caller—hey, he's a doctor—Osborne's zaniest play has been the "fumblerooskie." It begins with the center falling to the ground with the ball between his legs, having faked a hike to the quarterback. The entire team except for a guard runs one direction as if the play were a sweep, to draw the defense that way. Then the guard picks up the ball and runs the other way. Deception City.

Dr. Tom Davis BASKETBALL

Davis has built winners everywhere he has been. He coached at Lafayette, Boston College and Stanford before moving to Iowa. In his tenure with the Hawkeyes he has led them to six NCAA tournaments.

Dr. Gil Morgan GOLF

Perhaps Dr. Gil's most notable moment in the sun was when he took a commanding lead in the windy 1992 U.S. Open at Pebble Beach only to fall way into the pack on the final day. The eventual winner of the tournament was Tom Kite.

Dr. Bobby Brown BASEBALL

A cardiologist by training, Brown played eight seasons at third base for the New York Yankees and spent even more time as president of the American League. He had a respectable career .279 batting average—and an outstanding .439 in World Series play.

Dr. Sammy Lee SWIMMING

A Korean-American Army doctor, Lee was Olympic Games gold-medal winner in platform diving in both 1948 and 1952. In '48, on his last dive, he felt a tingling sensation and thought he had done a belly flop. When he got out of the water, he was pleasantly surprised to find out that the judges thought his dive was close to perfect. The U.S. virtually ruled Olympic platform diving from 1920 to 1952—winning the gold in every Games.

"Doctor Death," Oscar Edwards FOOTBALL

Edwards was a member of the 1975-76 UCLA team that won the school's first Rose Bowl in a decade. Noted for tucking into his pants a small black towel with a skull-and-crossbones emblem, Edwards led an inspired defense that upset Ohio State 23-10, after losing to the Buckeyes by a wide margin earlier in the season.

"Doctor Dunkenstein," Darryl Griffith BASKETBALL

When you talk about a guy who could fire up his team, you talk about Darryl Griffith.

Griffith was an instant hit with the Louisville Cardinals his first year. In one game against UCLA he came off the bench with his team trailing and the Louisville crowd relatively quiet. In less than a minute, at the end of a fast break, he tried to throw down a big time high riser over the Bruins' 6-foot-9 David Greenwood. Using his superior vertical leap, the 6-4 Griffith soared over Greenwood and, while missing the jam, drew a foul and drove the fans wild. Electricity City! In his senior year he led the Cards to the 1980 NCAA title—a team nicknamed "The Doctors of Dunk"—and was the second player picked in the 1980 NBA draft. He became the league's 1980-81 Rookie of the Year with the Utah Jazz.

When you talk about Frank House, you're talking about a backstop for some of the great hurlers of the fifties—Jim Bunning, Frank Lary, Billy Hoeft, and Paul Foytack, among them.

21 | ALL-HOUSING AND CONSTRUCTION TEAM

Eligibility: Each team entry must include a first name, last name, nickname or sports expression that suggests a building tool or building material, a home or a part of a home.

Samples: Fred "The Hammer" Williamson (tool)
Art Wall Jr. (part of a home)

And your nominees are ...

_____   _____

_____   _____

_____   _____

_____   _____

_____   _____

_____   _____

_____   _____

_____   _____

Dick's Picks
All-Housing and Construction Team

Tools and Materials:

Fred "The Hammer" Williamson *FOOTBALL*

"The Hammer," John Milner *BASEBALL*

Tracy Caulkins *SWIMMING*

Jim O'Toole *BASEBALL*

Jerry Tarr *TRACK & FIELD*

Andy Toolson *BASKETBALL*

Allen Leavell *BASKETBALL*

Brad Gilbert *TENNIS*

Gary Bradds *BASKETBALL*

Dave Stapleton *BASEBALL*

▼ Note: For natural materials used in building: See All-Natural Materials Team (page 142)

Homes or Parts of Homes:

Art Wall Jr. *GOLF*

Everson Walls *FOOTBALL*

Ron LeFlore *BASEBALL*

Phil Roof *BASKETBALL*

Bobby Locke *BASEBALL*

Dan Gable *WRESTLING*

Leroy Keyes *FOOTBALL*

Bobby Doerr *BASEBALL*

Roger Bannister *TRACK & FIELD*

Brooke Steppe *BASKETBALL*

Matt Stairs *BASEBALL*

Jackie Collum *BASEBALL*

Gates Brown *BASEBALL*

Wally Post *BASEBALL*

Gerald Glass *BASKETBALL*

Bill Glass *FOOTBALL*

Frank Brickowski *BASKETBALL*

Frank House *BASEBALL*

Rowland Office *BASEBALL*

Gerald Paddio *BASKETBALL*

Matt Bahr *FOOTBALL*

Chris Bahr *FOOTBALL*

Joe B. Hall *BASKETBALL*

Tommy John *BASEBALL*

Joe Garagiola *BASEBALL*

Tom Chambers *BASKETBALL*

Curtis Kitchen *BASKETBALL*

Phil Sellars *BASKETBALL*

Brad Sellars *BASKETBALL*

Clarence "Bighouse" Gaines *BASKETBALL*

Trivial Tidbits

Tools and Materials:

"The Hammer," John Milner   BASEBALL

Milner hit .249 for 12 major-league years, but he had moments of glory. In 1973, he led the Yogi Berra-coached Mets into the World Series with 23 home runs and 72 RBIs. There, he swung for a lofty .296 in a losing effort against the A's. With the "we are family" Pirates in 1979, where finally he won his World Series ring against the O's, it was virtually deja vu all over again at the plate. Milner batted a sizzling .333 for that series. In 10 World Series games (1973, with the Mets, and 1979, with the Pirates) he hit .306.

Tracy Caulkins   SWIMMING

The John Wooden of swimming, Caulkins won 48 titles between 1977 and 1984, an American record. The next closest aquatic ace is Johnny Weissmuller—of Tarzan fame—with 36 titles. Yes, Tracy was the predominant superstar of women's swimming.

Jim O'Toole   BASEBALL

O'Toole pitched 10 years in the National League and compiled a 98-84 record, with a 3.57 ERA. Virtually his entire career was spent in a Cincinnati Reds uniform, back in the days when the big lumber in the lineup was wielded by Frank Robinson, Vada Pinson and Wally Post. O'Toole was 17-7 in 1963 with a 2.88 ERA, and 19-9 in the Reds' World Series year of 1961. In the Series—won in five games by the Yankees—he pitched well, allowing only four runs in 12 innings.

Jerry Tarr   TRACK & FIELD

Not to be confused with Mel Farr, Jerry Tarr was NCAA Champion for Oregon in both the 120-yard and 440-yard hurdles in 1962. He also was a member of the Ducks' 4x110-yard relay team that set a world record of 40 seconds flat in 1962. He passed up an opportunity to compete in the 1964 Olympics, choosing to try out for professional football instead.

Allen Leavell   BASKETBALL

A guard with the Houston Rockets during the 1980s, Leavell was a good playmaker with superb foot speed, a guy who enjoyed passing the rock. He averaged 4.8 assists per game for his career, often coming off the bench. He played on Houston's Western Conference Championship team in 1986, which featured the Twin Towers of Hakeem Olajuwon and Ralph Sampson inside, and the capable J-shooting of Robert Reid, Lewis Lloyd and Mitchell Wiggins on the perimeter.

Houses or Parts of a Homes:

Art Wall, Jr.   GOLF

In 1959, Wall won the Masters Tournament and was the PGA Tour's leading money winner for the year—with about $53,000.

Ron LeFlore   BASEBALL

A player who turned his life around, LeFlore was found by Billy Martin in prison and given the chance to play major league baseball—and he responded. In 1980, LeFlore led the National League with 97 stolen bases for the Montreal Expos. His career batting average was .288, and he stole 455 bases over the course of his nine years in the major league.

Phil Roof   BASEBALL

A 15-year veteran of the majors, Roof played on the first-year squads of three different teams: the 1968 Oakland A's, the 1969 Milwaukee Brewers, and the 1977 Toronto Blue Jays.

Dan Gable   WRESTLING

When you talk about great wrestlers, you talk about Dan Gable. Gable was undefeated as a high school wrestler and for the first 118 matches of his college career—twice winning NCAA Championships in his weight class. Gable went on to win an Olympic gold medal in the 1972 Munich Olympics, and then he became the most successful college wrestling coach of all time. From 1978 until 1986, his Iowa team won the NCAA tournament every year, and they won again under his guidance in 1991 and 1992. HIs 18-year career coaching record includes a dual meet record of 309-20 with five ties, 18 Blg Ten Championships and 12 NCAA Championships. This guy knows how to find the winner's circle.

Roger Bannister *TRACK & FIELD*

An athlete with class, Bannister was the first person to break the 4-minute-mile barrier, running a historic 3:59.4 in Oxford, England, in 1959. He retired at the end of the same year to become a physician, but only after competing in the 1500-meter run in the European Championships. There, he both won the race and defeated rival John Landy—who had broken his mile record by running a 3:58.

Gates Brown *BASEBALL*

Who can ever forget Gates Brown? One of baseball's supreme pinch hitters, Brown spent 13 seasons with the Tigers. He pinch hit 414 times and had 107 hits—both top-10 stats on the all-time list.

Frank Brickowski *BASKETBALL*

This guy is a solid NBA performer—a guy who came to play. From 1985 through 1992, the 6-foot-10 Brickowski averaged 9.4 points per regular-season game, shooting 52 percent from the floor and averaging 12 ppg in the playoffs. He is currently with the Sacramento Kings.

Frank House *BASEBALL*

Let me tell you about an excellent defensive catcher with a .988 lifetime fielding average. Frank House was a part-time catcher with the Detroit Tigers and Kansas City A's and had a .248 lifetime batting average.

Rowland Office *BASEBALL*

Office was a .259 lifetime hitter and was often inserted into the lineup in the late innings for defensive purposes. He spent most of his 11-year career in Atlanta and Montreal.

Tommy John *BASEBALL*

Here's a guy who had heart, soul and spirit when he took to the mound. A superior competitor who pitched for 26—count 'em—years in the major leagues, Tommy John makes my All-Longevity Team, along with George Blanda and Nolan Ryan. John relied on control and an assortment of breaking pitches to put up big numbers, winning 288 games. He was a clutch pitcher, compiling a 6-2 won-loss record with an ERA below 2.50 in League Championship and World Series competition.

Tom Chambers *BASKETBALL*

A player who knows where the basket is, Chambers has consistently averaged over 20 points per game since entering the NBA 13 years ago, and he's still bouncing the rock. He holds the Phoenix Suns season-scoring record with 2,201 points. He also has the distinction of having played for the only NBA team I know of, the Seattle Supersonics, who had to postpone a home game because of rain (a leaky roof).

Clarence "Bighouse" Gaines *BASKETBALL*

One of the great coaches—All-Rolls Royce on the bench. A member of the NAIA Hall of Fame, Gaines was the winningest active college-division coach during his final years coaching. His best team was the 1967 Winston-Salem College squad, led by Earl "The Pearl" Monroe, that finished 31-1. In 1981 he became the first African-American coach to be inducted into the Basketball Hall of Fame. When he finished his career he was second to Adolph Rupp on the all-time list of coaching victories with 848.

22 | ALL-WEAPONS AND AMMO TEAM

Eligibility: Each team entry must include a first name, last name, nickname or sports expression that suggests a weapon or type of ammunition.

Samples: Billy Cannon
Raghib "Rocket" Ismail

And your nominees are ...

_____   _____

_____   _____

_____   _____

_____   _____

_____   _____

_____   _____

_____   _____

_____   _____

Dick's Picks
All-Weapons and Ammo Team

Billy Cannon *FOOTBALL*

"The Toy Cannon," Jimmy Wynn *BASEBALL*

Larry Cannon *BASKETBALL*

Calodeis Cannon *BASKETBALL*

Paul Derringer *BASEBALL*

Chris Gatling *BASKETBALL*

"The Polish Rifle," Ron Jaworski *FOOTBALL*

"The Rifleman," Chuck Person *BASKETBALL*

Kennard Winchester *BASKETBALL*

"Pistol" Pete Maravich *BASKETBALL*

Lance Larson *SWIMMING*

Lance Rentzel *FOOTBALL*

Lance Mehl *FOOTBALL*

"Bullet" Bob Turley *BASEBALL*

Don Beebe *FOOTBALL*

Frederick Beebe *BASEBALL*

Larvell Blanks *BASEBALL*

"Matti Nukes," Matti Nykanen *SKIING*

Bennie Blades *FOOTBALL*

Don "The Blade" Blasingame *BASEBALL*

Razor Ruddick *BOXING*

"The Destroyer," George Foster *BASEBALL*

The Bronx Bombers *BASEBALL*

Raghib "Rocket" Ismail *FOOTBALL*

Maurice "The Rocket" Richard *HOCKEY*

Henri "The Pocket Rocket" Richard *HOCKEY*

Trivial Tidbits

Billy Cannon *FOOTBALL*

Cannon, the 1959 Heisman Trophy winner, led LSU to a national championship. His sparkling career featured a memorable game against Mississippi. During the days when defense ruled, Mississippi was holding a 3-0 lead, and, not taking any chances, was opting to punt to LSU on second—and even first—down. In the fourth quarter, Cannon burst free for a spectacular 89-yard punt return and LSU prevailed, 7-3. Fans claimed that the noise in Tiger Stadium could be heard all the way back in Oxford, Mississippi. Cannon went on to play both running back and tight end in the pros, finishing his 11-year career—split between Houston and Oakland—with 64 touchdowns and an average of 15.5 yards per reception.

"The Toy Cannon," Jimmy Wynn *BASEBALL*

For his size, this guy was unbelievable, baby. A relatively short man by home-run-hitter standards, Wynn blasted 291 home runs during his 15-year career and also knocked in over 100 RBIs four times. A longtime Houston Astro, he led the Los Angeles Dodgers into the 1974 World Series with 32 home runs and 104 RBIs.

Larry Cannon *BASKETBALL*

Cannon was a legend in the streets of Philadelphia. He starred for Tom Gola at La Salle when the Big Five (La Salle, Villanova, St. Joseph's, Pennsylvania and Temple) was something special. Cannon lived up to his shooter surname during his five or so years in the ABA. He flat out liked to shoot the J. Larry averaged more than 14 shots per game—about one for every two minutes of playing time—and had a per game scoring average of 16.6 points.

"The Rifleman," Chuck Person *BASKETBALL*

Person is resoundingly an All-Weapons and Ammo Team guy. His full name is Chuck Connors Person—he is named after "The Rifleman" of TV fame. As if that weren't enough to qualify him for this team, he also has been an accurate gunner in the NBA, sometimes sinking J's at will. In his first pro season, 1986, he was the NBA Rookie of the Year. He can do it all—stroke the J, jam the rock and clean the glass. Now his brother Wesley is entering the NBA, so it's family showtime.

"Pistol" Pete Maravich *BASKETBALL*

One of the great outside shooters of all-time, Maravich scored an average of 44.2 ppg in three college seasons—all without the benefit of the three-point shot. Can you imagine his numbers if the trifecta rule had been in effect? A true showboat with exceptional dribbling ability, Maravich pulled the trigger at every opportunity—once putting up 57 shots in a Southeastern Conference tilt. He once scored 69 points in a college game and 68 points in a pro game—Unconscious City if ever it existed. In the NBA, he played mostly for the Jazz and the Hawks, and he was selected to the All-Rookie team in 1971. He also set NBA free-throw shooting records—one for most free throws attempted in a quarter (16) and another for most free throws made in a quarter (14). Yes, Pete Maravich was a magician with the rock in his hands.

Lance Larson *SWIMMING*

Larson was involved in one of the most controversial races in Olympic Games history. Swimming for the U.S. in the 100-meter freestyle at the 1960 Rome Olympics, he was clocked by the three timers assigned to his lane in 55.1 seconds. Australian swimmer John Devitt put in at 55.2 seconds.

Judges sitting to the side of the pool, at a distance to the finish, claimed Devitt was the winner because, from their angle, it appeared that he had touched the wall first.

Lance Mehl FOOTBALL
Mehl was the heart of the New York Jets defense from 1980-87. The former Penn State linebacker had 15 career interceptions for the Jets and led them into the AFC play-offs in 1981, 1982, 1985 and 1986.

"Bullet" Bob Turley BASEBALL
Pitcher Turley finished his 12-year career with a record of 101-85 and a 3.64 ERA. He allowed just over seven hits per nine innings. His best years were with the New York Yankees, where he posted an American League-leading 21-7 record in 1958. During Turley's tenure with the Bombers, the team played in five World Series. He pitched to a 4-3 mark in the fall classic, finishing third all-time in World Series pitching appearances.

Frederick Beebe BASEBALL
Beebe's seven-year major-league career was spent as a pitcher in the National League. His lifetime record was 63-84, but he finished with an ERA of 2.86 and led the league in 1906 with 171 strikeouts.

"Matti Nukes," Matti Nykanen SKIING
Here's a guy who had sensational air time. Nykanen was another in a long line of champion Finnish ski jumpers. He was the 1984 and 1988 Olympic Champion in the 90-meter ski jump. In 1988, he also won the gold on the short hill and a gold in the team jumping.

Bennie Blades FOOTBALL
A former star with the perennially powerful Miami Hurricanes, Blades has played defensive back for the Detroit Lions since 1988. It would be easy for his agent to argue that Blades can help a team find the winner's circle. During his first four seasons, the Lions went from last in their division (1988), to third (1989), to second (1990), to first (1991).

Don "The Blade" Blasingame BASEBALL
A 12-year major-league veteran, second-baseman Blasingame was a dependable player who finished with a .258 batting average—leading the National League with 680 at bats in 1957.

Maurice "The Rocket" Richard HOCKEY
Talk about a guy with grace, class and agility, Richard is one of hockey's all-time greats. He played 18 years (1942-1960) for the Montreal Canadiens. He still holds the team record for most goals (544) and hat tricks (26). Winner of the Hart Memorial Trophy in 1947, Richard also holds the NHL playoff records for points scored in one period (4) and goals scored in a game (5).

Henri "The Pocket Rocket" Richard HOCKEY
Let me tell you about Maurice Richard's younger brother, Henri. He holds the Montreal team record for most games played (1256), a mark set between 1955 and 1975. During the 21-year period Henri suited up for the Montreal Canadiens, they won the Stanley Cup twelve times.

One of the best pure shooters ever and a guy with a hair-trigger release, Pistol Pete Maravich was Mr. Unconscious City when he was in a rock-and-roll mode on the court.

Mr. Greg "Cadillac" Anderson also makes my All-General Motors Team, joining Bill Olds and Jesus Vega.

23 | ALL-AUTO TEAM

Eligibility: Each team entry must include a first name, last name, nickname or sports expression that suggests a car or some specific make or model of car.

Samples: Lou Hudson
               "Hot Rod" Hundley

And your nominees are ...

_____   _____

_____   _____

_____   _____

_____   _____

_____   _____

_____   _____

_____   _____

_____   _____

Dick's Picks
All-Auto Team

Antoine Carr	BASKETBALL	John Stearns	BASEBALL
Austin Carr	BASKETBALL	Willis Reed	BASKETBALL
Henry Carr	TRACK & FIELD	LaSalle Thompson	BASKETBALL
Phil Ford	BASKETBALL	Bill Olds	FOOTBALL
Don Kaiser	BASKETBALL	Fritz Crisler	BASKETBALL
Greg "Cadillac" Anderson	BASKETBALL	Bob Nash	BASKETBALL
Eugene "Mercury" Morris	FOOTBALL	Joe Morgan	BASEBALL
Rich Dotson	BASEBALL	Jesus Vega	BASEBALL
Lou Hudson	BASKETBALL	"Hot Rod" Hundley	BASKETBALL
Don Hutson	FOOTBALL	"Hot Rod" Williams	BASKETBALL
Trent Tucker	BASKETBALL		

Trivial Tidbits

Antoine Carr *BASKETBALL*
A consistent scorer for each team he has played for in the NBA, Carr averages over 10 points per game—often off the bench—while shooting 51 percent from the field in the regular season and almost 60 percent in the playoffs. No relation, as far as I know, to Austin Carr, M.L. Carr, Kenny Carr, Lydell Carr, Carl Carr, Reggie Carr, Chetti Carr, Fred Carr, Earl Carr, Roger Carr, or Henry Carr—all of them on my All-Carr Team.

Austin Carr *BASKETBALL*
Carr was one of the great NCAA Tournament performers and one of the best players ever to come out of Notre Dame. At March's Big Dance, he holds the record for highest scoring average for career play (41.3 points, 1969 through 1971) and for a single tournament (52.7 points in 1970), and he also has the scoring record for a single game (61 points in 1970). In NBA play, he racked up over 10,000 points during his 10-year stay, averaging 15.4 ppg. His uniform has been retired by the Cleveland Cavaliers, the club he was with for nine of his 10 pro seasons.

Henry Carr *TRACK & FIELD*
Carr was the gold-medal winner in the 200-meter dash at the 1964 Tokyo Olympic Games, setting an Olympic record of 20.3 seconds. He also won gold in the 4x400-meter relay. Unfortunately, his NFL career was almost as fleeting. He played only three years as a defensive back with the New York Giants, finishing his career with seven interceptions.

Phil Ford *BASKETBALL*
Phil Ford was the greatest point guard ever to play for Dean Smith. He was the heart, soul and spirit of his UNC team. Although North Carolina normally was successful protecting a lead with Ford at the helm, they were unable to do so in the 1977 NCAA title game, when Al McGuire's Marquette Warriors overcame a second-half deficit to win 67-59. Ford averaged 11.5 points per game in six NBA seasons. He is currently assistant coach at UNC under Dean Smith.

Greg "Cadillac" Anderson *BASKETBALL*
During his first five NBA seasons, Anderson traveled more miles after being traded than most Caddy owners drive their cars in a year. He played for five different teams—including three in 1990-91. Should his wheels ever wear out, Anderson should feel free to call on Gail Goodrich—one of my All-Auto Accessories Team guys—for some new rubber. And if he needs a tuneup, he can turn to Oil Can Boyd, another All-Auto Accessories Team great.

Rich Dotson *BASEBALL*
Dotson had a superb year in 1983, winning 22 games and losing only seven. For his career—most of which was with the White Sox—he finished only 111-109, with a 4.16 ERA. Dotson averaged one shutout for every 10 wins.

Don Hutson *FOOTBALL*
Hutson was one of the best players ever to wear a football uniform. His statistics as an NFL pro are staggering: over 100 touchdowns, a career 488 passes caught for 7,991 yards, tops in the league in scoring five consecutive seasons and in touchdowns eight seasons, and, hey, baby, I'm just giving you the highlights! Joining the Packers in 1935, Hutson is credited as being the first player to create pass patterns. Before he came on the scene, receivers lined up tight to the line, with little room to maneuver. Hutson, who had 9.5 (100-yard-dash) speed and liked the open field, didn't buy into this arrangement at all, and essentially

developed what we know today as the "wide receiver" position to showcase his talents.

Trent Tucker   BASKETBALL
Tucker joined the NBA in 1983. Playing for the Knicks his first nine years, he was extremely effective from behind the three-point line—making about 40 percent of his shots. Still in the NBA, he averages about nine points and a little over two assists per game coming off the bench.

John Stearns   BASEBALL
Named like the Touring Car, John Stearns' 11-year career—10 of which were with the New York Mets—was a dandy. While this Colorado grad never put up breathtaking numbers, he was a steady performer and finished the majors with a .260 average. It is particularly interesting that he stole 91 bases—including 25 in 1978—an unusually high number for a catcher.

Bill Olds   FOOTBALL
A blocking fullback while at Nebraska, Olds played four NFL seasons. He helped the Baltimore Colts turn their fortunes around, as the team rebounded from 4-10 and 2-12 records during Olds' first two seasons (1974 and 1975) to 10-4 his third season.

He finished his career with 985 yards gained rushing, 372 yards receiving, and 14 touchdowns.

Jesus Vega   BASEBALL
Vega was a designated hitter who had neither a high batting average (.246) nor, just like his namesake car, much raw power—only 11 extra-base hits in 236 at bats. He finished his 87-game, three-year major-league career in 1982.

"Hot Rod" Hundley   BASKETBALL
Who can ever forget this crowd pleaser and court wizard? Mr. Excitement! Hundley was a mustard-laden hot-dog's hot dog at West Virginia University, where he preceded "Mr. Clutch," Jerry West, as the star. At the end of some home games, when the Mountaineers had a big lead, he would showboat with acrobatic shots and his ballhandling wizardry. In a six-year NBA career that spanned the 1958-1963 period, Hundley scored fewer than 10 ppg and shot only 35 percent from the field. Perhaps his most interesting NBA stat is fouling out only once in 431 games played. After his career as a player, he took advantage of his bent for showmanship and went on to a successful career in broadcasting.

24 | ALL-MUSIC TEAM

Eligibility: Each team entry must include a first name, last name, nickname or sports expression that suggests music or a musical instrument.

Samples: George Bell
Noel Carroll

And your nominees are ...

_____   _____

_____   _____

_____   _____

_____   _____

_____   _____

_____   _____

_____   _____

_____   _____

_____   _____

Dick's Picks
All-Music Team

Jim Musick *FOOTBALL*

Frank Viola *BASEBALL*

Steve Sax *BASEBALL*

Don Horn *FOOTBALL*

Phil Villapiano *FOOTBALL*

Brian Piccolo *FOOTBALL*

Theopolis "T" Bell *FOOTBALL*

Buddy Bell *BASEBALL*

Michel Jazy *TRACK & FIELD*

Doug Flutie *FOOTBALL*

Gerald Harp *FOOTBALL*

Derek Harper *BASKETBALL*

Joe Bugel *FOOTBALL*

Lute Olson *BASKETBALL*

Bill Singer *BASEBALL*

John Hummer *BASKETBALL*

Al Toon *FOOTBALL*

Bernard Toone *BASKETBALL*

Otis Birdsong *BASKETBALL*

Carl Birdsong *FOOTBALL*

Vijay Singh *GOLF*

David Humm *FOOTBALL*

Clay Carroll *BASEBALL*

Carroll Dale *FOOTBALL*

Noel Carroll *TRACK & FIELD*

Pat Rapp *BASEBALL*

Jimmy Arias *TENNIS*

Matt Bahr *FOOTBALL*

Chris Bahr *FOOTBALL*

Jimmy Key *BASEBALL*

Sterling Sharpe *FOOTBALL*

Don Highnote *FOOTBALL*

Trivial Tidbits

Jim Musick   *FOOTBALL*

In 1933, the second year of the NFL's existence, Jim Musick led the league in rushing, gaining 809 yards in 173 tries. He eclipsed the old standard set a year earlier. The next season, Musick's mark was shattered by Beattie Feathers of the Chicago Bears, who ran for over 1,000 yards and at an unbelievable 9.9 yards-per-carry clip—a feat no rushing leader has even come close to matching since then. Feathers, of course, ran to further glory by racking up a starting slot on my All-Bird Anatomy Team.

Frank Viola   *BASEBALL*

Viola's glory days were with the Minnesota Twins from 1984 to 1988. In '88 he won the Cy Young Award, posting a 24-7 record. The same year he also was a combined 3-1 in the American League Championship Series and World Series, winning the seventh game of the World Series and its MVP Award, while leading the Twins to their first Series victory.

Steve Sax   *BASEBALL*

Infielder Sax has been wearing a major-league uniform since 1981 when he broke in with the Dodgers as a second baseman. Among his career highlights are leading the National League in at bats in 1988 (632) and 1989 (651), and going 6-for-20 in the 1988 World Series for the Dodgers as they dismantled the A's in five games. Some critics knock his defensive ability, but he has not made any errors in the 25 postseason games he has played.

Don Horn   *FOOTBALL*

A former San Diego State quarterback, Horn played for several NFL teams from 1967 to 1974. Used mostly as a backup, he finished his career with just under a 50 per-cent completion rate. He was prone to interceptions, however, throwing one about every 13 passes attempted. Horn was a member of the 1967 Green Bay Packers Super Bowl-winning team.

Phil Villapiano   *FOOTBALL*

Villapiano played 12 NFL seasons as linebacker, averaging one interception per year. He was a member of the Oakland Raiders Super Bowl XI championship team. There, the fortunes of the Bay Area team rested on the arm of Ken "The Snake" Stabler, an All-Reptiles Team first selection.

Brian Piccolo   *FOOTBALL*

Brian Piccolo led the nation's collegiate running backs in rushing in 1964. In four NFL seasons he rushed for 927 yards for the Bears, averaging 3.6 yards per carry. He died of cancer in 1970. His friendship with Gayle Sayers was given an emotional portrayal in the movie *Brian's Song*.

Buddy Bell   *BASEBALL*

Buddy Bell is the son of the legendary Gus Bell, a longtime star National Leaguer. The younger Bell, who played 18 years—mostly with the Cleveland Indians and Texas Rangers—was himself a star in his own right. He batted a lifetime .279, only two salami-thin percentage points lower than his dad. With the Indians in the early 1970s, Buddy Bell was tall in the saddle and arguably the Tribe's main man.

Michel Jazy   *TRACK & FIELD*

In 1964, Michel Jazy of France was one of the favorites to win the 5000 meters. He was leading the pack with only 50 meters to the tape when he faulted badly and lost the race to American Bob Schul. Jazy finished a disappointing fourth.

Doug Flutie   FOOTBALL

This 1984 Heisman winner took part in one of the most aerially oriented college football games ever played. On Thanksgiving weekend of 1984, the 5-foot-10 Flutie's Boston College Eagles faced the 6-5 Bernie Kosar's Miami's Hurricanes in a contest that was billed "The Battle of the Quarterbacks." The PR hype was only exceeded by the game itself—truly one of the most awesome ever. BC won, 47-45, on Flutie's last-second Hail Mary pass. Flutie went 34-for-46 (472 yards); Kosar, 25-for-38 (447 yards).

Derek Harper   BASKETBALL

Harper, from Lou Henson's Illinois program, has been in the NBA since 1984, first with the Dallas Mavs, then with the New York Knicks. He was on track to be the most valuable player for the 1994 NBA Championship Finals, what with his pickpocketing of Houston guards and his point scoring. It was showtime for him. But his Knicks came up short, and the series MVP went to a very deserving Hakeem Olajuwon.

Lute Olson   BASKETBALL

Robert Luther Olson is in the front rank of today's college basketball coaches. He began his career on the California JuCo circuit, then moved on to Long Beach State, Iowa and Arizona—where he is now. Lute guided Arizona to the Final Four in 1988 when they were led by Sean Elliott. His team also surprised everyone last year when it marched to the Final Four, led by the dynamic backcourt of Khalid Reeves and Damon Stoudamire.

Bill Singer   BASEBALL

The Singer Throwing Machine pitched 14 years in the majors, nine of them with the Dodgers. Despite a fine career ERA of 3.39 and two outstanding seasons (20-12 in 1969 and 20-14 in 1973), he finished his career with a record of 118-127. He pitched a no-hitter in 1970, carrying the Dodgers over the Phils, 5-0.

John Hummer   BASKETBALL

If you can't be a singer, be a hummer, I always say. This 6-foot-9 Princeton graduate and protege of Pete Carril played in the NBA in the early 1970s, averaging about seven ppg for his career. In college, he was on the same Tiger team as Geoff Petrie, who eventually went on to be an NBA Rookie of the Year and one of the first big stars for the Portland Trail Blazers.

Al Toon   FOOTBALL

Toon averaged almost 70 catches for each of his first seven NFL seasons, all with the New York Jets. He led the AFC in receiving in 1987 and 1988. In 1988, he caught 93 passes for 1,067 yards and was the lead player in the Jets' offense, as the rest of the team gained only 2,817 yards receiving and rushing. Toon retired in 1993 due to a series of injuries.

Bernard Toone   BASKETBALL

One of the most highly recruited players from the New York City area in the 1970s, Bernard Toone played forward on the Al-McGuire-coached 1977 Marquette team that won the NCAA tournament. Other leading scorers on the team included tournament MVP Butch Lee, Jerome Whitehead, and Bo Ellis.

Otis Birdsong   BASKETBALL

Birdsong was one of the great players to come out of Houston between the Elvin Hayes and Hakeem Olajuwon eras. His NBA career—where he averaged about 18 ppg and shot about 51 percent from the field—lasted more than a decade. He was second-team All-NBA for the Kansas City (now Sacramento) Kings in the 1980-81 season, leading the club into the NBA playoffs—the only time that franchise qualified for postseason play.

Carroll Dale   FOOTBALL

A former Virginia Tech Hokie, Carroll Dale played 14 NFL seasons as a wide receiver on the great Green Bay Packer teams of the

1960s. He averaged almost 19 yards per catch and scored 52 touchdowns during his illustrious career, including putting up Green Bay's first score in the 1965 NFL title game—a 23-12 defeat of the Cleveland Browns. Along with Boyd Dowler and Max McGee, The Vince Lombardi-coached Packers of the 1960s had one of the most feared corps of receivers in the history of the pro game.

Noel Carroll *TRACK & FIELD*
Sounds Christmasy, doesn't it? Carroll, an Irishman, was a middle distance runner for some of the great Villanova track teams under Jumbo Jim Elliot in the 1960s.

Matt Bahr *FOOTBALL*
A longtime placekicker in the NFL, Bahr's capstone acheivement to a brilliant career was booting a last-second field goal in the 1990 NFC title game to give his New York Giants a 15-13 win over the San Francisco 49ers and send New York to Super Bowl XXV, where the Giants beat favored Buffalo, 20-19. Matt is the younger brother of Chris Bahr, another highly successful NFL kicker and the guy who preceded him as the chief scoring toe with Joe Paterno's Penn State Nittany Lions.

Jimmy Key *BASEBALL*
Jimmy Key has been pitching in the major leagues since 1984 and has been one of the better pitchers around since he arrived. He was the winning hurler in Game 4 of the 1992 World Series, shutting down the Atlanta Braves in a 2-1 win, as the Toronto Blue Jays marched to the first major-league *baseball* championship ever won by a Canadian team. His most recent accolade was starting the 1994 All-Star Game for the American League.

The New York Giants picked up Joe Don Looney in the first round of the 1964 NFL draft.

25 | ALL-STATE-OF-MIND TEAM

Eligibility: Each team entry must include a first name, last name, nickname, or sports expression that suggests moods or states of mind.

Samples: Orville Moody
Dizzy Dean

And your nominees are ...

_____   _____
_____   _____
_____   _____
_____   _____
_____   _____
_____   _____
_____   _____
_____   _____
_____   _____

Dick's Picks
All-State-of-Mind Team

Jamie Quirk *BASEBALL*

Dizzy Dean *BASEBALL*

Joe Don Looney *FOOTBALL*

Orville Moody *GOLF*

Helen Wills Moody *TENNIS*

Earl Battey *BASEBALL*

Johnny Sain *BASEBALL*

Curtis Strange *GOLF*

Kelly Downs *BASEBALL*

Pepe Mangual *BASEBALL*

Bob Purkey *BASEBALL*

"The Mad Hungarian," Al Hrabosky *BASEBALL*

"Sad" Sam Jones *BASEBALL*

Les Shy *FOOTBALL*

Russ Grimm *FOOTBALL*

Billy Loes *BASEBALL*

"Happy" Chandler *BASEBALL*

"Happy" Hairston *BASKETBALL*

Greg Joy *TRACK & FIELD*

Dave Bliss *BASKETBALL*

Bob Rush *BASEBALL*

Dave Jolly *BASEBALL*

Tom Fears *FOOTBALL*

Dean "The Dream" Meminger *BASKETBALL*

Steve Tensi *FOOTBALL*

Tim Beamer *FOOTBALL*

Anthony Pleasant *FOOTBALL*

Buzz Capra *BASEBALL*

"Mean" Joe Greene *FOOTBALL*

Wimp Sanderson *BASKETBALL*

Dave "The Rave" Stallworth *BASKETBALL*

Johnny High *BASKETBALL*

Hector "Macho" Camacho *BOXING*

Eric Comas *AUTO RACING*

Eric "Sleepy" Floyd *BASKETBALL*

Rickey Sobers *BASKETBALL*

John Jurkovic *FOOTBALL*

Trivial Tidbits

Jamie Quirk *BASEBALL*
Quirk's major-league career stretched out 15 years. His most productive season was 1987, when he batted 296 times and got 70 hits. He lasted so long in baseball because of his fielding ability. Quirk made himself indispensible by wearing many gloves—he caught, played the outfield, and took on every infield position during his pro career.

Dizzy Dean *BASEBALL*
The last pitcher in the National League to win 30 games—he went 30-7 in 1934—Dean led the senior circuit in strikeouts and complete games four times. He finished the bigs with 150 wins in a career cut short by having his toe broken by a line drive during an All-Star game. If you think the name Dizzy is a nutty handle, try his brother Paul's nickname on for size—Daffy. Nicknames nothwithstanding, the brother tandem was effective. When Dizzy was a combined 58-19 for St. Louis in 1934 and 1935, Daffy was 38-23 over the same period for the same club. A true baseball philosopher like Yogi Berra and Casey Stengel, Dizzy Dean was credited for coining the expression (paraphrased), "it ain't bragging if you did it."

Orville Moody *GOLF*
A retired U.S. Army officer, Moody won the U.S. Open Championship in 1969. Not to be confused with Charles Coody, another pro golfer, or The Moody Blues.

Helen Wills Moody *TENNIS*
In the 1920s and 1930s, H.W.M. was the Martina Navratilova of her day. Check out these stats on her singles titles: Eight Wimbledons, seven U.S. Opens, and four French Opens.

Earl Battey *BASEBALL*
This catcher played with the Chicago White Sox, Washington Senators and Minnesota Twins in the late '50s and early 60's. A career .270 hitter, at the height of his career he was considered one of the better backstops in the American League.

Johnny Sain *BASEBALL*
In a pitching career that spanned more than a decade in the 1940s and 1950s, Sain pitched for the Boston Braves, New York Yankees and Kansas City Athletics. Because the rest of the staff was notoriously weak, after he and teammate Warren Spahn pitched in a series, Braves fans were fond of saying, "Spahn and Sain, then pray for rain." Sain finished his career with a 139-116 record and went on to become a pitching coach. Introducing methods such as not having pitchers run between starts, he developed such stars as former Detroit Tiger Denny McClain, the last American League pitcher to win 30 games (31-6 in 1968).

Curtis Strange *GOLF*
Strange won the 1988 U.S. Open in a play-off with Nick Faldo, then successfully defended his title in 1989. He is the first player on the U.S. PGA Tour to win over $1 million in a single season. An early star, he played for the U.S. Walker Cup Team at age 20.

Pepe Mangual *BASEBALL*
One of the many baseball players coming from Ponce, Puerto Rico, Mangual roamed the infield for the Expos and Mets in the 1970s, batting a light .242 lifetime with a total of 16 homers.

Bob Purkey *BASEBALL*
Pitcher Purkey played a dozen years in the majors in the 1950s and 1960s with Pittsburgh, Cincinnati and St. Louis. He finished with 129 wins and 115 losses. He lost his only World Series start for Cincy against the Yanks in 1961. It was a complete game for Purkey—he was sent downtown in the ninth inning in a 3-2 loss by Mister 1961, himself, Roger Maris. Purkey also started the

second 1961 All-Star Game for the National League—a game that ended in a 1-1 tie in the ninth inning when rain fell. This was one of the years when two baseball All-Star games were played during the same season.

"Sad" Sam Jones BASEBALL
Right—in case you didn't have *The Baseball Encyclopedia* handy, this is also Sam "Toothpick" Jones. This 15-year pitching veteran of the 1950s and '60s played for seven ball clubs and finished his career winning only one more game than he lost. He led the National League in wins, bases on balls, and ERA in 1959, and in strikeouts in 1955, 1956 and 1958.

Billy Loes BASEBALL
This native of Queens, New York, had a pitching career that lasted more than a decade, most of it in the 1950s. In his salad days, he wore Dodger blue. Despite a 4.14 ERA, his best year was 1954, when he posted a 13-5 won-loss record, benefiting, you can bet your bottom Happy Felton cap, from a lineup that included the explosive lumber of Duke Snider, Gil Hodges, Carl Furillo, and Jackie Robinson.

"Happy" Chandler BASEBALL
Chandler—who was also the governor of Kentucky and a U.S. senator—became the commissioner of baseball when the venerable "Mountain" Landis died in 1945. Chandler's term lasted until 1951. Chandler also loved University of Kentucky basketball. You could see him at Wildcat games on a regular bases.

"Happy" Hairston BASKETBALL
Hairston, who went to NYU with the highly-touted and later forgotten Barry Kramer, spent close to a decade in the NBA, his best years coming with the Lakers in the early 1970s. Hairston had a fine pro career, averaging about 15 ppg. A highlight was the 1971-72 season, when he teamed with Wilt Chamberlain, Jerry West and Gail Goodrich

and company to win 33 straight games, shattering the old record of 20 set a year earlier by the Milwaukee Bucks. LA then cruised through its three playoff series, winning a dozen games and dropping only three. In the Championship series against the Knicks, Hairston was the second-leading rebounder on the floor—behind Chamberlain.

Greg Joy TRACK & FIELD
Canada's Joy won the silver medal in the high jump in the 1976 Olympic Games in Montreal. He leaped 7 feet, 3 3/4 inches, to finish behind Poland's Jacek Wszola, who set an Olympic record of 7-4.

Dave Bliss BASKETBALL
Dave Bliss learned his basketball under the guidance of The General, Robert Montgmery Knight. He served as an assistant with Knight in the mid 1970s at Indiana and helped to form some of the greatest college basketball teams of all time. He has recently revived basketball tradition at New Mexico by leading the Lobos to victory in the WAC tournament in the 1992-93 season and then winning the regular-season WAC crown in 1993-94. Before New Mexico, Bliss put in an impressive coaching stint at Oklahoma and SMU.

Bob Rush BASEBALL
Robert Ransom Rush's pitching career spanned three decades, starting in 1948 and finishing in 1960. About 10 seasons were spent in a Cub uniform, and he completed his career with a 3.65 lifetime ERA and a 17-win season in 1952.

Tom Fears FOOTBALL
From 1948-50, the Rams' Fears was the leading receiver in the NFL. In one game in 1950 against Green Bay he caught 18 passes—a mark that's still a record. He was named to the Pro Football Hall of Fame in 1960 and had a short stint in 1970 as the skipper of the New Orleans Saints.

Dean "The Dream" Meminger BASKETBALL

"The Dream" played at Marquette under Al McGuire and then packed his bags for the Big Apple, where he threw in with the New York Knicks for several seasons in the 1970s. In college he was MVP of the NIT in 1970, playing for a strong club that chose to enter the smaller tournament rather than The Big Dance.

Buzz Capra BASEBALL

Capra pitched for the New York Mets from 1971-73 and the Atlanta Braves from 1974-77. For his career, he won 31 games and lost 37. His best year was 1974 with the Braves, when he went 16-8 with a league-leading 2.28 ERA.

"Mean" Joe Greene FOOTBALL

A five-time All-Pro in the 1970s, this North Texas State star led the Steelers to four Super Bowl championships. Greene played his entire career (1969-81) with Pittsburgh. When negotiating his first contract, Greene went to the management asking for $600,000. His logic was that it "would take a $600,000 man to stop O.J. Simpson."

Dave "The Rave" Stallworth BASKETBALL

This pre-Xavier McDaniels Wichita State star played for the New York Knicks at the time they were putting the pieces together for their great teams of the late '60s and early '70s. "The Rave" was a respectable forward, but with the likes of Bill Bradley and Dave DeBusschere on the payroll, he mostly had to come off the bench for his scores. One of those occasions was the fifth game of the 1970 playoffs against the Lakers. Center Willis Reed was injured and the Knicks trailed by a bakers dozen at the half. Inserting Stallworth as a forward and going without a center—thereby forcing Wilt Chamberlain to play away from the basket—the Knicks rallied for a dramatic 107-100 victory. Stallworth made one outstanding offensive play in which he drove around Chamberlain for a hoop, making New York fans go wild.

A great shooting touch and a superior ability to collect garbage off his own glass made Bernard King one of the primo scorers and offensive rebounders in NBA history.

26 | ALL-ROYALTY AND HEADS OF STATE TEAM

Eligibility: Each team entry must include a first name, last name, nickname or sports expression that suggests royalty or head of state.

Samples: Stacey King
Duke Snider

And your nominees are ...

_____   _____

_____   _____

_____   _____

_____   _____

_____   _____

_____   _____

_____   _____

_____   _____

Dick's Picks
All-Royalty and Heads of State Team

Bernard King BASKETBALL

Stacey King BASKETBALL

Don King PROMOTER

Mel Queen Jr. BASEBALL

Cozell McQueen BASKETBALL

Duke Snider BASEBALL

Duke Maas BASEBALL

Walter Dukes BASKETBALL

"The Count," John Montefusco BASEBALL

Marquis Grissom BASEBALL

Acie Earl BASKETBALL

Earl Monroe BASKETBALL

Earl Gros FOOTBALL

Ali Haji-Sheikh FOOTBALL

"The Sultan of Swat," Babe Ruth BASEBALL

John Tudor BASEBALL

"The Chief," Robert Parish BASKETBALL

Roger Kingdom TRACK & FIELD

Margaret Court TENNIS

Darrell Royal FOOTBALL

Reggie Royals BASKETBALL

Don Kaiser BASEBALL

Eddie LeBaron FOOTBALL

Bob Prince ANNOUNCER

Trivial Tidbits

Bernard King *BASKETBALL*

King was one of the game's great scorers and offensive rebounders. He averaged about 23 points per game for his career, with a league-leading 32.9 average in the 1984-85 basketball season. King is also in the top 20 scorers on the all-time NBA list, having put up 19,432 points for his career. Who can ever forget the Ernie and Bernie Show, when he teamed up with Ernie Grunfeld at the University of Tennessee? Ernie would feed Bernie who took it to the goal.

Mel Queen Jr. *BASEBALL*

After beginning his major-league career as a fielder, Queen follow his father's footsteps and become a pitcher. He fared better from the mound, posting a lifetime 20-17 record and a 3.14 ERA. With the Angels in 1971, he appeared in 44 games, mostly in relief.

Cozell McQueen *BASKETBALL*

A stellar performer for Jim Valvano, McQueen played on the N.C. State team that shocked the Phi Slama Jamas of Houston in the 1984 NCAA Championship game. His job was to clean the glass and play the tough D. Other players on that team included Lorenzo Charles, Sidney Lowe, Derrick Whittenburg and Thurl Bailey.

Duke Maas *BASEBALL*

Maas had a so-so seven-year career, finishing the bigs with a 45-44 record and completing 21 of his 91 starts. He has one very unusual statistic—an 81.00 ERA for the 1958 World Series. He only appeared in the second game of that fall classic and only pitched a third of an inning, relieving starter Bullet Bob Turley, who was sent to the showers after only going a third of an inning himself. Johnny Kucks finally came in to apply cold water to the Milwaukee Braves, who, when all was said and done, had put up seven runs in the inning and were well on their way to a 13-5 rout.

Walter Dukes *BASKETBALL*

Walter Dukes was a collegiate All-American. This center led Seton Hall to prominence and became the NCAA all-time leader for rebounds in a single season, having pulled down 734 in 1953. The 7-foot Dukes, who was in the NBA in the 1950s and '60s, played eight seasons. He averaged about 10 points per game shooting 37 percent from the field. With an average playing time of only 27 minutes per game, he fouled out about 20 percent of the time. Dukes played with the Harlem Globetrotters before joining the New York Knicks.

"The Count," John Montefusco *BASEBALL*

Although he won 31 combined games his second and third seasons in the majors with the Giants, The Count of Montefusco won only 56 more his next 10 years in the major leagues. His best outing was a 9-0 no-hitter against the Braves in 1976.

Marquis Grissom *BASEBALL*

Grissom is one of the great players of the game today. For the 1994 season he finished second in the National League in runs scored (96), third in stolen bases (36), and eighth in hits (137). This Montreal Expos star, whose name is the title of a noble ranking between a duke and earl or count, was not named for nobility. Instead, he was named for a car, the Mercury Grand Marquis, which his father was working on in the auto factory when his son was born.

Earl Gros *FOOTBALL*

Gros was a running back—first at LSU and then for nine seasons in the NFL (1962-70). As a pro, he accounted for over 4,400 yards rushing and receiving , and scored 38 touchdowns. At 6-foot-3 and 224 pounds, he was a big man. Early in his career, while playing for the Green Bay Packers, a series of game-related injuries caused the Pack to be left with only two healthy linebackers at halftime. So, the 224-pound fullback was inserted into the defense for much of the second half.

Ali Haji-Shikh *FOOTBALL*
This ex-New York Giant of the 1980s had his best season in 1983 when he made 35 of 42 field goal attempts. If I had an All-Foreign Named Field Goal Kickers team, he'd be right up at the top along with Garo Yepremian, Jan Stenerud, Rolf Benirschke, Fuad Reviz, Luis & Max Zendejas, Carlos Huerta, Efren Herrera, Pete Stoyanovich, Rafael Septien, Horst Muhlmann, Uwe von Schamann, Raul Allegre, Donald Igwebuike, Danny Villanueva, Ben Agajanian, and Toni Fritsch. Did I leave anyone out?

John Tudor *BASEBALL*
Tudor pitched for 11 years in the majors, most of them with Boston and St. Louis. His best year by far was 1985 when he was 21-8 and sported a stingy 1.93 ERA. Tudor had an excellent winning percentage—105 wins and only 68 losses (.607). One reason he was so successful was that he walked fewer than three batters per game.

"The Chief," Robert Parish *BASKETBALL*
How many NBA stars can you name that went to Centenary College? I can only think of one, myself—Robert Parish. The Chief is one of the most durable players in the history of the NBA, seemingly lasting forever. Who knows, he may have a 20-year career. Parish started with Golden State in 1977 and has played with the Celts since 1981. During the '80s, the Celts made it into the NBA finals five times, winning the championship three times. The frontline of Bird, Parish and McHale will go down in history as one of the best ever. The Chief is consistent—a guy who does it all on a regular basis. He recently signed with the Charlotte Hornets who are seeking winning experience.

Roger Kingdom *TRACK & FIELD*
Pittsburgh's Roger Kingdom won a gold medal in the 110-meter hurdles in both the Los Angeles (1984) and Seoul (1988) Olympic games, setting Olympic records both years.

Darrell Royal *FOOTBALL*
One of the great college coaches, Royal's Texas teams won about 75 percent of their games. He rarely called for a pass, and he introduced the wishbone offense that has been taken up with a vengeance by Texas' hated rival—the Oklahoma Sooners. Royal's teams won 30 straight games between 1968 and 1970.

Eddie LeBaron *FOOTBALL*
LeBaron quarterbacked in the NFL, CFL and AFL in the 1950s and in the early 1960s. Diminutive by today's NFL quarterbacking standards, the 5-foot-9 tosser played ten NFL seasons. He completed about 50 percent of his passes, 104 of which went for touchdowns.

Bob Prince *BASEBALL*
A longtime announcer for the Pittsburgh Pirates, Bob Prince has also manned the mike at times on national television.

27 | ALL-NATURAL MATERIALS TEAM

Eligibility: Each team entry must include a first name, last name, nickname, or sports expression that suggests a natural material.

Samples: Dwight Stones
Mercury Morris

And your nominees are ...

_____   _____

_____   _____

_____   _____

_____   _____

_____   _____

_____   _____

_____   _____

_____   _____

Dick's Picks
All-Natural Materials Team

Rocky Colavito *BASEBALL*

Rocky Bridges *BASEBALL*

Dwight Stones *TRACK & FIELD*

Steve Stone *BASEBALL*

Alberto "Hands of Stone" Duran *BOXING*

Wilbur Wood *BASEBALL*

Al Wood *BASKETBALL*

Sandy Koufax *BASEBALL*

Sandy Amoros *BASEBALL*

Clay Dalrymple *BASEBALL*

Clay Carroll *BASEBALL*

Dwight Clay *BASKETBALL*

Earl "The Pearl" Monroe *BASKETBALL*

Pearl Washington *BASKETBALL*

Calvin Peete *GOLF*

Rodney Peete *FOOTBALL*

Horace Ivory *FOOTBALL*

Alice Marble *TENNIS*

Roy Marble *BASKETBALL*

Art Shell *FOOTBALL*

"Iron" Mike Ditka *FOOTBALL*

Gerald Irons *FOOTBALL*

Bobby Orr *HOCKEY*

"The Silver Queen,"
Merlene Ottey *TRACK & FIELD*

Charlie Silvera *BASEBALL*

Golden Richards *FOOTBALL*

Corky Calhoun *BASKETBALL*

Eugene "Mercury" Morris *FOOTBALL*

Charlie Waters *FOOTBALL*

Salty Parker *BASEBALL*

Don "Air" Coryell *FOOTBALL*

Note:
▼ For names that suggest foliage: See All-Foliage Team (page 24)

Trivial Tidbits

Rocky Colavito *BASEBALL*

Rocco Domenico Colavito—a product of Bronx, New York—was one of the most popular players to ever don a Cleveland Indians uniform, Gus Bell and Super Joe Charbonneau notwithstanding. Playing throughout most of the 1950s and 1960s, he hit 374 home runs for his career. He was also involved in one of the highest profile trades in baseball history, when Cleveland sent him to Detroit for Harvey Kuenn.

Rocky Bridges *BASEBALL*

Bridges kicked around the majors for about a decade, most of it in the 1950s, playing for non-contenders. He had almost 2,300 at bats and hit a lifetime .247. The name Rocky Bridges makes me think that this athlete would be a fine selection for my All-Scenic Americana Team.

Dwight Stones *TRACK & FIELD*

Dwight Stones won a bronze medal in 1972 and again in 1976 in the Olympic high jump. In the '76 Olympics, he had to quit early in the competition because of slippery conditions. The eventual gold and silver winners kept competing, as their straight-on approaches to the bar were less dangerous than Stones' side approach. In the 1984 Los Angeles Olympics, Stones leaped higher than he ever had in Olympic competition, but so did three other competitors and he did not win a medal.

Steve Stone *BASEBALL*

In 1980, while playing with Baltimore, Steve Stone won the Cy Young Award. His record that year was 25-7, but his ERA was 3.23—one of the highest ever in the history of the award. Stone's lifetime record was 107-93 with a 3.96 ERA compiled with the Giants, White Sox, Cubs and Orioles. He now forms an outstanding broadcasting team with Harry Cary for the Chicago Cubs.

Alberto "Hands of Stone" Duran *BOXING*

This Panamanian boxer held four different world titles from 1972 to 1990—lightweight, welterweight, junior middleweight, and middleweight. His pro record was 86-9-0 and 60 knockouts in 1980, the year of his famous "no mas" fight with Sugar Ray Leonard. After that bout, he announced his retirement, but recently has resumed fighting.

Wilbur Wood *BASEBALL*

Wood, who won 164 games in a 17-year career, was one of the premier knuckleballers of all time. Once, for the White Sox, he started both games of a doubleheader. His workhorse ethic is demonstrated by his leading the American League three times in pitching appearances, four times in games started, and two times in innings pitched. In 1972 and 1973 he led the American League in wins, both times with 24 victories.

Al Wood *BASKETBALL*

Wood was one of the North Carolina Tar Heels' main go-to guys in the early 1980s and went on to a short pro career, playing for Atlanta, San Diego, Seattle and Dallas. In college, when he was hot, he could really can the J with the best of them. Who can ever forget him lighting up the boards for 39 in the 1981 NCAA semifinal against Virginia?

Sandy Koufax *BASEBALL*

One of the greatest pitchers in the history of baseball, Koufax wound up with 165 career wins, 2,396 strikeouts, and four no-hitters. He was a lifetime Dodger. For the 1963-1966 seasons his ERA was 1.88, 1.74, 2.04 and 1.73 for each season, respectively.

Sandy Amoros BASEBALL

This native Cuban spent played most of his career in the 1950s, in a Dodger uniform. His lifetime batting average was .255. He starred in the 1955 World Series, the first time the Dodgers came away with the whole enchilada. In that fall classic, Amoros batted .333 and made a spectacular catch to start a double play in the deciding seventh game, which the Dodgers won 2-0.

Clay Dalrymple BASEBALL

Dalrymple caught over 1,000 games from 1960 to 1971, most of them for the Phillies. He finished up his career with a .233 average and 327 RBIs.

Clay Carroll BASEBALL

Carroll pitched for Cincinnati in the mid-70s and was around when the "Big Red Machine" beat the Boston Red Sox in the chillingly close 1975 World Series. He was the winner of the seventh game, decided by a bloop single by Joe Morgan in the top of the ninth inning. The series, watched by 71 million people, was not supposed to be as close as it was, and things looked bleak for the Reds. One of their earlier wins was on a disputed, extra-inning interference call, and the Sox had just won the sixth game on a dramatic 12th-inning homer by Carlton Fisk. In Game 7, Boston scored three runs early and the 4-3 Reds victory had to be pulled from the jaws of defeat.

Dwight Clay BASKETBALL

On January 19, 1974 Dwight Clay hit one of the most memorable winning shots in the history of college basketball. With UCLA on an 88-game winning streak, and the Bruins up by eleven points with only moments to go, Notre Dame rallied to score the last 12 points—Clay hitting the corner J as the final seconds ticked off for a 71-70 Irish victory.

Pearl Washington BASKETBALL

Pearl Washington was heralded as a New York City legend. He entered Syracuse University in the mid '80s with his shake and bake moves and dazzled them at the Carrier Dome. He went on to a two-year career in the NBA, playing for the New Jersey Nets and the Miami Heat.

Horace Ivory FOOTBALL

This Oklahoma Sooner back played five seasons in the NFL starting with the 1977-78 season. He put up 108 points for his career, most of the scoring coming with the New England Patriots. His best season was 1978, when his 693 yards put him second in rushing for the Pats—right behind Sam "The Bam" Cunningham, a member of my All-Rhymes team, along with Mel Parnell and Tony Barone (last name rhymes with baloney).

Alice Marble TENNIS

Alice Marble was one of the dominant forces on the women's tennis scene in the late 1930s and early 40s, winning four U.S. championships and one Wimbledon.

Roy Marble BASKETBALL

Marble had spectacular leaping ability. He played guard on several super Iowa teams along with Chicago Bulls star B.J. Armstrong. He went on to play one year in the NBA with the Atlanta Hawks.

Art Shell FOOTBALL

This guy personifies the Al Davis Raider tradition. Shell, the current Los Angeles Raiders head coach, was a heavily accoladed offensive tackle for the Raiders, playing from 1968 to 1982. He was extremely effective blocking with Gene Upshaw in the 1977 Super Bowl, a game in which the Raiders rushed for 266 yards in a 32-10 hammering of the Vikings.

"Iron" Mike Ditka   *FOOTBALL*

Ditka was the man "Papa" George Halas personally picked to take over the reins of the Bears upon his retirement. He found the winner's circle, leading his team to a victory in Super Bowl XX. As a tight end, Ditka was outstanding—an All-American at Pitt and a three-time All-Pro in the NFL. Ditka also makes my All-Sweater Team with Lou Carnesseca and Bob Knight.

Charlie Silvera   *BASEBALL*

The Yankees' third-string catcher of the '50s—behind Yogi Berra and Elston Howard—Silvera was seen more on Topps baseball cards than he was at the plate. In nearly 500 total plate appearances over a decade, he hit a very respectable .282. He also collected quite a few World Series checks.

Salty Parker   *BASEBALL*

Parker was the manager of the New York Mets in 1967, two years before their championship season. His career stats as a player: one season with Detroit in 1936, 25 at bats. A few years back, the Mets used to refer to Lenny Dykstra and Wally Bachman, who were at the top of their lineup card, as their table setters. In this scholarly tome, I prefer a table setting that includes Salty Parker placed alongside Pepper Martin.

Reggie Jackson was not just Mr. October, he was Mr. Tape Job and Mr. Clutch all rolled into one.

28 | ALL-CALENDER AND TIME TEAM

Eligibility: Each team entry must include a first name, last name, nickname or sports expression that suggests a calendar or time concept.

Samples: Rick Monday
Chuck Daly

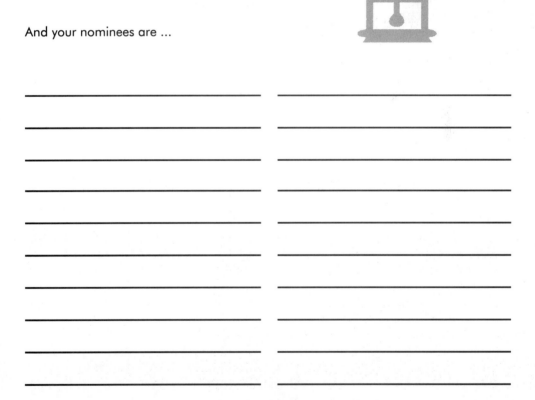

And your nominees are ...

_____   _____

_____   _____

_____   _____

_____   _____

_____   _____

_____   _____

_____   _____

_____   _____

_____   _____

Dick's Picks
All-Calendar and Time Team

Brian Winters *BASKETBALL*

Summer Sanders *SWIMMING*

Jim Summer *FOOTBALL*

Champ Summers *BASEBALL*

Dawn Fraser *SWIMMING*

Rick Monday *BASEBALL*

Early Wynn *BASEBALL*

Alonzo Mourning *BASKETBALL*

Daley Thompson *TRACK & FIELD*

Chuck Daly *BASKETBALL*

John Daly *GOLF*

Boots Day *BASEBALL*

Darren Daye *BASKETBALL*

Bob Knight *BASKETBALL*

Billy Knight *BASKETBALL*

Ray Knight *BASEBALL*

Jack Spring *BASEBALL*

Larry Friday *FOOTBALL*

Paul Westphal *BASKETBALL*

Steve Weeks *HOCKEY*

Joe Auer *FOOTBALL*

Scott May *BASKETBALL*

Lee May *BASEBALL*

Mr. October," Reggie Jackson *BASEBALL*

Don January *GOLF*

Steve August *FOOTBALL*

June Jones *FOOTBALL*

Trivial Tidbits

Brian Winters *BASKETBALL*
A nine-year NBA veteran, Winters spent most of his career with the Milwaukee Bucks, where he scored more than 16 points per game. Between the 1975-76 and 1979-80 seasons he started at guard, and in each of those five campaigns there was a different starting center—Elmore Smith, John Gianelli, Kent Benson, Bob Lanier and Swen Nater. Turnstile City. No wonder the Bucks never went anywhere. Nater, incidentally, has the distinction of being the only NBA first-round draft choice never to have started a game in college.

Summer Sanders *SWIMMING*
In the 1992 Summer Olympics at Barcelona, Sanders won the gold medal in the 200-meter butterfly. She also won a silver and bronze in the 200-meter and 400-meter individual medleys, respectively.

Dawn Fraser *SWIMMING*
Fraser, an Australian swimmer, won the gold medal in the 100-meter freestyle in three consecutive Olympic Games—1956, 1960 and 1964. She was the first woman to break the 1-minute barrier in the event.

Rick Monday *BASEBALL*
He made thousands of catches in 19 years of patrolling major-league outfields, but perhaps Monday's most famous snatch was in 1976 when he grabbed an American flag from two protesters who jumped out of the stands to burn it. For weeks thereafter he was a hero to fans—the guy who stood up for his country. They ate him up. Monday was a very respectable and feared hitter in his day. His career numbers were a .264 batting average with 241 home runs and 1,619 hits.

Early Wynn *BASEBALL*
Pitcher Wynn won exactly 300 games during a sparkling career that began in 1939 and ended in 1963. He was 43 when he won number 300. While a player, he wrote a sports column for a Cleveland newspaper.

Alonzo Mourning *BASKETBALL*
The Charlotte Hornets' Mourning is one of three active NBA centers—all of them athletes that other teams would love to get their mits on—to hold a Georgetown sheepskin. The other two players are the Knicks' Patrick Ewing and the Nuggets' Dikembe Mutombo. No surprise that Georgetown attracts centers. Coach John Thompson played that position at Providence College in the early 1960s. Mourning set an NCAA career record for number of shots blocked, 453, while at Georgetown.

Daley Thompson *TRACK & FIELD*
Great Britain's Thompson won the gold in the decathlon in the 1980 and 1984 Olympic Games. In 1976, at age 18—the youngest contestant in the decathlon field—Thompson also represented the Brits and finished 18th.

Chuck Daly *BASKETBALL*
Chuck Daly piloted the Detroit Pistons to two consecutive NBA titles in 1989 and 1990 before taking over to coach the New Jersey Nets. He also coached the USA's "dream team" to a gold medal in the 1992 Summer Olympic Games.

John Daly *GOLF*
John Daly came from virtual obscurity to win the 1991 PGA Championship. He is known on the tour as one of golfing's long-ball hitters—the Dave "King Kong" Kingman of his sport. Off the links, his life has been a bit of a soap opera.

Darren Daye *BASKETBALL*
A product of UCLA in the post-Wooden era, Daye played for three NBA teams in the mid- to late-1980s. During his five-year career, he averaged 6.8 ppg.

Billy Knight *BASKETBALL*
One of the first major stars to come out of the Pitt basketball program, Knight played in the pros for more than a decade, many them in the old ABA. He made the adjustment from the ABA to the NBA hardly missing a step, averaging more than 28 points with Indiana of the ABA in 1975-76 and 26.6 the next year when the team entered the NBA. His numbers placed him second among all scorers in his first NBA season.

Ray Knight *BASEBALL*
For many years, Ray Knight's wife—golfer Nancy Lopez—grabbed the lion's share of the family headlines. That all changed in the 1986 World Series when Knight could barely be stopped at the plate and was voted Series MVP. Besides getting nine hits, more than any other Met, his leadoff homer in the seventh inning of the seventh and deciding game, with the score tied, proved to be both the game- and Series-winning hit.

Paul Westphal *BASKETBALL*
A little bit of a stretch for this list, but, hey, fall is a season and it's part of this former USC Trojan's name. Westphal was a first-team All-NBA selection three times in the late 1970s when he played for the Suns. He began his career with the Celtics, where he came off the bench to relieve Jo Jo White and Don Chaney. Westphal is now coach of Charles Barkley and the Phoenix Suns, one of the NBA's premier teams.

Scott May *BASKETBALL*
Forward Scott May had a 23.5 ppg scoring average in 1976, leading the Indiana Hoosiers to a perfect 32-0 record and the NCAA Championship. They beat Big-10 rival Michigan in the final, 86-68. He also starred for the 1976 Olympic team that won gold in Montreal.

Lee May *BASEBALL*
"The Big Bopper" played for four major-league teams in a career that spanned from 1965 to 1982. He finished with 354 home runs, 1,244 RBIs and a respectable .267 batting average. Some of his best years were with the Cincinnati Reds, where he was one of the main men for a long time. In 1971 he was dealt away in a multiplayer arrangement with the Houston Astros that involved the Reds getting Joe Morgan, Jack Billingham and Cesar Geronimo—not to mention Denis Menke and Ed Armbrister. The rest is history.

"Mr. October," Reggie Jackson *BASEBALL*
Reggie Jackson, who hit 563 home runs during his 20 years in the major leagues, hit only one in his rookie season in 118 times at bat. One of the best ever to grace a major-league lineup, his highlight film easily rivals Dominique Wilkins' collection of celluloid. And then some. No baseball fan can ever forget Jackson's three consecutive homers for the Yankees in Game 6 of the 1977 World Series—a tilt that immediately sent the Dodgers bopping and slopping straight back to la-la land. Each of those blasts was on a first pitch and each of them off a different pitcher. Unbelievable, baby. Mr. October was the guy with the "S" on his chest that day.

29 | ALL-SIZES, MEASUREMENTS, AND DISTANCES TEAM

Eligibility: Each team entry must include a first name, last name, nickname or sports expression that suggests an absolute or comparative size, measurement or distance.

Samples: Frank Shorter
Mark Minor

And your nominees are ...

_____   _____

_____   _____

_____   _____

_____   _____

_____   _____

_____   _____

_____   _____

_____   _____

_____   _____

Dick's Picks
All-Sizes, Measurements, and Distances Team

Floyd Little FOOTBALL

Chris Short BASEBALL

Purvis Short BASKETBALL

Frank Shorter TRACK & FIELD

Ed "Too Tall" Jones FOOTBALL

Dale Long BASEBALL

Verlon Biggs FOOTBALL

"Big Daddy" Lipscomb FOOTBALL

Gerald Small FOOTBALL

Doug Small HOCKEY

Mel Farr FOOTBALL

Les Josephson FOOTBALL

Pee Wee Reese BASEBALL

Sidney Lowe BASKETBALL

Nate "Tiny" Archibald BASKETBALL

Kelvin Ransey BASKETBALL

James "Jumbo" Elliot TRACK & FIELD

John "Jumbo" Elliot FOOTBALL

Jumbo Ozaki GOLF

Fatty Taylor BASKETBALL

Wiley Peck BASKETBALL

George Yardley BASKETBALL

Foots Walker BASKETBALL

Major Harris FOOTBALL

Mark Minor BASKETBALL

Mary T. Meagher SWIMMING

Minnie Minoso BASEBALL

Bob Pettit BASKETBALL

Jim Nill HOCKEY

Jearl Miles TRACK & FIELD

Trivial Tidbits

Floyd Little   *FOOTBALL*

Floyd Little was one of the great running backs at Syracuse University, wearing the same No. 44 as did Jim Brown and Ernie Davis. While at Syracuse he played in the same backfield with Jim Nance, and later with Larry Csonka. For his career with the Broncos he rushed for 6,323 yards, had 215 pass receptions and scored 52 TDs.

Frank Shorter   *TRACK & FIELD*

In 1972, Frank Shorter won the Olympic marathon, missing the world record held by Abebe Bikila by less than 10 seconds. He became the first American to win the event since 1928 and was virtually unchallenged. In 1976, Shorter tried to repeat his victory, but came in second to German Waldemar Cierpinski in a very close race.

Ed "Too Tall" Jones   *FOOTBALL*

At 6 feet 9 inches, Ed "Too Tall" Jones was, during his day, the tallest player in the history of the National Football League. He terrorized opposing quarterbacks so much throughout his 15-year career that the Dallas Cowboys' report for his activity for a game included not only tackles and sacks, but "scares." Intimidation City!

Dale Long   *BASEBALL*

This man is aptly named, because he's in the record books for his long ball. In 1956, Long set a major-league record by clobbering a home run in eight consecutive games. His bid for nine was thwarted by Don Newcombe, the Dodger great. Long's record was tied by Don Mattingly in 1987.

"Big Daddy" Lipscomb   *FOOTBALL*

Tipping in at 6 feet 6 inches and 284 pounds, Eugene "Big Daddy" Lipscomb is not completely out of whack by today's standards of human slab, but he was an absolute giant when he played defensive line in

the NFL 40 years ago and was regularly an All-Pro. He played with the Rams three seasons, the Colts five seasons and the Steelers two seasons. Perhaps his most significant play came late in the fourth quarter of the 1958 NFL Champioship game when he stopped Frank Gifford on third down. That forced the Giants to punt and the Colts took the ball and drove for a game-tying field goal in the final seconds, then won the game in overtime, 23-17.

Pee Wee Reese   *BASEBALL*

Longtime Dodger shortstop Reese finished his 16-year career with 2,170 hits. He played in 44 World Series games and had a total of 169 at bats and 46 hits in those fall classics—numbers that put him in the all-time top 10 in all three categories. He threw out Elston Howard for the very last out in the 1955 Series, giving the Brooklyn Dodgers their first Series victory.

Sidney Lowe   *BASKETBALL*

Lowe was on the North Carolina State team that won the 1983 NCAA Championship in the wild finish over Houston. This game, in which State was a huge underdog, had such an exciting finish that my good friend Coach Jim Valvano had the last few seconds of the audio portion of it recorded so that it would play when someone rang the doorbell to his home. Lowe, a true student of the game, followed in Valvano's footsteps and went on to coach.

Nate "Tiny" Archibald   *BASKETBALL*

A genuine superstar, Nate Archibald could hang, twist and dance in the aisles with the best. This UTEP product had a brilliant, 13-year NBA career, which included being named to the NBA All-Star Team several times. Breaking into the pros with the Cincinnati Royals, Tiny Archibald didn't take long to adjust to the NBA. By his second year he was second in the league in scoring (28.2) and third in assists. The next season, 1972-1973, he accomplished something no other basketball player has done—leading the league in both scoring (34.0 points per game) and assists (11.4 per game). By then the Royals had become the Kansas City-Omaha Kings, later dropping Omaha, and are now the Sacramento Kings. Archibald played for five teams in his pro career.

Kelvin Ransey BASKETBALL
Ransey played on some super teams at Ohio State coached by Eldon Miller. He had his moments in the NBA. He started in his first year and made the NBA All-Rookie Team. He played in the NBA for six seasons, averaging more than 11 points per game.

James "Jumbo" Elliot TRACK & FIELD
"Jumbo" Elliot was the longtime coach of the Villanova University track team and the man who built it into a national powerhouse in the 1960s. Many of his athletes won Olympic gold medals, including Charles Jenkins in the 400 meters (1956), Don Bragg in the pole vault (1960), and Larry James in the 400 meters and 4x400-meter relay (1968).

George Yardley BASKETBALL
George Yardley was a superb scorer. Playing for the Fort Wayne Pistons before they moved to Detroit, Yardley became the first NBA player to score more than 2,000 points in a single season—scoring 2,001 in the 1957-58 campaign, an average of 27.8 points per game. Think about it—if they ever make a movie of his life, they can call it *2001: A Hoops Odyssey.*

Mary T. Meagher SWIMMING
In 1980, when she was only 15 years old, Meagher (pronounced Ma-her) held the world record in the 200-meter butterfly at 2 minutes, 7.01 seconds—almost 3 1/2 seconds better than the winning time in the boycotted 1980 Olympics in Moscow. In the 1984 Olympics, she finally got her chance to showcase herself to the world, dominating the butterfly events and winning the gold in the 100- and 200-meter races.

Minnie Minoso BASEBALL
Born Saturnino Orestes Armas Minosoy Arietta Minoso—you can see why he goes by Minnie—this Havana-born athlete is the only big-leaguer to have played in five different decades, although he had to "cheat" a little to do it. He came up in 1949 and played until 1964, then made brief appearances in a handful of games—five total—in 1976 and 1980. During the meaty part of his career, he was the season leader in the American League at one time or another in hits, doubles, triples and stolen bases.

Bob Pettit BASKETBALL
Bob Pettit was premier forward with a velvet touch. Dominique Wilkins notwithstanding, Hall of Famer Pettit is the Hawks' career- and single-season leader in rebounds and single-season leader in scoring. During Pettit's day, the Hawks were in St. Louis. He was twice the NBA's MVP and a member of the All-NBA team 10 times. He averaged 26.4 points and 16.2 rebounds for his 11-year career.

Today, in the era of PC, we'd have to call him "Vertically Impaired" Reese—somehow it just doesn't have the same ring, does it?

Robert Montgomery Knight, one of my favorite generals both on and off the court, has had the magic touch for developing hustling, championship-level teams.

30 | ALL-MILITARY TEAM

Eligibility: Each team entry must include a first name, last name, nickname or sports expression that suggests a military term or a famous military leader.

Samples: Walt Garrison (military term)
Horace Grant (famous military leader)

And your nominees are ...

_____   _____

_____   _____

_____   _____

_____   _____

_____   _____

_____   _____

_____   _____

_____   _____

Dick's Picks
All-Military Team

Military Terms:

Wally Bunker *BASEBALL*

Paul Warfield *FOOTBALL*

Kenny Battle *BASKETBALL*

Chet Forte *FOOTBALL*

Wally Post *BASEBALL*

Vic Power *BASEBALL*

Walt Garrison *FOOTBALL*

"The Admiral," David Robinson *BASKETBALL*

"The Aircraft Carrier," Jerome Whitehead *BASKETBALL*

"The General," Bob Knight *BASKETBALL*

Major Harris *FOOTBALL*

Bobby Majors *FOOTBALL*

Trooper Washington *BASKETBALL*

Marshall Bridges *BASEBALL*

Tom LaGarde *BASKETBALL*

Terry Furlow *BASKETBALL*

Dave Rader *BASEBALL*

Military Leaders:

Name *SPORT*	Military Leader
Napoleon McCallum *FOOTBALL*	Napoleon Bonaparte
Napoleon Lajoie *BASEBALL*	Napoleon Bonaparte
Wellington Mara *FOOTBALL*	Duke of Wellington
Horace Grant *BASKETBALL*	Ulysses S. Grant
Greg Lee *BASKETBALL*	Robert E. Lee
Mark Jackson *BASKETBALL*	Stonewall Jackson
Sherman Plunkett *FOOTBALL*	William Sherman

Pat Sheridan *BASEBALL*	Philip Sheridan
Charlie Scott *BASKETBALL*	Winfield Scott
Dick Stuart *BASEBALL*	J.E.B. Stuart
Larry Eisenhauer *FOOTBALL*	Dwight D. Eisenhower
McArthur Lane *FOOTBALL*	Douglas McArthur
Jim Marshall *FOOTBALL*	George C. Marshall
Mel Patton *TRACK & FIELD*	George S. Patton
Bill Bradley *BASKETBALL*	Omar Bradley
Roosevelt Grier *FOOTBALL*	Theodore Roosevelt
Kermit Washington *BASKETBALL*	George Washington
Steve Howe *BASEBALL*	William Howe
Cleon Jones *BASEBALL*	John Paul Jones
Gaylord Perry *BASEBALL*	Oliver Perry

Note:
▼ For names suggesting weapons or ammunition: See All-Weapons and Ammo Team

Trivial Tidbits

Wally Bunker *BASEBALL*

Bunker broke into the American League in 1964, going 19-5 as a 19-year old with the O's and tossing a World Series shutout for them two years later. 1966 was the year the Birds stuck it to the Dodgers in the fall classic, four games to none—especially in the pitching department. The O's hurlers had a combined 0.50 ERA. Yup, that's not a printing error—it's a piddly half of a run per game. Bunker's outing was a 1-0 sparkler, in which he only gave up one extra-base hit.

Paul Warfield *FOOTBALL*

Warfield, one of the all-time-great NFL wide receivers, was a PTPer for a decade. His best year was 1968 when he played for the Browns. Stats: 50 receptions for 1,067 yards and 12 touchdowns. Awesome, baby. Unfortunately, the Browns got coldcocked 34-0 by the Colts in the playoffs that year, so that was all she wrote for 1968. Warfield was traded to the Dolphins and picked up a couple of championship rings with Miami in the early 1970s. When he retired, he was fourth on the all-time yardage list. Interestingly, Warfield played defensive back at Ohio State but switched to WR when he joined the NFL. He was also a world-class long jumper in his day.

Vic Power *BASEBALL*

Nobody who grew up closely following baseball in the '50s could forget Vic Power and his pendulumlike batting stance and flamboyancy on and off the field. He was a graceful but flashy fielder, known for snagging thrown or hit balls with a sweeping glove hand. He finished his career as a first baseman with a .992 fielding average—that's fewer than one error every 100 chances. In a career spanning a dozen years, Power was a lifetime .284 hitter, but didn't live up to his name—hitting one home run in every 50 at bats.

Walt Garrison *FOOTBALL*

This workhorse Dallas Cowboy back carried the ball for the club during the Calvin Hill-Roger Staubach era. When Walt Garrison ran, it took more than one defender to bring him down.

"The Admiral," David Robinson *BASKETBALL*

Robinson—known as "The Admiral" for his stint at the U.S. Naval Academy and two-year Naval career—was the 1989-90 NBA Rookie of the Year. He is still the make-it-happen guy for the San Antonio Spurs, winning the 1993-1994 NBA scoring title. Robinson set the Spurs' career rebounding record after playing only four seasons, and when he slams, it's a rim rattler!

"The General," Bob Knight *BASKETBALL*

Bob Knight is a member of the National Basketball Hall of Fame. He has had a brilliant coaching career both at West Point and at Indiana University. He's had amazing success at Indiana, leading the Hoosiers to National Championships in 1976, 1981 and 1987. He has compiled 640 coaching wins and certainly has developed a reputation that is of national stature. He is a flat out legend in the world of sports. Nicknamed "The General", Knight's teams play with discipline. You can rest assured if competing against Indiana you will be in a battle. His teams always give 110 percent, which is a reflection of his tenacity.

Major Harris *FOOTBALL*

The scrambling Major Harris quarterbacked the West Virginia Mountaineers in the late 1980s. He finished third in the 1989 Heisman voting behind winner Andre Ware of Houston and runner-up Anthony Thompson of Indiana.

Trooper Washington BASKETBALL

Washington spent about six seasons playing pro ball. He averaged about 10 points and 10 rebounds a game, and he was almost as accurate shooting from the field (53 percent) as he was from the foul line (61 percent).

Marshall Bridges BASEBALL

Nearly all of Bridges' career was spent as a relief pitcher. He appeared in 201 games, winning 23 and losing 13, with 25 saves. He was a fastball pitcher, with 302 strikeouts in 345 innings.

Jim Marshall FOOTBALL

Few players in NFL history can match the longevity of this famed member of the Purple People Eaters. Marshall played 20 seasons—just about every one of them for Minnesota's Vikings—and had a stunning career.

Tom LaGarde BASKETBALL

This North Carolina star played with four NBA teams in the late '70s and early '80s. He was also on the 1978-79 Seattle SuperSonics championship team, although he was sidelined with a knee injury.

Terry Furlow BASKETBALL

This former Michigan State star under Coach Gus Ganakas played four seasons in the NBA in the late '70s. He averaged 10.7 points per game for his career. He tragically lost his life at a young age in an automobile accident in 1980.

Dave Rader BASEBALL

A catcher who toiled for five teams, Rader was used primarily for defensive purposes. In his 10 years in the bigs, he had 149 extra-base hits.

Napoleon Lajoie BASEBALL

In an outstanding 21-year career that began in 1896 and ended in Cooperstown in 1951—the latter being the year that Sweetwater Clifton and Al McGuire were coming off the bench for basketball's Knicks—Lajoie batted .338 lifetime and hit safely 3244 times. His stats include hitting .422 in 1901—one of the highest averages by any major leaguer this century. Baby boomers can take heart that Lajoie hit .368 at age 38.

Mel Patton TRACK & FIELD

Patton won the gold in the 200-meter dash in the 1948 Olympic Games after finishing a disappointing fifth in the 100 meters. He won by 2 feet over Barney Ewell of the U.S., both runners finishing in 21.1.

Rudy "T"—a great player in his prime—took the Houston Rockets to their first NBA Championship in 1994, downing the Knicks in a tough, seven-game series.

31 | ALL-INITIALS TEAM

Eligibility: Each team entry must be the name of someone who is either (1) known by his or her initials or (2) has a nickname that is an initial.

Samples: O.J. Simpson
"The Big O," Oscar Robertson

And your nominees are ...

_____   _____

_____   _____

_____   _____

_____   _____

_____   _____

_____   _____

_____   _____

_____   _____

_____   _____

Dick's Picks
All-Initials Team

"The Big E," Elvin Hayes *BASKETBALL*

"The Big O," Oscar Robertson *BASKETBALL*

"X Man," Xavier McDaniel *BASKETBALL*

Tony "C," Tony Conigliaro *BASEBALL*

Ernie "D," Ernie DiGregorio *BASKETBALL*

Rudy "T," Rudy Tomjanovich *BASKETBALL*

J.R. Rider *BASKETBALL*

L.C. Greenwood *FOOTBALL*

E.J. Junior *FOOTBALL*

I.M. Hipp *FOOTBALL*

J.W. Porter *BASEBALL*

A.J. Foyt *AUTO RACING*

Y.A. Tittle *FOOTBALL*

J.R. Reid *BASKETBALL*

A.J. Kitt *SKIING*

T. Bell *FOOTBALL*

K.C. Jones *BASKETBALL*

M.L. Carr *BASKETBALL*

J.C. Caroline *FOOTBALL*

R.C. Owens *FOOTBALL*

C.R. Roberts *FOOTBALL*

J.R. Richard *BASEBALL*

D.J. Dozier *FOOTBALL*

A.C. Green *BASKETBALL*

B.J. Armstrong *BASKETBALL*

T.R. Dunn *BASKETBALL*

J.D. Hill *FOOTBALL*

C.J. Kupec *BASKETBALL*

P.J. Carlesimo *BASKETBALL*

C.M. Newton *BASKETBALL*

Trivial Tidbits

"The Big E," Elvin Hayes   *BASKETBALL*
One of the many superstars to wear jersey number 44—like Hank Aaron, John Riggins, Floyd Little, the list goes on and on—University of Houston's "Big E" averaged 36.8 ppg in 1968, the year the Cougars challenged UCLA for the crown as the country's best college team. They finished the regular season 30-0 that year, only to be stomped by 25-1 UCLA in a rematch in the NCAA semifinals. Trivia buffs often quiz each other on the rest of the starting Cougar five that year. They are: Ken Spain, Theodis Lee, Don Chaney and George Reynolds.

"The Big O," Oscar Robertson   *BASKETBALL*
Oscar Robertson is widely regarded as one of the most complete basketball players ever. He could score, rebound, dribble, pass and play defense with the best of them. In 1958, 1959 and 1960—playing at the University of Cincinnati—he was the nation's Division I scoring leader. What is less known about Robertson is that he averaged 15.2 rebounds per game while in college, a mark that is still a Bearcat career record. As a pro he was just as outstanding—nine years in a row he was first-team All-NBA.

"X Man," Xavier McDaniel   *BASKETBALL*
In 1985, Wichita State's Xavier McDaniel led the nation's Division I schools in scoring (27.2 ppg) and rebounds (14.8 rpg). He also led the nation in rebounds in 1983 (14.4). McDaniel later went on to a respectable NBA career which is still going strong—playing for the Sonics, Knicks and Celtics—averaging about 20 points and seven rebounds per game.

Tony "C," Tony Conigliaro   *BASEBALL*
No Red Sox fan will ever forget the night of August 18, 1967, when Tony Conigliaro—talented, handsome and a local boy—was hit in the head by a pitch from Jack Hamilton and was never the same again. Tony C had been off to what looked like a great baseball career. At 20, he became the youngest player ever to lead the American League in homers (32), and he was the youngest ever to hit 100.

Ernie "D," Ernie DiGregorio   *BASKETBALL*
Ernie DiGregorio was known as Ernie "D" during an outstanding career as a point guard for Providence College where he was coached by Dave Gavitt. This little guy created excitement galore when he had the rock in his hands. He was brilliant during the 1973 NCAA Tournament, when, playing alongside teammates Marvin Barnes and Kevin Stacom, the Friars made a run for the title. They were stopped in the semis 98-85 by a gritty Memphis State team that sported Larry Kenon and Larry Finch. The contest—which was close for a long time—could have swung in the Friars' favor had not Barnes gotten injured in the game.

L.C. Greenwood   *FOOTBALL*
Greenwood was a defensive end on the great Pittsburgh Steeler teams of the 1970s and a member of their "Steel Curtain" defense. Back in the mid-1970s, he was one of the many NFL stars who played in the fledgling World Football League (WFL). Using the lure of big bucks and taking advantage of the NFL players' strike, the WFL had been picking off some of the senior league's top stars—Larry Csonka, Paul Warfield and Calvin Hill, to name a few. But by August 1974, the strike had ended and the party was over for the WFL. Teams

in the new league were folding their tents left and right, and players like L.C. Greenwood saw the writing on the wall and canceled their future contracts. Early in the fall of 1975, about halfway into its season, the WFL folded.

E.J. Junior FOOTBALL

Junior was a defensive end on the 1979 Alabama team that went 12-0 under Coach Bear Bryant. He later enjoyed an NFL career that lasted more than a decade, playing with St. Louis, Phoenix and Miami.

I.M. Hipp FOOTBALL

This guy was "hip" when it came to toting the pigskin. Hipp was a star in the Nebraska Cornhuskers backfield in the late 1970s. Then it was on to the pros. There, he filled out the roster one year for the Oakland Raiders (1980), barely touching the ball and not scoring a single point. 1980, of course, was the year that the Raiders—led by the ever-resourceful Jim Plunkett—stunned the Philadelphia Eagles in the Super Bowl and thus become the first wild-card team ever to win the big one.

A.J. Foyt AUTO RACING

This four-time Indy 500 winner was a fixture in racing cockpits throughout the 1960s and 1970s. He is the only driver in history to win both the Indy and Daytona 500s as well as the 24-hour LeMans.

Y.A. Tittle FOOTBALL

Yelberton Abraham Tittle—I like Y.A.— quarterbacked the New York Giants in the 1960s. In 1963, he was the NFL's leading passer—221 completions for 367 attempts (3,145 yards and 36 TDs). He was traded to the Giants by the 49ers for Lou Cordileone—an offensive guard—in the early '60s. The Niners were going to a running offense and Tittle didn't fit in their plans. It turned out to be one of the best trades ever for the Giants. In one game against the Redskins in 1962, Tittle threw seven TDs—still an NFL record.

J.R. Reid BASKETBALL

One of the most highly recruited players to come out of the state of Virginia in the 1980s, this wide-bodied center-forward had a brilliant career at North Carolina under Coach Dean Smith before playing with the NBA Charlotte Hornets and the San Antonio Spurs. Today, he is used mostly as a role player coming off the bench.

A.J. Kitt SKIING

Kitt was a member of the United States Olympic downhill ski teams in 1992 and 1994. In 1994, he finished way in the back of the pack as teammate Tommy Moe captured the gold.

K.C. Jones BASKETBALL

Jones played for the Boston Celtics for eight seasons and coached them for another four. He was one of the great winners of all time, along with his college and Celtic teammate, Bill Russell. Jones played on the University of San Francisco team that won 56 consecutive games and two NCAA championships, the 1956 gold medal-winning U.S. Olympic team, and eight NBA championship Celtic teams in his nine NBA seasons. A superior athlete, Jones was drafted by the Los Angeles Rams and actually played an exhibition season with them before joining the Celts in 1959. He was recently hired by Don Chaney to be assistant coach with the Detroit Pistons.

R.C. Owens FOOTBALL

This 6-foot-3 receiver from—where else?— The College of Idaho patented the Alley Oop Pass in the late 1950s. When this play was pulled out of the book, Owens—who had a David Thompsonlike vertical leap— would run deep, turn and jump high into the air, and attempt to catch a pass that, if all went according to Hoyle, was going to be too high for lead-footed defenders to knock down. It worked well on occasion, especially when Owens was on the San Francisco 49ers, back in the days when John Brodie was flinging the pigskin.

J.R. Richard BASEBALL

James Rodney Richard, sometimes called "High Rise" because of his towering 6-foot-8 height, pitched for 10 years—almost all of them in the 1970s—with the Houston Astros. In back-to-back years—1978 and 1979—he struck out more than 300 batters. Four years in a row he won 18 or more games. His promising career was cut short by blood clots in his shoulder.

A.C. Green BASKETBALL

Green played his college ball at Oregon State, and in the pros, with the L.A. Lakers and Phoenix Suns. He has been a solid player who shoots the rock well and plays the good D.

B.J. Armstrong BASKETBALL

This Iowa Hawkeye is just starting to come into full bloom with the Chicago Bulls. During his first couple of seasons, he came off the bench to relieve Michael Jordan and John Paxson. Now, with Michael gone and Paxson hobbled by injury, Armstrong is having a chance to show the all-star quality stuff he's made of.

J.D. Hill FOOTBALL

In eight NFL seasons in the 1970s, Hill was a deep threat as a wide receiver, averaging more than 15 yards per catch. He scored 21 touchdowns on only 185 receptions. One of his best years was 1975, when he put up seven TDs for the Bills. Hill knew where to find the end zone.

P.J. Carlesimo BASKETBALL

Carlesimo, who had outstanding success as the basketball coach of Seton Hall, has now moved on to the NBA as head coach of the Portland Trail Blazers. His best year was 1989, when the Andrew Gaze-led Pirates went 31-7 and lost to Michigan in overtime by a single point in the final game of the NCAA championships. He now will be called upon to take over the Portland team and blend the talents of stars such as Clyde "The Glide" Drexler, Cliff Robinson and company.

C.M. Newton BASKETBALL

A class guy all the way, Newton is presently the athletic director at his alma mater, the University of Kentucky, where he once played for Adolph Rupp on a championship Wildcat team. Newton is now putting together an outstanding athletic program. He is responsible for bringing Rick Pitino to Kentucky.

Not to be confused with Fly Williams of All-Insect Team fame, Sly Williams—along with Rick Wise and Katarina Witt—is a solid member of my All-Intelligence Team.

32 | ALL-INTELLIGENCE TEAM

Eligibility: Each team entry must include a first name, last name, nickname or sports expression that suggests high or low intelligence or something having to do with intelligence.

Samples: Rick Wise
Katarina Witt

And your nominees are ...

_____   _____

_____   _____

_____   _____

_____   _____

_____   _____

_____   _____

_____   _____

_____   _____

_____   _____

Dick's Picks
All-Intelligence Team

Harry Bright *BASEBALL*

Keith Smart *BASKETBALL*

Rick Wise *BASEBALL*

Willie Wise *BASKETBALL*

Harvey Kuenn *BASEBALL*

Katarina Witt *SKATING*

Mike Witt *BASEBALL*

Luke Witte *BASKETBALL*

Mike Quick *FOOTBALL*

Sterling Sharpe *FOOTBALL*

Shannon Sharpe *FOOTBALL*

Mike Sharperson *FOOTBALL*

Sly Williams *BASKETBALL*

"Tricky" Dick McGuire *BASKETBALL*

Ken Trickey *BASKETBALL*

Billy Cunningham *BASKETBALL*

Bimbo Coles *BASKETBALL*

Charles "Booby" Clark *FOOTBALL*

Bob Learn Jr. *BOWLING*

Trivial Tidbits

Harry Bright *BASEBALL*

Sounds like the name of a man with a 1,000-watt brain. Bright played for five teams in eight major-league seasons in the late 1950s and early 1960s. He was used mostly as a reserve infielder and only played 336 games in his career. The one year he was given an opportunity to play regularly, 1962, he responded by batting .273 with 17 home runs and 67 RBIs.

Keith Smart *BASKETBALL*

Smart was one of the first junior college players to be offered a scholarship by Bob Knight. He is best remembered for making the winning basket for Indiana University in the 1987 NCAA championship game against Syracuse, sending Hoosier fans into Excitement City. Smart played one year in the NBA.

Rick Wise *BASEBALL*

Wise pitched 18 years in the majors, winning 188 games and losing 181 with a 3.69 ERA. Probably his best years were 1971, when he pitched a no-hitter, and 1975, when he was 19-12. He was almost invisible in relief as the winning pitcher in a contest that some people call the most exciting World Series game ever played—Game 6 of the 1975 fall classic, when Boston beat Cincinnati 7-6 on Carlton Fisk's 12th-inning home run off the foul pole. How many times have we seen replays of Fisk using body english to coax the ball fair and then jumping for joy afterward? It was sweet music in Beantown.

Willie Wise *BASKETBALL*

In his nine pro seasons spent among six teams, Wise was a productive scorer and rebounder. Some of his best years were spent with the Utah Stars of the old ABA, playing alongside Zelmo Beatty and Gerald Govan on the front line. In the early '70s, he was often in the top 10 in the league in scoring. By the '74 season, Wise was off the Utah team and playing elsewhere. The Stars had acquired a new starting forward— a much-heralded but wet-behind-the-ears high-schooler named Moses Malone.

Harvey Kuenn *BASEBALL*

Kuenn was an excellent contact hitter who averaged .303 for his 15-year major-league career. He led the American League in hits four times, doubles three times, and at-bats twice. In 1960 he was involved in one of the biggest trades ever in the world of baseball—going from the Tigers to the Indians for slugger Rocky Colavito. Kuenn's only World Series was with the San Francisco Giants in 1962 in which he had one hit in 12 plate appearances. The Giants lost it in the seventh game to the Yankees on Ralph Terry's 1-0 four-hitter.

Katarina Witt *SKATING*

Witt was the 1984 gold medal winner in figure skating at the Sarajevo Winter Olympics, and repeated her achievement four years later in Calgary. In the 1994 Winter Olympics in Lillehammer, Norway, Witt tried again for the gold after a six-year Olympics hiatus. She gave a classy performance and finished close behind the medal winners.

Mike Witt *BASEBALL*

Mike Witt has pitched in the majors since 1981, mostly with the California Angels. His best year was 1986 when he was 18-10 with a 2.84 ERA. He was the complete-game winner of Game 1 of 1986's dramatic American League Championship Series, pitting the Angels against the Boston Red Sox. The Angels had won three of the first four games and in Game 5 had the Sox just a gnat-hair strike away from elimination. It looked like Gene Autry was finally back in the saddle again. Then, with millions ready to turn off their tubes, Dave Henderson's famous two-run homer off Donnie Moore put the Sox ahead in the game. They won it and the series.

Mike Quick FOOTBALL

Quick was an excellent wide receiver who scored 61 touchdowns in his nine NFL seasons, averaging 17.8 yards per catch. At the height of his career, he was scoring about 10 touchdowns per season. His best year was 1983 when he caught 13 TD passes for 1,409 yards—all of them thrown, as far as I can remember, by "The Polish Rifle," Ron Jaworski.

Mike Sharperson BASEBALL

An above-average hitter who joined the Los Angeles Dodgers in 1987, Sharperson has shown little power. He had no home runs in his first three seasons and averages less than one per 100 at bats. Although he was on the Dodgers bench in the 1988 World Series, he saw no action. That was the year that Orel Hersheiser and Mickey Hatcher were on my All-World Team and stopped the A's in five.

Sly Williams BASKETBALL

Sly Williams is often confused with Fly Williams—the Austin Peay man who makes my All-Insect Team. Fly lasted a year in the NBA; Sly, about seven. The latter played guard and forward, averaging one point for every two minutes played. He earned the nickname "Garbage Man," a term usually used for a guy who stands under the basket and picks up refuse known as unsuccessful shots. He knew how to penetrate in the paint.

Billy Cunningham BASKETBALL

Because of his unusual leaping ability, this forward was known as "The Kangaroo Kid," a nickname that gets him a spot on my All-Marsupials Team. When he entered the NBA in 1966, Cunningham gained the reputation of being an excellent "sixth" man. Coming off the bench, he averaged 16-18 points per game with the Philadelphia 76ers. His average climbed to about 25 ppg as a starter. Twice he pulled down more than 1,000 boards in a season. During his zenith he was first-team All-NBA three years in a row. He was a genuine all-star talent and a fierce competitor. Cunningham was just as successful as a coach. In eight years at the Sixers' helm he compiled a record of 520-235, leading them to the NBA title in 1983 and the Finals in 1980 and 1982. His winning percentage of .689 is second on the all-time list. He's now a part owner of the Miami Heat.

Bimbo Coles BASKETBALL

Bimbo Coles was an excellent guard at Virginia Tech and played on the 1988 U.S. Olympic basketball team. With the Miami Heat early in his career, he has alternated between being a starter and a reserve.

Charles "Booby" Clark FOOTBALL

One of the more interesting nicknames to surface in the world of sports. Clark, however, was neither a boob nor a booby prize when it came to carrying the pigskin. He was a bruising runner who knew where the hole was for eight NFL seasons (1973-80), most of them with the Bengals. He ran for almost 1,000 yards in 1973, helping the team into the playoffs. He was the Bengals' rushing leader in both 1975 and 1976.

Bob Learn Jr. BOWLING

Learn was the 1992 winner of the Fair Lanes Open, defeating Dave D'Entremont in the final—263-163. The 100-pin difference was the largest winning margin in a PBA finals event on the 1992 Winter Tour.

33 | ALL-THREE NAMES TEAM

Eligibility: Each team entry must be a person who is commonly addressed by his or her first, middle, and last name. (Note: The person must be addressed by all three names on a consistent basis; e.g., Joe Willie Namath disallowed. For women, no married names; e.g., Florence Griffith Joyner disallowed.)

Samples: Joe Barry Carroll
Billy Joe Dupree

And your nominees are ...

_____   _____

_____   _____

_____   _____

_____   _____

_____   _____

_____   _____

_____   _____

_____   _____

Dick's Picks
All-Three Names Team

Joe Barry Carroll *BASKETBALL*

Jean Pierre Coopman *BOXING*

Billie Jean King *TENNIS*

Mary Jo Fernandez *TENNIS*

Billy Joe DuPree *FOOTBALL*

Joe Don Looney *FOOTBALL*

Billy Joe Tolliver *FOOTBALL*

John David Crow *FOOTBALL*

John Henry Johnson *FOOTBALL*

Billy Ray Brown *GOLF*

Michael Dean Perry *FOOTBALL*

Michael Ray Richardson *BASKETBALL*

Bobby Joe Conrad *FOOTBALL*

Eddie Lee Wilkins *BASKETBALL*

Billy Ray Barnes *FOOTBALL*

Jim Ray Hart *BASEBALL*

Jack Kent Cooke *FOOTBALL*

Sugar Ray Leonard *BOXING*

Ni Chin Chin *TRACK & FIELD*

Mary Lou Retton *GYMNASTICS*

Trivial Tidbits

Joe Barry Carroll   *BASKETBALL*

Joe Barry Carroll played at Purdue from 1975-1980. He led the Big Ten in scoring in 1979 and was an All-American the following year, when he led his team to the NCAA Final Four. Carroll was the No. 1 pick in the 1980 NBA draft and made the NBA's All-Rookie Team during the 1980-81 season. In 11 NBA campaigns, he averaged almost 18 points and eight rebounds a game. In the 1986-87 season, as the team's leading scorer at 21.2 ppg, he led the Warriors into the playoffs for the first time in a decade.

Jean Pierre Coopman   *BOXING*

Coopman, the heavyweight champion of Belgium in the 1970s, fought Muhammad Ali for the World Heavyweight crown in 1976. The fight was a mismatch from the get go. Ali finally put the Belgian and viewers out of their misery in the fifth round with a TKO.

Billie Jean King   *TENNIS*

Before Chrissie, Martina and Steffi, there was Billie Jean—six-time Wimbledon singles champ and winner of four U.S. Opens. In one of her last crowning achievements, in 1973, she knocked off Bobby Riggs in a much ballyhooed, battle of the sexes, $100K winner-take-all match in the Houston Astrodome. It was Hustle City. King finished Riggs off with ease in straight sets.

Mary Jo Fernandez   *TENNIS*

Mary Jo Fernandez is a rising star among U.S. tennis players. In all of the big tournaments she is increasingly becoming a threat to go all the way. More importantly for my All-Three Names Team, she is one of the few female tennis players sporting three names who does not have the surname of her main squeeze stuck in there somewhere,

living as she does in a world populated by the Yvonne Goolagong Cawleys, Margaret Court Smiths, and Arantxa Sanchez Vicarios.

Billy Joe DuPree   *FOOTBALL*

A durable, dependable tight end for the Cowboys from 1973-1983, DuPree played alongside such standout receivers as Drew Pearson, Drew Hill and Tony Hill. He had 267 career receptions for 42 touchdowns. He was on the Cowboys when they faced the Steelers in the quarterback shootout of Super Bowl XIII, with Roger Staubach and Terry Bradshaw going one-on-one. DuPree caught a 7-yard pass from Staubach in the fourth quarter, but it was not enough. Pittsburgh edged Dallas, 35-31.

Billy Joe Tolliver   *FOOTBALL*

The former Texas Tech Red Raider—Texas Tech being the only Southwest Conference school never to play in a Cotton Bowl game—Tolliver had an excellent 1990 season. Then it was on to the Chargers. In only his second year with San Diego he threw for 3,526 yards while completing over 52 percent of his passes. The next year he was traded to Atlanta.

John Henry Johnson   *FOOTBALL*

John Henry Johnson—even the name sounds tough as nails and mythical—was the leading rusher for the Detroit Lions in the 1957 National Football League Championship game. For his nine-year career he accounted for over 8,000 yards rushing and receiving and scored 55 touchdowns.

Michael Dean Perry   *FOOTBALL*

Michael Dean Perry is an All-Pro defensive lineman who followed the path of his brother—William "The Refrigerator" Perry—to the NFL through Clemson. Michael has become a big-league sack man.

Michael Ray Richardson BASKETBALL
Richardson played at Montana under Jud Heathcote, current coach at Michigan State. He was a talented, clutch performer whose NBA numbers included averaging over 15 points and seven assists in more than 100 playoff games.

Bobby Joe Conrad FOOTBALL
In 1963, playing with the St. Louis Cardinals, Conrad was the NFL's leading receiver, with 73 catches and 967 yards. That may not sound so impressive today, but the NFL season was only 14 games back then—just up from 12, which it was in 1960, and not yet 16, which it is today.

Billy Ray Barnes FOOTBALL
A member of the 1960 NFL Champion Philadelphia Eagles, Barnes was a tough runner who scored 38 career touchdowns while rushing for almost 3,500 yards. Back in the early '60s, the Eagles backfield featured Barnes, Clarence Peaks, and Ted Dean.

Jack Kent Cooke FOOTBALL
After earning a fortune in broadcasting and publishing, Cooke began purchasing professional sports franchises. He presently owns the Washington Redskins and has owned at one time or another both the Los Angeles Kings and the Los Angeles Lakers. He also invested his own money to promote the first Muhammad Ali-Joe Frazier heavyweight championship fight.

Sugar Ray Leonard BOXING
Many claim that pound for pound, inch for inch, Sugar Ray Leonard was the best fighter of all time. Winner of five world titles, Leonard won an Olympic gold medal in boxing in the light welterweight class in 1976. One of his most memorable fights occurred in 1980 when he beat Alberto Duran in the famous "no mas" welterweight bout, which was stopped in the eighth round when the Panamanian decided he'd had enough. That night Leonard taunted and talked so much you would have needed a cast on his tongue to keep him quiet, but he won the big fight.

Ni Chin Chin TRACK & FIELD
A candidate for my All-Anatomy Team, Chin once high jumped 7 feet, 6 inches. He once said "When I read the thoughts of Chairman Mao, I feel I could jump higher than a fireman's ladder." I wonder how high he would jump if he ever read this book?

34 | ALL-TWO SPORTS TEAM

Eligibility: Each team entry must be a person that has participated in at least two sports at a world-class level.

Samples: Deion Sanders
               Bo Jackson

And your nominees are ...

_____   _____

_____   _____

_____   _____

_____   _____

_____   _____

_____   _____

_____   _____

_____   _____

_____   _____

Dick's Picks
All-Two Sports Team

Dave DeBusschere *BASKETBALL/BASEBALL*

Gene Conley *BASKETBALL/BASEBALL*

Deion Sanders *FOOTBALL/BASEBALL*

John Lucas *TENNIS/BASKETBALL*

Danny Ainge *BASKETBALL/BASEBALL*

Bo Jackson *FOOTBALL/BASEBALL*

Bob Hayes *FOOTBALL/TRACK & FIELD*

James Jett *FOOTBALL/TRACK & FIELD*

Renaldo Nehemiah *FOOTBALL/TRACK & FIELD*

Charlie Ward *FOOTBALL/BASKETBALL*

Henry Carr *FOOTBALL/TRACK & FIELD*

Ray Norton *FOOTBALL/TRACK & FIELD*

Dick Groat *BASEBALL/BASKETBALL*

Herschel Walker *FOOTBALL/BOBSLED*

Willie Gault *FOOTBALL/BOBSLED*

Jim Thorpe *FOOTBALL/TRACK & FIELD*

Michael Carter *FOOTBALL/TRACK & FIELD*

Richmond Flowers *FOOTBALL/TRACK & FIELD*

Ollie Matson *FOOTBALL/TRACK & FIELD*

Babe Didrikson *GOLF/TRACK & FIELD*

Jim Hines *TRACK & FIELD/FOOTBALL*

Wilt Chamberlain *BASKETBALL/TRACK & FIELD*

Michael Jordan *BASKETBALL/BASEBALL*

Tim Stoddard *BASKETBALL/BASEBALL*

Trivial Tidbits

Dave DeBusschere *BASKETBALL/BASEBALL*
In 1962 and 1963, DeBusschere had a combined 3-4 pitching record (2.90 ERA) for the Chicago White Sox in a total of 36 games. He certainly wasn't known for his baseball exploits, but he was far more successful on the NBA hardwood, as we all know. DeBusschere was with the New York Knicks' championship teams in 1969 and 1973—starting at forward with Bill Bradley—and was a second-team All-NBA pick during their first championship year. He was an outstanding defensive player with great rebounding ability.

Gene Conley *BASKETBALL/BASEBALL*
The 6-foot-8 Conley was the tallest pitcher in the major leagues at the time he was active. In an 11-year career—spent mostly in Milwaukee (when the Braves were there) and Boston—he compiled a 91-96 win-loss record. In 1955 he was the winning pitcher for the National League in the All-Star Game, coming on in relief in the 12th inning and striking out the side. He played a couple of seasons for Boston in the NBA prior to his baseball career.

Deion Sanders *FOOTBALL/BASEBALL*
"Neon Deion" was a two-time All-American in football at Florida State and, later, an All-Pro cornerback with the Atlanta Falcons. On D, he is truly one of the best on the gridiron. In 1992, he had the highest batting average of any Atlanta Brave in the World Series.

John Lucas *TENNIS/BASKETBALL*
Before becoming an NBA coach with the San Antonio Spurs, Lucas was a playmaker in the NBA for 14 seasons, averaging seven assists and 10 points per game. In college he was terrific. Contributing about 20 ppg, he led the 1974 University of Maryland Terrapins to a 23-4 record and a national No. 4 ranking. That team also featured future NBAers Tom McMillan, Len Elmore and Mo Howard. Lucas also played on the Maryland tennis team where he was an NCAA standout. He has recently been named coach and general manager of the Philadelphia 76ers. However, his best work might be with the John Lucas Treatment and Recovery Center in Houston, Texas, where he helps many people turn their lives around.

Danny Ainge *BASKETBALL/BASEBALL*
Danny Ainge had an ever-so-brief fling with the Toronto Blue Jays before going on to a fine basketball career. As an infielder, he played 211 games in three years, winding up with an anemic .220 batting average. Basketball was a different story. Ainge starred for the Boston Celtics—where he collected two well-deserved championship rings—and then later played for the Sacramento Kings, Portland Trail Blazers and Phoenix Suns. His lifetime "highlight film" would have to include him going end-to-end to score the winning basket at the buzzer for Brigham Young against a favored Notre Dame squad in an early round NCAA Tournament game a little over a dozen years ago.

Bo Jackson *FOOTBALL/BASEBALL*
One of the most gifted athletes ever, Jackson won football's Heisman Trophy in 1985 and was the most valuable player in the 1989 major-league All-Star Game. A severe injury sustained while playing football for the Raiders in early 1991 cut short what could have been one of the most successful two-sport careers in the history of pro sports. But Bo is still swinging the lumber and lighting up the scoreboard for the California Angels.

Bob Hayes *FOOTBALL/TRACK & FIELD*
Hayes took the gold medal in the 100-meter dash in the 1964 Olympic games—winning by a margin of 7 feet, at that time the wid-

est in Olympic history. Later, he was a two-time all-pro wide receiver for the Dallas Cowboys.

Renaldo Nehemiah
FOOTBALL/TRACK & FIELD

In the 1980s, when he was the world's best hurdler, Nehimiah decided to cut short a promising track career for a football jersey. Unfortunately, his brief career with the San Francisco 49ers did not pan out as hoped and the U.S. briefly lost its dominance in the world's hurdling scene.

Charlie Ward   FOOTBALL/BASKETBALL
The 1994 Heisman Trophy winner while at Florida State, Ward recently signed a contract with the New York Knicks. In the NBA, he joins former FSU teammate Sam Cassel, who plays for the Rockets. Ward was a no-brainer choice for the Heisman—he was the hands-on favorite from the opening game of the season to get the prize and never disappointed.

Dick Groat   BASEBALL/BASKETBALL
Groat is probably best remembered as a very capable baseball shortstop in the 1950s and '60s—first with the Pirates, then with the Cards. He has two World Series rings and was the National League MVP in 1960. Less known: his basketball life. He was a two-time All-American at Duke and college Player of the Year in 1951. Groat has widely been credited as pioneering basketball's one-handed jump shot. Before the J came along, the "set" shot was used, with players rarely leaving their feet when firing the rock some distance from the basket.

Herschel Walker   FOOTBALL/BOBSLED
Few people have ever won a Heisman Trophy with the competition that Herschel Walker had in 1982, having to outdistance

the likes of John Elway and Eric Dickerson, who respectively came in second and third. In the 1990 Winter Olympic Games, Walker tried to parlay his fast starts on the gridiron into a fast start in the bobsledding competition.

Willie Gault   FOOTBALL/BOBSLED
Willie Gault has competed in three different sports at a world-class level—pro football, Olympic bobsledding, and track and field (sprinting and hurdling). He was a wide receiver on the Chicago Bears squad that won Super Bowl XX, a 46-10 pummeling of the New England Patriots. At the beginning of the first half, he caught a 60-yard bomb from Jim McMahon, setting up a 1-yard quarterback sneak.

Jim Thorpe   FOOTBALL/TRACK & FIELD
Probably the most acclaimed athlete in the history of sports, Thorpe won the decathlon and pentathlon in the 1912 Olympics, was a college football All-American, and was a professional football and baseball player. He was stripped of his medals after the Olympics when it was discovered that he had accepted a small amount of money for playing professional baseball. Many, many years later—after his death—his medals were restored.

Michael Carter   FOOTBALL/TRACK & FIELD
In addition to playing nose tackle for three Super Bowl Champion 49er teams, Carter was an NCAA Champion in the shot put. Most likely, he would have competed in the 1980 Moscow Olympics had the U.S. not boycotted the Games.

Ollie Matson   FOOTBALL/TRACK & FIELD
This 14-year, 12,000-plus yards veteran of the NFL was a four-time All-Pro in the 1950s for the Chicago Cardinals, and before that, a football All-American at San Francisco.

He also won a bronze medal in the 400-meter dash in the 1952 Olympic Games. Talk about valuable, he was traded for nine players! When Ollie Matson had the ball in the open field, it was show time.

Babe Didrikson Zaharias   *GOLF/TRACK & FIELD*

When she was 18 years old Babe Didrikson Zaharias won three medals—two gold and a silver—in the 1932 Olympics. Three years later she took up golf and won 55 pro and amateur events, 10 of them major tournaments, including the U.S. Open three times, and helped found the LPGA in 1949. She may have been the greatest female athlete ever.

Jim Hines   *TRACK & FIELD/FOOTBALL*

Hines was the Olympic gold medal winner in the 100-meter dash in the 1968 Mexico City Games. He also anchored the 4x100-meter relay team to victory, the team setting a world record. Drafted as a wide receiver by the Miami Dolphins, Hines had difficulty holding onto passes and was given the nickname "Oops" by his Dolphin teammates. Hines actually helped nickname himself—he would say "oops" every time he mishandled a flying pigskin in practice. In his only season with the team, 1969, he caught two passes for 23 yards.

Wilt Chamberlain

BASKETBALL/TRACK & FIELD

After winning the Big Eight high jump championship and having an outstanding college basketball career at Kansas, Chamberlain became one of the NBA's all-time greats. Among his NBA records are most points scored in a single game (100) and most points scored in a season (4,029). In his best season, he averaged more than 50 ppg. After retiring from hoops, Chamberlain kept on jamming, playing professional volleyball.

No wonder Ty Cobb is a baseball legend—almost 70 years ago he retired and he's still in the all-time top five in games played, career batting average, at bats, hits, doubles, triples, runs, RBIs and stolen bases.

35 | ALL-SHORTEST NAME TEAM

Eligibility: Each team entry must consist of a person with no more than a combined seven letters in his or her first and last names.

Samples: Ed Ott
                Ray Guy

BOB

And your nominees are ...

_____   _____

_____   _____

_____   _____

_____   _____

_____   _____

_____   _____

_____   _____

_____   _____

Dick's Picks
All-Shortest Names Team

Pele *SOCCER*

Mel Ott *BASEBALL*

Ed Ott *BASEBALL*

Bob Rule *BASKETBALL*

Bill Lee *BASEBALL*

Sam Huff *FOOTBALL*

Jack Ham *FOOTBALL*

Bob Boyd *FOOTBALL*

Bob Buhl *BASEBALL*

Fred Cox *FOOTBALL*

Jim Mora *FOOTBALL*

Guy Drut *TRACK & FIELD*

Jim Otis *FOOTBALL*

Max Baer *BOXING*

Jim Otto *FOOTBALL*

Mel Hein *FOOTBALL*

Jim Ard *BASKETBALL*

Jim Frey *BASEBALL*

Joe Foy *BASEBALL*

Eli Grba *BASEBALL*

Al Smith *BASEBALL*

Art Howe *BASEBALL*

Ty Cobb *BASEBALL*

Ty Cline *BASEBALL*

Art Monk *FOOTBALL*

Les Moss *BASEBALL*

Ron Mix *FOOTBALL*

Ray Ilg *FOOTBALL*

Hank Iba *BASKETBALL*

Ron Cey *BASEBALL*

Bob Dee *FOOTBALL*

Ray Guy *FOOTBALL*

Tom Gola *BASKETBALL*

Tom Kite *GOLF*

Don King *BOXING*

Don Ohl *BASKETBALL*

Trivial Tidbits

Pele SOCCER
Hey, this guy could shake and bake with his feet the way Earl Monroe could when driving to the hole. One of the most famous athletes in the history of sport, Pele led Brazil to the World Cup in soccer in 1958 (at age 17), 1962 and 1970.

Mel Ott BASEBALL
Ott was one of the first five elected to the Baseball Hall of Fame. When he retired in 1947, Ott had the most career home runs (511) of any player in the history of the National League.

Ed Ott BASEBALL
A utility catcher for most of his career—with a .259 batting average and only 195 RBIs in eight years—Ott was somewhat of a surprise as a hitting star in the 1979 World Series victory by the Pirates over the Orioles. For the Series, he hit .333 for the Bucs, with two runs scored and three RBIs.

Fred Cox FOOTBALL
This Minnesota Vikings field-goal kicker was the NFC scoring leader in 1969 and 1970. He is still in the top 10 list of career scorers. Cox was from the old school of field-goal kicking, booting 'em from straight-on rather than soccer-style, which is the standard today.

Jim Mora FOOTBALL
Known for his ultraconservative play calling, Mora was the NFL's 1987 Coach of the Year at New Orleans. In '87, he improved the "Aint's" from a 7-9 record to 12-3, and the team became one of the more respected in football. From 1987 to 1992 his teams won 62 regular season games, only losing 33.

Guy Drut TRACK & FIELD
Frenchman Guy Drut won the gold in the 110-meter hurdles in the 1976 Olympic Games, having settled for a silver behind USA's Rod Milburn in the same event four years earlier. He was the first person ever from a non-English-speaking country to win the high hurdles.

Jim Otis FOOTBALL
The height of Otis' nine-year NFL career came in 1975, when, as a St. Louis Cardinal, he led the NFC in rushing with 1,076 yards. That same year, the team took first in a strong NFC Eastern Division.

Max Baer BOXING
Not to be confused with Max Baer Jr.—his son—who played Jethro Clampett on *The Beverly Hillbillies*, Baer was the heavyweight boxing champion of the world in 1934 and 1935. He held the crown for about a year.

Jim Otto FOOTBALL
The only pro football Hall of Famer to wear the number 00, Jim Otto played center for the Oakland Raiders throughout the 1960s and the first half of the 1970s. Many rank him as one of the finest centers to ever play the game. Otto also makes my All-Palindronic Surnames Team—players whose last name is spelled the same backwards and forwards. The guy is so palindronic, in fact, that even his jersey number reads the same backwards and forwards. Incidentally, baseballers Toby Harrah and Mark Salas join Otto on the said surnames team, as well as footballer John Hannah.

Mel Hein FOOTBALL
This former New York Giant from over a half century ago was Mr. Consistency—the Cal Ripken Jr. of his day: NFL All-Pro for eight straight years and didn't miss a game for 15 seasons.

Jim Frey BASEBALL
Frey, who managed the Royals and Cubs in the 1980s, was legendary for his reasoning abilities. Once, when pitcher Lee Smith had to face Rusty Staub—a .280 lifetime hitter with almost 3,000 hits—Frey pointed out to Smith that those numbers meant

Staub made "8,000 outs." The point was well taken. Smith then proceeded to strike Staub out.

Eli Grba *BASEBALL*
Grba was the winning pitcher in the first game ever played by the Los Angeles (now California) Angels in 1961. The hurler's performance prompted compliments from the club's proud boss, Gene Autry.

Ty Cobb *BASEBALL*
"The Georgia Peach" had the highest career batting average (.367) in the history of baseball. He led the American League in hitting 12 times and stolen bases six times. Until Pete Rose broke his record, Cobb was also baseball's all-time hits leader.

Ty Cline *BASEBALL*
An outfielder for seven major-league teams in the 1960s and 1970s, Cline batted .238 for his career.

Ron Mix *FOOTBALL*
Mix, a tackle, was one of the first big stars of the AFL—before the AFL and NFL became one. He was an All-Pro his first nine years and played in five of the first six AFL championship games.

Hank Iba *BASKETBALL*
Notching 767 wins in a superb coaching career, Iba led Oklahoma State (then known as Oklahoma A&M) to two straight NCAA titles in 1945 and 1946, a runnerup finish in 1949 and a fourth-place finish in 1951, and the U.S. Olympic team to two gold medals (1964, '68). Hank Iba was a coach who won and who taught many other coaches how to take their teams to the winner's circle.

Ron Cey *BASEBALL*
Few third baseman saw duty in as many seasons (17) and as many games (2,073) or had as many RBIs (1,139) as "The Penguin," Ron Cey. He's sixth all-time, in fact, in games played. Starting in the early 1970s, Cey was an integral part of one of the longest-intact infields in modern major-league history. Joining him were Davey Lopes at shortstop, Bill Russell at second base, and Steve Garvey at first.

Ray Guy *FOOTBALL*
One of the best punters in the history of football, Guy was a fixture in the Raiders lineup for over a dozen years in the 1970s and 80s. His 1,052 punts rank him third on the all-time NFL list. One other noteworthy fact about his career was that he scored one running point—scooting into the end zone on a bobbled extra-point snap for which he was the holder.

Tom Gola *BASKETBALL*
One of basketball's main men in the 1950s and '60s, Gola was a four-time All-American at La Salle and a four-time NBA All-Star. In his personal scrapbook are NBA, NCAA and NIT championships.

Tom Kite *GOLF*
Although his first major tour victory was the 1992 U.S. Open at Pebble Beach, Kite entered 1992 as the all-time PGA Tour money winner with close to $7 million. Among his golfing accolades are NCAA champion (1972), PGA Rookie of the Year (1973), and PGA Player of the Year (1989).

36 | ALL-UNOFFICIAL TEAMS TEAM

Eligibility: Each team entry must be an unofficial group—either a set of fans or players or an entourage that is associated with a team or an athlete.

Samples: Gerela's Gorillas
The Fearsome Foursome

And your nominees are ...

_____   _____

_____   _____

_____   _____

_____   _____

_____   _____

_____   _____

_____   _____

_____   _____

_____   _____

Dick's Picks
All-Unofficial Teams Team

Arnie's Army *GOLF*

Gerela's Gorillas *FOOTBALL*

The Dawg Pound *FOOTBALL*

The Nasty Boys *BASEBALL*

The No-Name Defense *FOOTBALL*

The Killer B's *FOOTBALL*

The Louie and Bouie Show *BASKETBALL*

The Ernie and Bernie Show *BASKETBALL*

The Jana and Hannah Show *TENNIS*

The Three Amigos *FOOTBALL*

The Doomsday Defense *FOOTBALL*

The Fearsome Foursome *FOOTBALL*

The Steel Curtain *FOOTBALL*

The Purple People Eaters *FOOTBALL*

The Posse *FOOTBALL*

The Whiz Kids *BASEBALL*

Murderer's Row *BASEBALL*

The Four Horsemen of Notre Dame *FOOTBALL*

Mr. Inside and Mr. Outside *FOOTBALL*

The Bleacher Bums *BASEBALL*

The Coneheads *BASEBALL*

Phi Slama Jama *BASKETBALL*

The Hogs *FOOTBALL*

The Big Red Machine *BASEBALL*

The Electric Company *FOOTBALL*

The Monsters of the Midway *FOOTBALL*

Chinese Bandits *FOOTBALL*

The Fun Bunch *FOOTBALL*

The Smurfs *FOOTBALL*

Orange Crush *FOOTBALL*

The Fab Five *BASKETBALL*

Trivial Tidbits

Arnie's Army GOLF
Fans, that's all they were. A few papparazzi, too. Just Arnold Palmer groupies. They followed this legendary golfer around the links in the '60s and '70s, oohing and aahing with each stroke. Of course, there was a lot to ooh and aah about—Palmer was one of the best golfers the world has ever seen and the winner of over a half dozen major tournaments. When he was making birdies he was Mr. Electricity on the links.

Gerela's Gorillas FOOTBALL
More fans. The Gorillas sat in the end zone of Three Rivers Stadium and whooped it up every time Steeler place kicker Roy Gerella would part the uprights in the 1970s.

The Dawg Pound FOOTBALL
Still more fans. With doggie masks and costumes, yet. These "bleacher bums" cheer on the Browns in their home park and make sure their presence is felt by opponents when they drop into Cleveland to play the home team.

The Nasty Boys BASEBALL
This feared bullpen of the 1990 World Series-winning Cincinnati Reds featured Randy Meyers, Rob Dibble and Norm Charlton. In the 1990 fall classic, the Oakland A's were supposed to make mincemeat of the Reds. There was even talk over in Northern California that Commissioner Fay Vincent should just mail the World Series trophy to Oakland and dispense with the Series. But the Reds surprised the experts and won in four straight.

The No-Name Defense FOOTBALL
In the early 1970s, when the Miami Dolphins won back-to-back Super Bowls, someone noticed that all the marquee players—

Griese, Csonka and Morris, to name just a few—were on offense. So the guys whose job it was to keep opponents from scoring became known as the No-Name Defense. Some of the more famous faces included Dick Anderson, Jake Scott, Nick Buoniconti, and Bill Stanfill. They played the tenacious team D for their great coach, Don Shula.

The Killer B's FOOTBALL
The Killer B defense played for Miami in 1985. Nine of the 11 defensive starters had a last name beginning with the letter "B"— Bob Baumhower, Kim Bokamper, Glenn and Lyle Blackwood, etcetera. Good as they were, they didn't stop San Francisco from scoring 38 points in Super Bowl XIX.

The Louie and Bouie Show BASKETBALL
During the mid-1970s, the Syracuse Orangemen relied heavily on an inside-outside game that featured guard Louis Orr and center Roosevelt Bouie. It was J time, then yoke time. The L&BS led the Orangemen into the 1975 Final Four, where they were rudely stopped by Kentucky.

The Ernie and Bernie Show BASKETBALL
Guard Ernie Grunfeld and forward Bernard King starred for Tennessee in the mid-1970s. Both later spent time in the N.Y. Knicks organization—King as an exceptional scoring machine and Grunfeld in management. King racked up 19,432 points in the NBA and is in the top 20 all-time in points scored.

The Jana and Hannah Show TENNIS
Two great Central European tennis stars, Jana Novotna and her coach, Hannah

Mandlikova. Mandlikova won the Australian Open in 1980, the French Open in 1981 and the U.S. Open in 1985. Novotna is still waiting for her first big win. She almost got it at Wimbledon in 1993, making the final, but lost to Steffi Graf. She has all the shots and should make it to Center Court for Breakfast at Wimbledon again.

The Fearsome Foursome   FOOTBALL

In the 1960s, the Los Angeles Rams sported a crack frontline defensive unit that featured Merlin Olsen, Deacon Jones, Lamar Lundy and Roosevelt Grier. Collectively, they became The Fearsome Foursome.

The Steel Curtain   FOOTBALL

One of the finest defensive lines in gridiron history belonged to the Pittsburgh Steelers of the 1970s. At the hub of the unit were Mean Joe Greene, L.C. Greenwood, Dwight White and Ernie Holmes. The "Curtain" helped the Steelers make eight consecutive playoff appearances and win four Super Bowls. They were hostility, agility and mobility personified.

Murderer's Row   BASEBALL

Murderer's Row consisted of the heart of the 1927 New York Yankee batting order—Babe Ruth, Lou Gehrig, and Tony Lazzari, to name just three players. The Yanks that year won a record 110 games.

The Four Horsemen of Notre Dame   FOOTBALL

This Rockne-era (1924) senior backfield consisted of Jim Crowley, Elmer Layden, Don Miller and Harry Stuhldreher. The idea for the horsemen began with a student sportswriter who suggested the players mount horses and pose for a photo. When the photo later appeared in papers all over the country, the concept stuck.

Mr. Inside and Mr. Outside   FOOTBALL

While many dynamic duos have laid claim to this title over the years, the original Mr. Inside and Mr. Outside are Glenn Davis and Felix "Doc" Blanchard, who led Army to national football titles in 1944-45. Davis won the Heisman in 1945; Blanchard took it a year later.

The Bleacher Bums   BASEBALL

These denizens of the Wrigley Field bleacher section throw the ball back onto the field when a round tripper is hit to them by a player on an opposing team.

The Coneheads   BASEBALL

Fans revisited. This time it's a combination of David Cone, sort of a wild-and-crazy guy in his own right, and Saturday Night Live's Coneheads. The Coneheads of Flushing Meadows fame, when Cone was playing for the Mets, dressed with cone-shaped heads. They would often sit in the front row of Shea Stadium's mezzanine section and unfurl "K" banners every time pitcher Cone would whiff someone at the plate.

Phi Slama Jama   BASKETBALL

Basketball's premier dunking fraternity, the 1982-83 Houston Cougars. They loved to rock 'n roll, to knock down major rim rattlers. Most of the playing time on that team went to Hakeem "The Dream" Olajuwon, Clyde "The Glide" Drexler, Michael Young, Larry Micheaux, Benny Anders and Alvin Franklin.

The Hogs   FOOTBALL

The offensive line of the Redskins in the 1970s and '80s. Members included Joe Jacoby, Len Hauss, Terry Hermeling, Ron Saul and Dan Nugent. They paved the way for runners like John Riggins to rack up monster real estate.

The Big Red Machine   BASEBALL

In the 1970s the Cincinnati Reds accumulated one of the best offensive lineups in the history of baseball; so good that fans still often mention it in the same breath as the '27 Yankees. Big bats included at one time or another: Pete Rose, Joe Morgan, Johnny Bench, Tony Perez, George Foster and Ken Griffey.

The Monsters of the Midway   FOOTBALL

The defensive unit of the Chicago Bears in the 1950s gave up yards so grudgingly that they took on this name. Led by Bill George, the group included Bill Atkins, Earl Leggett and Joe Fortunato.

Chinese Bandits   FOOTBALL

In 1958, during the era of platoon football—when a coach could substitute one or a group of players only a few times each quarter—LSU coach Paul Dietzel's defensive group became known as the Chinese Bandits.

Hey baby, who can ever forget those annual Saturday afternoon wars featuring Bo Schembechler's Michigan Wolverines against Woody Hayes' Ohio State Buckeyes?

37 | ALL-BO AND MO TEAM

Eligibility: Each team entry must include a person with a first name, last name or nickname of Bo, Mo or Moe.

Samples: Tommy Moe
Bo Jackson

And your nominees are ...

_____   _____

_____   _____

_____   _____

_____   _____

_____   _____

_____   _____

_____   _____

_____   _____

_____   _____

Dick's Picks
All-Bo and Mo Team

Bo Jackson *BASEBALL*

Bo Belinsky *BASEBALL*

Bo Ellis *BASKETBALL*

Dwight "Bo Peep" Lamar *BASKETBALL*

Bo Kimble *BASKETBALL*

Bo Schembechler *FOOTBALL*

Bo Roberson *TRACK & FIELD*

Bo Diaz *BASEBALL*

Bobo Olsen *BOXING*

Bobo Newsom *BASEBALL*

Alva "Bobo" Holloman *BASEBALL*

Bo Erias *BASKETBALL*

Fitzgerald Bobo *BASKETBALL*

Moe Drabowski *BASEBALL*

Mo Rivers *BASKETBALL*

Mo Cheeks *BASKETBALL*

Doug Moe *BASKETBALL*

Mo Layton *BASKETBALL*

Mo Howard *BASKETBALL*

Tommy Moe *SKIING*

Moe Berg *BASEBALL*

Maureen "Little Mo" Connolly *TENNIS*

Mo Vaughn *BASEBALL*

Karen Moe *SWIMMING*

Trivial Tidbits

Bo Belinsky   *BASEBALL*

Probably no major-league pitcher with only 28 career wins ever got more media attention than Bo Belinsky. He was often seen in the company of movie stars and heiresses and was a familiar face at posh nightclubs and at chic Hollywood parties. Bo's roster of Robin Leach-league dates includes Ann-Margret, Tina Louise (Gilligan's Island anyone?), and heiresses to the DuPont and Weyerhauser fortunes. Also, Bo was once the main squeeze of actress Mamie Van Doren. Named after boxer Bobo Olsen, Belinsky pitched a no-hitter in 1962—his rookie year with the Angels.

Bo Ellis   *BASKETBALL*

Bo Ellis played forward on the Al McGuire-coached 1977 Marquette team that won the NCAA tournament. Ralph Lauren take note: He also helped design the Marquette uniforms. Later, Ellis went on to the NBA for a very short career with the Denver Nuggets.

Dwight "Bo Peep" Lamar   *BASKETBALL*

In 1972, Southwest Louisiana's Dwight Lamar led the nation's Division I schools with a 36.3 ppg scoring average. He was Mr. Shot Time—he loved to get the mustard out and hot dog. During his first three seasons as a pro he averaged 17.5, 20.9 and 18.3 points per game.

Bo Kimble   *BASKETBALL*

After his friend and teammate Hank Gathers died of a heart attack shortly before the 1990 NCAA tournament, Loyola Marymount star Kimble took out his frustration on New Mexico State in the opening-round game, going nuts for 45 points. His 35.8 ppg scoring average in the tournament tied for third-best ever. Late in that NM State game, Kimble, normally a right-handed shooter, took a foul shot with his left hand in Gathers' honor to the delight of Loyola fans in attendance. Gathers was a southpaw.

Bo Schembechler   *FOOTBALL*

When he retired in 1989, Michigan's Schembechler was the fifth-winningest Division I college coach of all time. His coaching career spanned 27 years (1963-1989). He retired with 234 coaching victories at Miami of Ohio and Michigan and was NCAA Coach of the Year in 1969. From 1970 through 1974, his Michigan teams were almost unbeatable, as he led them to 50 wins with only three losses and one tie.

Bobo Newsom   *BASEBALL*

Newsom pitched in four decades in the majors, starting in 1929 with the Brooklyn Dodgers and ending in 1953 with the Philadelphia Athletics—with a dozen trades or so scattered in between. In not letting sod grow under his feet, he set the standard for such well traveled folks as Harry "Suitcase" Simpson and Bob MacAdoo—members of my All-Frequent Fliers Team. Newsome played for the Senators no less than four separate times in his major-league career— 1935-37, 1942-43, 1946-1947, and 1952.

Alva "Bobo" Holloman   *BASEBALL*

Now this is really weird—even by sports standards. In his major-league pitching debut in 1953, Holloman spins a no-hitter, 6-0, against the Philadelphia Athletics. Guess how many games he wins next year? If you said "zero" you're correct. Holloman never pitched again in the bigs after '53.

Moe Drabowski   *BASEBALL*

Moe Drabowsky pitched in the big leagues for 17 seasons, appearing in 589 games.

His golden moment was winning the first game of the 1966 World Series for the Baltimore Orioles, pitching six innings of shutout relief against the Los Angeles Dodgers and fanning 11—racking up six K's in a row at one point. The Dodgers didn't score another run for the entire series, getting whitewashed in the next three games. The total carnage for LA: 33 scoreless innings and only two runs the entire Series.

Doug Moe   *BASKETBALL*
Here's a guy who knew how to work his way up. Moe has had one of the more unusual professional basketball careers. He was 30 years old as a rookie with New Orleans of the ABA when he was the league's second-leading scorer with a 24.2 ppg average. Despite his obvious scoring ability, he played for a different ABA team each of his first four years, then after two with the Virginia Squires, he became an NBA head coach. Here he was more popular with his players than his previous coaches, winning NBA Coach of the Year for the 1987-88 season. Some say his Denver team was perhaps the best NBA team not to make the NBA finals.

Mo Layton   *BASKETBALL*
This USC star of the early 1970s played for five teams in the NBA. He was playing for USC when all the basketball ink in town was being spent on the Bruins over in Westwood. USC had outstanding teams when Layton served as point guard. One of his teammates: Paul Westphal.

Mo Howard   *BASKETBALL*
This Maryland star played only a single season in the NBA—1977. He was a member of the great Terrapin team that featured John Lucas, Tom McMillen and Len Elmore.

Tommy Moe   *SKIING*
In the 1994 Winter Olympic Games, Tommy Moe of Alaska became only the second American ever to win a gold medal in the men's downhill.

Moe Berg   *BASEBALL*
Once described by Casey Stengel as the "strangest fella to ever put on a uniform," Morris "Moe" Berg was anything but your garden-variety jock. Graduating Phi Beta Kappa from Princeton University, Berg spoke a dozen languages fluently and—while he played in the majors—engaged in espionage activities against the Japanese in the 1930s.

Karen Moe   *SWIMMING*
In the 1972 Summer Olympic games, Karen Moe won the 200-meter butterfly in world-record time. She let two others set the pace for the race and then blew them both away after the final turn.

38 | ALL-TWO FIRST NAMES TEAM

Eligibility: Each team entry must have a last name that is commonly used as a first name.

Samples: Tommy John
Jeff George

WILLIAM PERRY

And your nominees are ...

_____   _____

_____   _____

_____   _____

_____   _____

_____   _____

_____   _____

_____   _____

_____   _____

Dick's Picks
All-Two First Names Team

Jeff George *FOOTBALL*

Bill George *FOOTBALL*

Tommy John *BASEBALL*

Rodney Peete *FOOTBALL*

Billy Joe *FOOTBALL*

Joe Christopher *BASEBALL*

Randy Beverly *FOOTBALL*

Bob Lilly *FOOTBALL*

Pete Rose *BASEBALL*

Connie Mack *BASEBALL*

Dick James *FOOTBALL*

Carlton Willey *BASEBALL*

Jeffrey Leonard *BASEBALL*

Horace Grant *BASKETBALL*

Lewis Lloyd *BASKETBALL*

Billy Brooks *FOOTBALL*

Byron Scott *BASKETBALL*

Lloyd Neal *BASKETBALL*

Ray Meyer *BASKETBALL*

Ed Charles *BASEBALL*

Larry James *TRACK & FIELD*

Jerry Lucas *BASKETBALL*

Marcus Allen *FOOTBALL*

Marv Albert *ANNOUNCER*

Phil Jackson *BASKETBALL*

Bill Bradley *BASKETBALL*

George Karl *BASKETBALL*

Butch Lee *BASKETBALL*

Rick Barry *BASKETBALL*

Mack Calvin *BASKETBALL*

Nate Archibald *BASKETBALL*

Walt Wesley *BASKETBALL*

Paul Silas *BASKETBALL*

Spencer Haywood *BASKETBALL*

Reggie Lewis *BASKETBALL*

Horace Clark *BASEBALL*

Mo Vaughn *BASEBALL*

Duane Ward *BASEBALL*

Bill Russell *BASKETBALL*

Walter Davis *BASKETBALL*

Trent Tucker *BASKETBALL*

Isiah Thomas *BASKETBALL*

Kevin Willis *BASKETBALL*

Sean Elliott *BASKETBALL*

Dale Ellis *BASKETBALL*

Joe Morris *FOOTBALL*

William Perry *FOOTBALL*

Joe Louis *BOXING*

Earl Anthony *BOWLING*

Amos Otis *BASEBALL*

Paul Blair *BASEBALL*

Rocky Nelson *BASEBALL*

Billy Martin *BASEBALL*

Jerry Manuel *BASEBALL*

Mike Glenn *BASKETBALL*

Joey Jay *BASEBALL*

John Salley *BASKETBALL*

Bob Oliver *BASEBALL*

Keith Lee *BASKETBALL*

Mike Lynn *BASKETBALL*

Ed Luther *FOOTBALL*

Frank Howard *BASEBALL*

Clifford Ray *BASKETBALL*

Trvial Tidbits

Bill George *FOOTBALL*
This Pro Football Hall of Famer—an All-American from Wake Forest—is often credited with defining the position of middle linebacker. When George first reported for to the pros at middle guard, it was customary in passing situations for those in his position to knock the center from his three-point stance before dropping back. George discovered, however, that if he neglected the center and just dropped back, he would intercept more passes. In short order, other teams were following his lead, and the position of middle linebacker was created.

Rodney Peete *FOOTBALL*
Here's a guy who can think as fast as he runs. This former USC star learned the Detroit Lions system quickly. In his first pro season, 1989, Pete completed more than 52 percent of his passes for five touchdowns. As the Lions' starter the next year, he again had a completion rate better than 52 percent but upped his numbers in the TD department—13. He now plays with the Cowboys.

Billy Joe *FOOTBALL*
Billy Joe What? Nothing—it's just Billy Joe. From 1963 to 1968 this Villanova fullback played for four NFL teams, gaining more than 2,600 yards rushing and receiving, and scoring 19 touchdowns. He put up a total of 118 points for his career.

Randy Beverly *FOOTBALL*
As a defensive back with the New York Jets, Beverly starred in Super Bowl III, intercepting two passes to stop Colt drives in the Jets' 16-7 upset win. He played in the NFL about four seasons.

Connie Mack *BASEBALL*
Talk about longevity, consistency and knowing how to manage! Connie Mack managed the Philadelphia Athletics for most of the first half of this century, retiring when he

was 87. His long shelf life got him a spot in the record books—he is the all-time leader in major-league wins for a skipper at 3,755.

Carlton Willey *BASEBALL*
One of the few major-leaguers from the state of Maine, Willey played eight years, some with the Amazing Mets whom he joined in 1963. Choo Choo Coleman, Marv Throneberry and Ed Kranepool were exciting to watch at the old Polo Grounds.

Jeffrey Leonard *BASEBALL*
A veteran of the bigs since 1977, "Hac-Man," or Jeffrey Leonard as he is more commonly referred to on the sports pages, was one of the main bats in the San Francisco Giants lineup in the 1980s. In 1987, his 19 homers and 70 RBIs led Roger Craig's Giants to an NL Western Division title and the playoffs. In the postseason, the Giants were expected to manhandle Whitey Herzog's light-sticking St. Louis Cardinals but they ran into great pitching. After taking a 3-2 game lead, the Giants couldn't buy a run in the last 22 innings of the series and lost.

Horace Grant *BASKETBALL*
Horace Grant played seven years for the Chicago Bulls after leaving Clemson. He was the main glass sweeper on the Bulls' three consecutive NBA championship teams and averaged more than 15 points, three assists and 11 rebounds per game. The Orlando Magic signed Grant before the 1994-95 season in the hope that he can perform the same tricks in Florida.

Byron Scott *BASKETBALL*
Scott has been a dependable scorer throughout his long NBA career, averaging more than 16 points per game. For many years, he was a starter with the Lakers. Recently dealt to the Indiana Pacers, he helped them in their surprise showing in the 1994 NBA playoffs. His three-point shot against

Orlando set the tone and provided the momentum that carried Indiana to within a few seconds of the NBA finals.

Ed Charles *BASEBALL*

Fondly known as "The Glider" for his smooth play in the field, Charles was on the roster of the 1969 "Amazing" Mets World Series champinship team. Despite his age (34) and part-time playing status, he tied for fourth on the team that year in stolen bases.

Jerry Lucas *BASKETBALL*

One of the most hyped players in the history of high school and college, Lucas was on nearly everybody's All-American team back in the 1950s and 1960s. As a center at Ohio State, he led the Buckeyes to three consecutive NCAA title games with a good supporting cast that included John Havlicek and Larry Sigfried. As a pro—playing at center and forward—he made All-NBA four years in a row, three times on the first team. He shot a very respectable 50 percent from the field and averaged more than 15 rebounds per game. Lucas has a photographic memory. Since retiring, he likes to do magic tricks and demonstrate his ability to memorize Manhattan phone numbers.

Phil Jackson *BASKETBALL*

With arms and elbows dangling randomly about like a mobile, Phil Jackson was one of the enforcers on the New York Knicks in the late 1960s and throughout the 1970s. He would come off the bench and score a quiet six or seven points, but his three main jobs—in order of importance—were defense, defense, defense. This man has always been a true master of his craft and you've got to give him credit where credit is due—he has one of the largest collections of NBA Championship rings of anyone active in the sport.

Bill Bradley *BASKETBALL*

Senator Bradley (D-New Jersey), one of only two Rhodes Scholars ever to play in the NBA (Tom McMillan was the other), scored 58 points against Wichita State in a 1965 NCAA tournament game. That same year he led Princeton to the Final Four where they were beaten in the semis by a Michigan team led by Cazzie Russell. Bradley was the tournament MVP and went on to play with Russell on the Knicks. He averaged more than 12 ppg in 10 seasons in New York. Bradley played on one Olympic gold medal-winning team and two NBA championship teams.

George Karl *BASKETBALL*

This courtwise North Carolina Tar Heel has made his greatest mark in basketball as a coach—most recently for the Seattle Supersonics. With their rip and run, led by Isolation Man Shawn Kemp, it could be NBA finals time for them very soon. Karl learned the game under Coach Dean Smith at Chapel Hill where Dean has produced so many great players.

Butch Lee *BASKETBALL*

Playing under Al McGuire, Butch Lee led Marquette University to the NCAA Championship in 1977 and was voted the tournament's MVP. He could hand and twist with anyone and loved to glide down the lane. Lee learned his moves on the playgrounds of New York City.

Rick Barry *BASKETBALL*

This five-time All-NBA first teamer was the only player to lead both the ABA and NBA in scoring. Barry averaged almost 25 points per game in14 years and led the San Francisco Warriors to the 1975 NBA title. He was great from the charity line, shooting the ball underhanded using both hands. He is the Warrior record holder for free-throw accuracy in a season (92.4 percent) and in a career (89.6 percent).

Paul Silas *BASKETBALL*

This 16-year NBA power forward from Creighton was on six pro teams before becoming a head coach. A player who knew how to win, Silas played on the 1974 and 1976 Celtics NBA championship teams as well as the 1979 Sonics championship team. To show you just how good this guy was at helping his teams score the W, note that he is third on the all-time list of playoff appearances—only Kareem Abdul-Jabbar and Dolph Schayes are ahead of him. He is now an assistant coach to Butch Beard with the New Jersey Nets.

Spencer Haywood   *BASKETBALL*
Haywood, who briefly attended the University of Detroit, entered the NBA in 1970. Almost as soon as he put on a uniform, he was a star. For two straight years he was first-team All-NBA and the next two he was a second-team pick. Careerwise, his numbers were big—he averaged about 20 points and 10 rebounds a game.

Bill Russell   *BASKETBALL*
Perhaps the greatest winner of all time in any professional sport, Russell's career was exemplary. He led his University of San Francisco team to 56 straight wins and back-to-back NCAA titles. He was a member of the gold medal-winning U.S. team at the 1956 Melbourne Olympics, then led the Boston Celtics to 11 NBA titles in 13 seasons, averaging 24.9 rebounds per game in the playoffs. Russell patented the move where he would block an opponent's shot to a Celtic teammate, thereby triggering the fast break.

Sean Elliott   *BASKETBALL*
Sean Elliott led Arizona to the Final Four in 1988 then won two symbols of college basketball excellence in 1989—the Wooden Award and the Rupp Trophy. After NBA stints with San Antonio and Detroit, he's back with San Antonio. He averages about 12 points per game.

Dale Ellis   *BASKETBALL*
He's on my All-Long Range J Team. One of the most prolific three-point shooters currently in the NBA, the Tennessee alum has played for the Mavs, Sonics, Bucks, Spurs and Nuggets. He's taken more than 2,000 three-point shots in the NBA and been successful on 40 percent of them.

William Perry   *FOOTBALL*
Coming into the NFL at 6 feet 2 inches and a hefty 325 pounds, Perry, whose athletic skills were such that he supposedly could dunk a basketball, became an instant hit with the Chicago Bears. Nicknamed "The Refrigerator," he not only played defensive line but also played in the offensive backfield at times when the Bears were near the goal line. In 1985-86, his rookie year and the year the Bears won the Super Bowl, Perry carried the ball six times and scored three TDs, one in the Super Bowl.

Joe Louis   *BOXING*
For 11 years and eight months (1937-49)—longer than anyone else before or after—Joe Louis ruled the heavyweight division of professional boxing. When he left the ring he was 63-3 with 49 KOs. From 1937-49 Louis defended his title 26 times, winning each bout.

Earl Anthony   *BOWLING*
This six-time PBA Bowler of the Year was the first bowler to earn $100,000 in a single year (1975) and the first to hit a million dollars in career earnings. Tough life, trying to pull in the cabbage down at the lanes.

Amos Otis   *BASEBALL*
Otis spent 17 years in the majors, mostly in a Kansas City Royals uniform. Lifetime, he batted .277 with more than 2,000 hits and more than 300 stolen bases. An excellent center fielder, he finished his career with a .991 fielding average.

Longtime Viking QB and now a Saints signal caller, Wade Wilson also makes my All-WW Team along with Wilbur Wood, Willie Wise, Willie Wilson and Wilson Washington.

39 | ALL-WATER TEAM

Eligibility: Each team entry must include a first name, last name, nickname or sports expression that suggests water or some type of structure or equipment that is found around water.

Samples: Mickey Rivers
Warren Wells

And your nominees are ...

_____   _____

_____   _____

_____   _____

_____   _____

_____   _____

_____   _____

_____   _____

_____   _____

Dick's Picks
All-Water Team

Ricky Watters *FOOTBALL*	Ron Springs *FOOTBALL*
Charlie Waters *FOOTBALL*	Glenn "Doc" Rivers *BASKETBALL*
Sweetwater Clifton *BASKETBALL*	Bill Wade *FOOTBALL*
"Ice Cube" McNeil *FOOTBALL*	Wade Wilson *FOOTBALL*
Bob Waterfield *FOOTBALL*	"Bubbles" Hawkins *BASKETBALL*
Mickey Rivers *BASEBALL*	Terry Puhl *BASEBALL*
Jose Rijo *BASEBALL*	Dock Ellis *BASEBALL*
Brooks Robinson *BASKETBALL*	Ulysses "Junior" Bridgeman *BASKETBALL*
Herb Brooks *HOCKEY*	Rocky Bridges *BASEBALL*
James Brooks *FOOTBALL*	Warren Wells *FOOTBALL*
Nick Eddy *FOOTBALL*	Pumpsie Green *BASEBALL*
Roland Lakes *FOOTBALL*	Derrick Coleman *BASKETBALL*
Bob Timberlake *FOOTBALL*	Emlen Tunnel *FOOTBALL*

Note:
▼ For names associated with fishing activities: See All-Fish Team (page 86)

Trivial Tidbits

Ricky Watters   *FOOTBALL*

A former Notre Dame star, Watters has led the San Francisco 49ers in rushing since the departure of Roger Craig. In what has to be his most memorable performance, he scored five touchdowns against the New York Giants in a middle-round NFC playoff game during the 1993-94 season—an annihilation if ever there was one. The celebration dance was short, however. The very next game, the 'Niners themselves got taken to the woodshed by the Cowboys in a no-contest tilt.

Charlie Waters   *FOOTBALL*

During the 1970s, Waters played defensive back for the Dallas Cowboys. He was a great one, playing in a great secondary—one that included Mel Renfro, Cliff Harris, and Benny Barnes. On the 'Pokes roster for close to a decade, Waters participated in two Super Bowl victories, three Super Bowl losses, and two losses in the NFC Championship Game.

Bob Waterfield   *FOOTBALL*

In his rookie season (1945), Waterfield's quarterbacking piloted the Cleveland Rams to the NFL championship, and he was voted the league's MVP. Later, when the Rams moved to Tinseltown, he was twice the league's leading passer—in 1946 and 1951, he threw for 1,747 and 1,566 yards, respectively.

Mickey Rivers   *BASEBALL*

This "make things happen" guy—sometimes called "Mick the Quick"—was sort of a low-calorie Rickey Henderson. In 15 major-league seasons, Rivers had 1,660 hits and 267 stolen bases. He played for the Angels and Yankees in the 1970s, and finished out his career with the Rangers in the 1980s.

Jose Rijo   *BASEBALL*

OK, so this name is a little bit of a stretch. Rio means river in Spanish. in case you didn't know, and the guy spells his name Rijo but pronounces it "rio." With that behind us, let it be said that Jose Rijo was the MVP in the 1990 World Series, in which the underdog Reds put it to the Oakland A's. Rijo went 2-0 in the series with a 0.59 ERA. He's still a solid pitcher and All-Star today.

Brooks Robinson   *BASEBALL*

Considered by many to be the greatest fielding third baseman of all time, Robinson was the American League MVP in 1964. Playing 23 years with the same team—the Orioles—he accumulated 2,848 hits, 16 consecutive Gold Glove awards, and finished with the highest fielding percentage of any third baseman in history—.971. At the Baseball Legends game before the 1993 All-Star game in Baltimore, Robinson thrilled local fans by making a terrific diving stop and starting a double play.

Herb Brooks   *HOCKEY*

While Brooks coached the Minnesota Golden Gophers to three NCAA titles and also led the Rangers and North Stars in the NHL, sports fans of all persuasions will never forget his crowning achievement—beating out the Russkies for the gold medal in the 1980 Winter Olympic Games.

Bill Wade   *FOOTBALL*

Bill Wade was one of the better running quarterbacks in the NFL. He rushed for 1,334 yards on 318 carries during his 13-year National Football League career. He played for the Rams in the 1950s and the Bears in the 1960s. In 1961, Wade was the third leading rusher in total yards gained, behind Willie Gallimore and Rick Casares. He had a higher yards per carry average than either Gallimore or Casares.

Wade Wilson   FOOTBALL

Wade Wilson has been a solid quarterback over the last several years, with most of his long career having been played in Minnesota. He rose to prominence during the 1987 season, when starter Tommy Kramer was hobbled by injury. Wilson led the Vikings past the highly favored San Francisco 49ers, 36-24—a snoozer in which the Vikes were up 20-3 at the half. In the NFC Championship Game against the eventual Super Bowl winner, the Washington Redskins, Wilson was sacked eight times—one shy of the game record—but almost pulled out a W anyway.

Terry Puhl   BASEBALL

A veteran of 15 major-league seasons, most of them with the Houston Astros, Puhl (pronounced "pool") had almost 5,000 at bats and finished with a fine .280 average. He was with the 'Stros in 1986 when the team made a valiant effort in the National League Championship Series to knock off the New York Mets, eventual winners of the World Series. The Mets won the Houston series in the 14th inning of Game 6, rallying from three down in the ninth. Had the series gone to a seventh game, the Astros were waiting in the wings with Mike Scott, the hottest pitcher in baseball that year and the man who beat the Mets twice already in the series, coughing up only a single run. Puhl had two singles in three at bats.

Dock Ellis   BASEBALL

Ellis had a long baseball career, the best part of it coming when pitching for the Pirates in the late '60s and early '70s. In 1971 he went 19-9—his most victories ever—with a 3.05 ERA. He started the All-Star Game for the National League, and lost it. Reggie Jackson literally lit Ellis up in the fourth, launching a missile deep downtown, off the light towers of Tiger Stadium. If Phil Rizzuto was announcing the game, for sure he'd have said, "Holy Cow." Maybe twice. It was a tape-measure job, for sure. The AL's W marked the first time the junior circuit had won the All-Star Game since 1962.

Ulysses "Junior" Bridgeman   BASKETBALL

Bridgeman, whose uniform number has been retired by the Milwaukee Bucks, came to that team in the trade with the Lakers that sent Kareem Abdul-Jabaar to Tinseltown in return for Bridgeman, Dave Meyers, Brian Winters and Elmore Smith. Bridgeman was a good shooter, popping in almost 50 percent from the field and over 85 percent from the foul line. He averaged nearly 14 ppg for his career.

Warren Wells   FOOTBALL

Wells was a wide receiver in the late 1960s. For his seven-year career, he had 42 touchdowns and averaged—and listen to this— a whopping 23.1 yards per catch.

Pumpsie Green   BASEBALL

Elijah Jerry Green played for five years in the majors, starting in 1959 and ending in 1963. His lifetime batting average of .246 was respectable for utility players of his day.

Derrick Coleman   BASKETBALL

This New Jersey Net forward has been a perennial All-Star over the last several years. He was a freshman on the 1987 Syracuse team that included Sherman Douglas and Rony Seikaly, which lost to Indiana on the famous buzzer beater by Keith Smart. One of the top power forwards in the NBA, the 6-foot-10 Coleman averages more than 20 points, three steals and 11 rebounds per game.

Emlen Tunnel   FOOTBALL

Emlen the Gremlin was a defensive back for the New York Giants in the late '40s and most of the '50s. His 79 career interceptions have put him in football's Hall of Fame.

40 | ALL-HOLLYWOOD TEAM

Eligibility: Each team entry must either have (1) pursued an acting career during his/her sports career or after retiring or (2) been associated with Hollywood or the Hollywood image in some way, or (3) have literally anything to do with Hollywood. Sports personalities with major TV appearances are OK for this list.

Samples: Jim Brown
Johnny Weismuller

And your nominees are ...

_____   _____

_____   _____

_____   _____

_____   _____

_____   _____

_____   _____

_____   _____

_____   _____

Dick's Picks
All-Hollywood Team

Tom "Hollywood" Henderson *FOOTBALL*

Jim Brown *FOOTBALL*

Sonja Henie *SKATING*

Esther Williams *SWIMMING*

Brian Bosworth *FOOTBALL*

Johnny Weismuller *SWIMMING*

Elroy "Crazylegs" Hirsch *FOOTBALL*

Ed Marinaro *FOOTBALL*

Rosey Grier *FOOTBALL*

Fred Dryer *FOOTBALL*

George Foreman *BOXING*

Bo Belinsky *BASEBALL*

"Broadway" Joe Namath *FOOTBALL*

Mark Harmon *FOOTBALL*

Oscar Schmidt *BASKETBALL*

Tony Kubek *BASEBALL*

Merlin Olsen *FOOTBALL*

Alex Karras *FOOTBALL*

Shaquille O'Neal *BASKETBALL*

Chuck Connors *BASEBALL*

O.J. Simpson *FOOTBALL*

Kareem Abdul-Jabbar *BASKETBALL*

Fred Williamson *FOOTBALL*

Carl Weathers *FOOTBALL*

Don Drysdale *BASEBALL*

Vera Hruba Ralston *SKATING*

Trivial Tidbits

Tom "Hollywood" Henderson *FOOTBALL*

This former Dallas Cowboy star earned his nickname by hiring limousines to take him around to social engagements. He was a big fish on some of the great Roger Staubach-era teams of the late 1970s. In the 1978 NFC title game against the LA Rams, he intercepted a Vince Ferragamo pass and bolted into 68 yards of daylight and six points. The Cowboys whitewashed the Rams that day, 28-0, but wound up falling to the Steelers in the Super Bowl. Were it not for Terry Bradshaw and Company hanging around the NFL, Hollywood Henderson might be wearing two more Super Bowl rings.

Jim Brown *FOOTBALL*

Perhaps best known in the movies for his role in *The Dirty Dozen*, Brown ran for 12,312 yards and scored 756 points in only nine pro seasons. This eight-time All-Pro joins such runners as O.J. Simpson and Walter Payton as one of the most prolific running backs in the history of the NFL—if not the best ever. Brown's movie credits are getting to be extensive. Other films he's been in include *Rio Conchos* (1964) and *The Running Man* (1987), just to name two. Who knows, one of these days there may even be a Jim Brown Film Festival.

Sonja Henie *SKATING*

Henie was a 10-time world figure-skating champion in the late 1920s and early 1930s and a gold medal winner in three straight Olympic games. Her first gold, won in her home country of Norway, prompted an Olympics rule change. There were five judges for figure skating and three of them were Norwegian. The three Norwegians picked Henie and the two other judges went with another competitor. Henie was into her stride by 1932, however, and was a unanimous choice for the gold. The-skater-turned-budding-actress packed her bags for Tinseltown and starred in numerous B-rated light musicals in the 30s and 40s. One her most memorable performances was in *Sun Valley Serenade* (1941), in which she played a war refugee traveling with the Glenn Miller band and manager Milton Berle.

Esther Williams *SWIMMING*

A former swimming champion, Williams carried her sports talent onto the silver screen, starring in several MGM musicals in the 1940s. In role after role after role she was cast as—naturally—a swimmer.

Johnny Weismuller *SWIMMING*

A five-time Olympic gold medalist and former world- and Olympic-record holder in the 100-meter freestyle, this hunk of the 1920s played Tarzan in the movies more than any other person. It was to start a trend—he was the first of four Olympics medalists to play the famous jungle do-gooder in the movies. In the 1930's, Weismuller had gotten a job with the BVD Underwear Company to model swimsuits. Hollywood liked what they saw and put a film conract under his nose. The underwear industry, not "one" to miss a trick, waited almost a half century before snagging Jim Palmer to pull a Johnny Weismuller on television audiences. Speaking of the tube, Weismuller also co-starred with a chimp named Tamba in the *Jungle Jim* television series in the 1950s.

Elroy "Crazylegs" Hirsch *FOOTBALL*

This star Rams back—named for his slashing moves—was one of the first gridiron hunks to migrate to the silver screen. He starred in three films, including the title role in the story of his life. Hirsch was one of the premier, "big play" performers in football—in nine seasons with the Rams he caught 343 passes for 6,299 yards and 53 TDs.

Ed Marinaro   *FOOTBALL*

At Cornell, Marinaro broke a slew of Ivy League rushing records and finished second in the Heisman Trophy balloting in 1971. While his pro football career at Minnesota was short-lived, he went on to fame as a movie star and a regular in the TV series *Hill Street Blues*.

Rosey Grier   *FOOTBALL*

Rosey Grier was a member of the L.A. Rams' touted Fearsome Foursome of the 1960s and was in a movie that film critic Michael Medved deemed the worst two-headed-transplant movie ever made—*The Thing with Two Heads* (1972). In this flick, Grier—through a medical experiment that looks borrowed from the playbook of Dr. Frankenstein—shares a neck with Ray Milland, whose character has a pathological hatred for blacks. One of the highlights of the film—in which both heads are on Grier's body—is Milland delivering a haymaker to Grier's head, which, of course, is actually Grier punching himself. With Grier's head down for the count, Milland tries to sever it, but, just in the nick of time, Grier's love interest arrives with a doctor, who instead detaches the Milland head, letting the former lineman traipse through the goalposts of love with his sweetie.

Fred Dryer   *FOOTBALL*

This former San Diego State, New York Giants, and Los Angeles Rams football star has gone on to great heights in the TV series *Hunter*. Measuring in at 6 feet 6 inches, Dryer played more than a decade in the NFL as a defensive end and was considered one of the best in his day.

"Broadway" Joe Namath   *FOOTBALL*

This swaggering star of Super Bowl III—where his Jets were 17-point underdogs to the Colts and wound up with the W—was also the first pro quarterback to pass for more than 4,000 yards in a single season (1967). Namath was never able to reproduce the success of that 1969 Super Bowl championship season on the silver screen. He starred in some lackluster films in the early 1970s, including *C.C. and Company* and *The Last Rebel*. As a pro footballer, though, Namath was hard to beat when he was on top of his game.

Mark Harmon   *FOOTBALL*

A former starting quarterback at UCLA, Harmon is one of today's busiest screen actors. Most recently, he was in the film *Wyatt Earp*. Harmon's father, Tom, was a two-time All-American at Michigan and the 1940 Heisman Trophy winner, and his sister was married to singer Ricky Nelson.

Oscar Schmidt   *BASKETBALL*

A longtime member of the Brazilian Olympic team and a familiar face on the world basketball scene, Schmidt has the same first name as Hollywood's ultimate award.

Tony Kubek   *BASEBALL*

Named the same as Hollywood's Tony Award, this nine-year veteran of the New York Yankees—with whom he spent his entire career—played shortstop on some of the powerhouse squads of the '50s and '60s. He was a superb player but regrettably he will always be remembered for the grounder that hit a pebble in the eighth inning of the seventh game of the 1960 World Series. A sure double-play out, the ball took a weird bounce, hit Kubek in the throat, and set the stage for a five-run Pirate rally and the unforgettable Bill Mazeroski homer in the ninth. The Yanks outscored the Pirates in that series 55-27, but came up on the short end of the most important stat—games won. Manager Casey Stengel said after the defeat: "I'll never make the mistake of being 70 again." Kubek went on to have a brilliant career in broadcasting as a baseball analyst.

Merlin Olsen   *FOOTBALL*

This gentle giant and Phi Beta Kappa from Utah State—and, with Grier, another member of the L.A. Rams' touted Fearsome Foursome of the 1960s—was a regular on television's *Father Murphy* and *Little House on the Prairie*. He is perhaps best known to the general public for his flower commercials on television.

Alex Karras   *FOOTBALL*

Karras—a perennial All-Pro at defensive tackle for the Detroit Lions in the 1950s and 60s—is probably best known in Hollywood for his roles in *Blazing Saddles* and *Babe*. He was also a color man on *Monday Night Football*, thrilling fans with his off-the-cuff humor.

Shaquille O'Neal   *BASKETBALL*

The rim rattler supreme—Mayor of Yoke City. He's got the body, the hands and the heart. He loves to go to the hoop and tell opponents, "Hello—here's my jam." He's learning to hijack on the defensive end as well. With Horace Grant, it might be Blowout City in Orlando. The Shaq made his movie debut in the Nick Nolte basketball flick, *Blue Chips*.

Chuck Connors   *BASEBALL*

Chuck Connors had a brief stint with the Dodgers and Cubs in the late 1940s and early 1950s as a first baseman before breaking into movies. Despite several film credits, he is probably best known for his portrayal of Lucas McCain on TV's *The Rifleman*, a popular series he starred in from 1957-1962.

Kareem Abdul-Jabbar   *BASKETBALL*

One of the best basketball players of all time, Kareem led his teams to three NCAA titles and six NBA titles. At his retirement after 20 pro seasons, he was the NBA frontrunner in more than 20 statistical categories. I remember that he did a cameo as a pilot in *Airplane*, a spoof of the Airport movies of the '70s and has signed on to executive produce a movie about civil rights pioneer Vernon Johns.

APPENDIX
KEEPING SCORE

You can play *Dickie V's Top 40* either by yourself or with other people.

Playing by Yourself: In the spaces provided, list as many team members as you can who meet the eligibility requirements. Give yourself three points for each new play on a name or idea and a single point for subsequent ones. For instance, if you are naming the All-Presidents Team, the first "Jackson" declared (say, Reggie Jackson) counts three points and each subsequent Jackson named (say, Phil Jackson, Chris Jackson, Jim Jackson, or Trenton Jackson) counts only a point.

Playing with Friends: With friends, the scoring works the same, but there are two different ways you can play, and also, some scoring modifications you may want to put in place.

The first way to play is, after selecting a team, each person playing takes 10-15 minutes to write down as many team members as he or she can think of. At the end of the allotted time, the person with the highest score is declared the winner for that team.

The second way is selecting the team, and then, instead of making separate written lists, each person playing takes turns at orally naming athletes. Scoring is done as the team is taking shape. (This second approach is ideal when one or more of the game players doesn't have use of his/her hands—like if you're on a long car trip and one of the players is driving. Alternatively, the players may be eating or chatting in a swimming pool, and writing is just plain inconvenient.)

There are two scoring modifications when 40 All-Star Teams is played in a group:

1. Several teams may be declared "open" for selection at the same time, making it possible for a single idea to score more than three points. For instance, if the All-U.S. Cities Team and All-Presidents Team are open for choices simultaneously, and the first participant names Trenton Jackson, there is a potential nine points with just this one name, since it covers two cities and one president.

2. To avoid people running up large, insurmountable scores by virtue of going first and picking the best name, you may wish to limit extra plays on a single name to a maximum of two points. Consequently, a person will get one or three points of base score for picking an eligible name and then one or two bonus points, depending on whether the name has one or two more extra plays in it.